I0884146

# THE URBAN PLAYS OF THE EARLY ABBEY THEATRE

*Irish Studies*
James MacKillop, *Series Editor*

OTHER TITLES FROM IRISH STUDIES

*Collaborative Dubliners: Joyce in Dialogue*
VICKI MAHAFFEY, ED.

*Ireland in Focus: Film, Photography, and Popular Culture*
EÓIN FLANNERY AND MICHAEL GRIFFIN, EDS.

*The Irish Bridget: Irish Immigrant Women in Domestic Service in America, 1840–1930*
MARGARET LYNCH-BRENNAN

*Irish Theater in America: Essays on Irish Theatrical Diaspora*
JOHN P. HARRINGTON, ED.

*Joyce, Imperialism, and Postcolonialism*
LEONARD ORR, ED.

*Making Ireland Irish: Tourism and National Identity since the Irish Civil War*
ERIC G. E. ZUELOW

*Memory Ireland. Vol. 1: History and Modernity; Vol. 2: Diaspora and Memory Practices; Vol. 3: The Famine and the Troubles; Vol. 4: James Joyce and Cultural Memory*
OONA FRAWLEY, ED.

*The Midnight Court/Cúirt an Mheán Oíche: A Critical Edition*
BRIAN MERRIMAN; DAVID MARCUS, *trans.*; BRIAN Ó CONCHUBHAIR, *ed.*

*Modern Irish Drama: W. B. Yeats to Marina Carr, 2nd ed.*
SANFORD STERNLICHT

# THE URBAN PLAYS OF THE EARLY ABBEY THEATRE

## BEYOND O'CASEY

ELIZABETH MANNION

*Syracuse University Press*

*Cover: From under O'Casey Bridge* © Nicholas Johnson


Syracuse, New York 13244-5290


First Edition 2014

14 15 16 17 18 19 6 5 4 3 2 1

∞ The paper used in this publication meets the minimum requirements of the American National Standard for Information Sciences—Permanence of Paper for Printed Library Materials, ANSI Z39.48-1992.

For a listing of books published and distributed by Syracuse University Press, visit our website at www.SyracuseUniversityPress.syr.edu.

ISBN: 978-0-8156-3367-9 (cloth) 978-0-8156-5304-2 (e-book)

**Library of Congress Cataloging-in-Publication Data**

Mannion, Elizabeth, author.

The urban plays of the early Abbey theatre : beyond O'Casey / Elizabeth Mannion. — First edition.

pages cm. — (Irish studies)

Includes bibliographical references and index.

ISBN 978-0-8156-3367-9 (cloth : alk. paper) — ISBN 978-0-8156-5304-2 (ebook)

1. Theater—Ireland—Dublin—History—20th century. 2. Irish drama—20th century—History and criticism. 3. English drama—Irish authors—History and criticism. 4. City and town life in literature. 5. Abbey Theatre—History. I. Title.

PN2602.D82M36 2014

792.09418'35—dc23 2014029022

*Manufactured in the United States of America*

*In memory of my grandmother, Kitty*

ELIZABETH MANNION is a senior lecturer in English at Temple University, where she teaches courses in drama and Irish literature. She received her PhD from Trinity College, Dublin.

# Contents

# Illustrations

# Acknowledgments

I OWE PARTICULAR THANKS to Steve Wilmer, who supervised the doctoral thesis on which this book is based, and to Brian Singleton, who examined it.

Thank you to Christopher Morash, Christopher Murray, Michael Pierse, and Nelson Ritschel, for invaluable comments on the introduction and early chapter drafts; to Hermann J. Real, Jim Rogers, and Roy Wolper, for editorial guidance on excerpts of chapters previously published; to Jennika Baines, Jim MacKillop, and their readers at Syracuse University Press, who improved the manuscript in every way; and to my colleagues at Temple University, particularly Chip Delany, Thom Guarnieri, and Steve Newman. And to Gabe Wettach, for keeping the faith and walking the walk. A very special thank-you to my little niece, Sarah, for the play breaks during final edits.

For their assistance during the research process: Abbey Theatre Archivist Mairéad Delaney; the manuscripts department at the National Library of Ireland; the Department of Early Printed Books at Trinity College, Dublin; Kristina DeVoe of the Paley Library, Temple University; and the staff of the New York City Public Library.

The feedback received at conferences was paramount in shaping this project. My gratitude to attendees at events hosted by The American Conference for Irish Studies, The Canadian Association for Irish Studies, and Glucksman Ireland House at New York University.

The author and publisher thank the editor of *Swift Studies Ehrenpreis Centre*, Westfälische Wilhelms-Universität, Münster, Germany, for permission to reproduce extracts from the following copyrighted material: "Swift Plays of the Abbey Theatre," which appeared in *Swift*

*Studies* 23 (2008); the editor of *New Hibernia Review/Iris Éireannach Nua* for permission to revise and publish material that appeared in issue 14.2 (Summer 2010); and the Trinity College Dublin Graduate Students' Union for permission to revise and publish material that appeared in the *Trinity College Dublin Journal of Postgraduate Research* 4.1–2 (2005).

*The Grand House in the City*, *Scrap*, *The Critic, or a Tragedy Rehearsed*, *The Suburban Groove*, and *The Leprechaun in the Tenement* are quoted courtesy of the National Library of Ireland. *The Dean of St. Patrick's Cathedral* and *The Slough* ©The British Library Board. All photographs, box office figures, and program notes courtesy of the Abbey Theatre Archives.

# Abbreviations

| | |
|---|---|
| DEF | Dublin Employers' Federation |
| ILT | Irish Literary Theatre |
| INDC | Irish National Dramatic Company |
| INTS | Irish National Theatre Society |
| ITC | Irish Theatre Company |
| ITGWU | Irish Transport and General Workers Union |
| IWDC | Irish Workers' Dramatic Club |
| NTSL | National Theatre Society Limited |
| TOI | Theatre of Ireland |
| ULT | Ulster Literary Theatre |
| WUI | Workers' Union of Ireland |

# Chronology of Urban Plays and Related Events

1899 First season of the Irish Literary Theatre

1901 Final season of the ILT

1902 *The Laying of the Foundations* by Frederick Ryan (INDC)

1903 The ILT merges with Willie Fay's INDC to form the Irish National Theatre Society (INTS)

1904 Horniman subsidy begins; Abbey Theatre opens

1905 The INTS is dissolved; replaced by the National Theatre Society Limited

1906 Founding of the Theatre of Ireland (TOI)

1908 Willie Fay steps down as manager, replaced briefly by Sara Allgood, then Norreys Connell (Conal O'Riordan); *The Man Who Missed the Tide* and *The Suburban Groove* by W. F. Casey

1909 *The Cross-Roads* by Lennox Robinson (Dublin-set prologue); *An Imaginary Conversation* by Connell (O'Riordan); Connell resigns as manager, succeeded by Lennox Robinson; death of Synge

1910 The Horniman subsidy is withdrawn

1911 *Mixed Marriage* by St. John Ervine

1912 The Irish Workers' Dramatic Club (IWDC) forms at Liberty Hall; *Victims* by A. Patrick Wilson (IWDC); final season of the TOI

1913 *The Dean of St. Patrick's Cathedral* by G. Sidney Paternoster; ITGWU strike and subsequent Lockout begins; *The Critics, or a New Play at the Abbey* by St. John Ervine

1914 *The Lord Mayor* by Edward McNulty; the Lockout ends; Lennox Robinson resigns as manager, A. Patrick Wilson appointed in his place; formation of the Irish Theatre Company (ITC); *The Orangeman* by St. John Ervine; *The Slough* by Wilson

1915 *The Dreamers* by Lennox Robinson; A. Patrick Wilson resigns as manager; St. John Ervine appointed in his place

1916 Easter Rising; St. John Ervine resigns, succeeded by J. Augustus Keogh

1917 *Blight: The Tragedy of Dublin* by Joseph O'Connor and Oliver St. John Gogarty; Fred O'Donovan replaces Keogh as manager

1919 *The Labour Leader* by Daniel Corkery; Lennox Robinson returns as Abbey manager

1920 The ITC stages its last production; *The Wooing of Julia Elizabeth* by James Stephens

1921 *The Revolutionist* by Terence MacSwiney

1922 *The Young Man from Rathmines* and *A Leprechaun in the Tenement* by M. M. Brennan

1923 *The Shadow of a Gunman* by Sean O'Casey; *Apartments* by Fand O'Grady (Kathleen Cruise O'Brien); *Kathleen Listens In* by O'Casey; Michael J. Dolan appointed manager

1924 *Juno and the Paycock* and *Nannie's Night Out* by O'Casey; *The Passing* by Kenneth Sarr (Reddin); Abbey receives subsidy from the Irish Free State

1926 *The Plough and the Stars* by O'Casey; opening of the Peacock Theatre at the Abbey

1927 *The Drapier Letters* by Arthur Power

1928 *Before Midnight* by Gerald Brosnan; first production of the Dublin Gate Theatre Studio at the Peacock Theatre

1929 *The Old Lady Says 'No!'* by Denis Johnston (for the Gate)

1930 *The Words upon the Window-Pane* by W. B. Yeats; opening of the Gate Theatre at the Rotunda

1931 *The Critic* by Lennox Robinson; *Money* by Hugh P. Quinn; *Scrap* by J. A. O'Brennan

1932 Death of Lady Gregory; *The Big Sweep* by M. M. Brennan
1935 *A Deuce O'Jacks* by F. R. Higgins
1936 *The Grand House in the City* by Brinsley MacNamara; *Blind Man's Buff* by Denis Johnston and Ernst Toller
1937 *The Man in the Cloak* by Louis D'Alton; *The Invincibles* by Hugh Hunt and Frank O'Connor; *Coggerers* by Paul Vincent Carroll
1938 *A Spot in the Sun* by T. C. Murray; *Moses' Rock* by Hunt and O'Connor; F. R. Higgins appointed managing director; *Time's Pocket* by Frank O'Connor; Hugh Hunt resigns as manager, succeeded by Louis D'Alton
1939 Death of Yeats; *Caesar's Image* by E. F. Carey; D'Alton resigns, succeeded by Frank Dermody
1940 *Birth of a Giant* by Nora MacAdam
1941 *Trial at Green Street Courthouse* by Roger McHugh; Ernest Blythe appointed managing director upon the death of F. R. Higgins; *Remembered For Ever* by Bernard McGinn
1943 *The O'Cuddy* by Anthony Wharton
1944 *The End House* by Joseph Tomelty
1945 *Rossa* by McHugh
1946 *Mungo's Mansion* by Walter Macken
1948 *The Drums Are Out* by John Coulter
1950 *Design for a Headstone* by Seamus Byrne
1951 Abbey Theatre destroyed by fire; company relocates to the Queens until 1966

# THE URBAN PLAYS OF THE EARLY ABBEY THEATRE

# Introduction

MY EXPERIENCE is that setting lingers. Character names and plot points often fade from memory over time, but what is seen on the stage to reflect the place and time of the action seldom does. A producer commenting on the shorter plays of Samuel Beckett observed that one is likely to mention the play with characters in urns, the one with the mouth or the one with the women on the bench immediately; but likely to say *Play*, *Not I*, or *Come and Go* only after giving it a bit more thought. When we recall *A Streetcar Named Desire*, we see a claustrophobic New Orleans apartment; memories of *Death of a Salesman* evoke a Brooklyn house divided by generations; and, of course, thinking back to the Trilogy of Sean O'Casey places a Dublin tenement room in the mind's eye. Studies of modern Irish drama, particularly those about the Abbey, often reflect a preoccupation with setting. Volumes have been devoted to the peasant play and its rural setting, to the mythically based works of W. B. Yeats and others, and to the symbolic component of these settings. Recent examination of the global presence in modern Irish drama strives, in part, to transcend setting. Doing so, however, emphasizes that location remains a driving concern.

This study of the urban repertoire of the early Abbey Theatre seeks to broaden the discourse on location in modern Irish drama generally, but at the Abbey specifically. It asks, Where is the city that was home to the Abbey and central to the political movements that emerged during the Abbey's early decades? It is an intervention of sorts on the dominant narrative of the early Abbey repertoire that asserts the urban location was not significant and largely limited to the works of Sean O'Casey. The urban repertoire of the early Abbey is defined here as plays set in Irish cities that premiered at the Abbey from its opening on December 27, 1904, until July 17, 1951, when the original structure was destroyed by fire at the same time that "the company who had first staged O'Casey's Dublin plays began to drift away" (Morash 2002, 198).

My interest in telling the early Abbey's urban story began with an interest in the O'Casey Trilogy—*The Shadow of a Gunman* (1923), *Juno and the Paycock* (1924), and *The Plough and the Stars* (1926)—and with an archival impulse to see how the Trilogy fit into the repertoire of the original Abbey, where its three parts were famously celebrated and vilified on the way to becoming among the most frequently performed plays at the National Theatre. In focusing on the early decades, the O'Casey works are central because they reflect how important they were and remain to the Abbey's history. By placing O'Casey in the middle, I tip my hat to the master of early Abbey urban drama while respectfully suggesting that we need to place him aside in order to see that the Irish city was represented by many Abbey playwrights and used as a setting to represent and interrogate multiple facets of Irish society. Examining the non-O'Casey urban plays, of which there are more than fifty, reveals an arresting picture of the Abbey's repertoire in terms of genre development and its canon. Reading all the plays produced by the Abbey in its early decades revealed much more than was expected. There are too many urban plays for the Trilogy settings to be considered an anomaly. These plays contain distinct patterns, and what emerges is a definitive Abbey urban genre with all the conventions and expectations the term *genre* implies.

The early urban repertoire can be read as a body of problem plays. The majority of these works adhere to this genre by thematically addressing contemporary social issues in a largely realistic tradition. There are occasional expressionistic episodes, but these are rare. Considering the high level of poverty in urban Ireland during the early decades of the twentieth century and the Abbey's predisposition toward depicting Irish cities in a realistic manner, it is not surprising that the dominant social concern is the institutional maintenance of a ghettoized working-class poor. What is unexpected is the extent to which the nationalist movement is portrayed as failing, and in some cases oppressing, the working classes. Such internal criticism of the shortcomings of the political arm of the nationalist movement was certainly under scrutiny in the O'Casey Trilogy, but cultural revivalism—a movement within which the Abbey was a central player—was, apart from Donal Davoren's satirical duality as a non-gunman/non-poet in *The Shadow of a Gunman*, largely omitted from his Trilogy.

In many of the urban plays, particularly those set in Dublin, the cultural project is singled out for derision as much or more than the political. As a result, the urban plays demonstrate that the Abbey was, through 1922, engaged in a more vibrant dialogue within revivalist dramatic literature than it is perhaps usually afforded. John Hutchinson argues that "cultural nationalists should be regarded as mediators, who, 'returning' to an imagined past in circumstances of confusion, are engaged in a project of self-discovery and collective definition that may lead them to experiment with several alternative visions of the nation over an extended period" (1999, 397). The more symbolic plays of Yeats are accepted as examples of the Abbey's willingness to experiment, but the urban plays should be included alongside his Noh-influenced dramas as equally emblematic of the Abbey's willingness to expand the boundaries of the dominant revivalist discourse it championed. Urban plays continued to be added to the repertoire after the close of the revivalist period in 1922, and they maintained a propensity to dramatize the ever-changing sociopolitical climate of Ireland.

The urban plays fit some standard Abbey conventions of the period, including a fair amount of idealization, characters written in a manner to maximize naturalism in performance, interior sets, and historical referencing. But the urban setting draws attention to the Abbey and its place in cultural revivalism in a way that makes many of these plays metadramatic to the institution's role in the movement. This canonical position of the urban plays within the Abbey's early repertoire calls to mind David Lloyd's examination of "minor" literature's relationship within nationalist movements. Lloyd's work is particularly relevant in articulating the irony of the urban repertoire's secondary status within the Abbey canon.

Minor literature is defined as possessing three primary characteristics: it is written in the majority language, with that language "effected by a strong co-efficient of deterritorialization"; it is inherently political; and it "has a collective value [that] constitutes a communal action" (Deleuze and Guattari 1983, 16–17). This definition applies to the major literature of the cultural nationalist movement, including the early Abbey's rural and ideological works, which follow the traditional model of minor literature in that they subvert the state through recurring thematic concerns of subverting authority. The urban repertoire serves a similar function *within* the Abbey canon, subverting the institution itself as well as its recurring tropes and themes on a local level. The plays often raise a civic voice to the detriment of a national voice. In this sense, one might read the urban repertoire of this period as serving an allegorical function in that it operates on both a local (Abbey) and a national scale. The early Abbey canon overwhelmingly conforms to the differentiating project of revivalism with primarily English-speaking characters, aspirational plots focusing on community over the individual, and rural or provincial settings. The urban plays deterritorialize the Abbey canon linguistically, by adopting urban syntax and idiom, but also politically through urban settings and reconfiguring of the "communal." The "communal" of the dominant repertoire is undermined in the urban plays by charging that the community of power is now feeding off its interests to the detriment of individuals who either opt out or cannot keep pace. Lloyd argues for the necessity "to grasp those criteria [that determine the constitution of a canon] in relation to the general ideological forms that legitimate domination in any given historical moment" (1987, 4). Although there was a theatrical tradition of touring, fit-ups, and variety halls in Irish cities and towns, in asserting itself as the National Theatre of Ireland, the Abbey carved out its own space as the dominant Irish theater. Its dominant ideological form is slightly less absolute. Moreover, 80 percent of its repertoire was set in the rural or provincial sphere and these settings were predominantly (albeit not exclusively, as several nonurban satires demonstrate) backdrops to narratives that were predisposed toward a notion of either self-sacrifice or self-promotion in search of a collective reward. By comparison, the urban-set plays often feel apart from their time and place within the Abbey repertoire. Here characters appear out of step with a swelling tide of a new, internal, emerging authority that was figuratively present in the dominant repertoire and, over time, literally present in the emerging nation's cultural and political power bases.

The Abbey was not alone in using the city setting to confront such problems. Other Dublin-based theater companies founded in the early twentieth century—including the Gate, the Theatre of Ireland, the Irish Theatre Company, and the Irish Workers' Dramatic Club—premiered works set in urban Ireland. Those that have bearing on the Abbey story are included here. The Gate, which got its start renting the Abbey's second stage, the Peacock, did not limit its urban settings to the realistic mode favored by the Abbey. From its first Dublin-set production, Denis Johnston's *The Old Lady Says "No!"* (1929), to its most commercially popular, Maura Laverty's *Liffey Lane* (1951), the Gate gave receptive audiences a more existential Dublin. The other companies did not enjoy the Gate's longevity, but they shared the Gate's willingness to stage urban plays.

The nomadic Theatre of Ireland (1906 to 1912) performed throughout the city, including at the Abbey and Molesworth Hall; the Irish Theatre Company (1914 to 1920) was based at Hardwicke Street Hall not far from the Abbey; and the Irish Workers' Dramatic Club (founded in 1912) operated out of Liberty Hall on the Dublin quays. The Theatre of Ireland was the first Dublin theater company to actively reject the Abbey's propensity for staging rural works. Many of its founding members (including Edward Martyn, Padraic Colum, and James Cousins) had relationships with the Abbey before starting the Theatre of Ireland and continued (with the notable exception of Martyn) to work with the Abbey and other companies. Ironically, in its six-year run, "the Anglo-Irish drama it produced was not markedly different from the Abbey's so-called peasant play" (Feeney 1980, 2). As will be discussed in chapter 1, its cofounder, Edward Martyn, left the

Abbey in large part because he "desired to use the stage for the presentation of modern plays by Irish authors concerned with the problems of ideas and of life" (Gwynn 1974, 136). Martyn's desire to develop Irish-authored and nonrural-set problem plays did not prevent him from supporting the staging of Ibsen and other European modernists. But, ironically, the Irish champion of the problem play, George Bernard Shaw, left him cold.

Martyn's work at the Theatre of Ireland carried over into his cofounding the Irish Theatre Company (ITC) with Joseph Plunkett and Thomas MacDonagh in 1914, specifically to stage "the production of non-peasant drama by Irishmen, of plays in the Irish language and of English translations from European master works for the theatre" (ibid., 167). Martyn's admiration for and emulation of Ibsen was apparent in the plays he wrote for the Irish Literary Theatre. As Christopher Morash notes, "If Martyn's *The Heather Field* had resembled Ibsen's *The Master Builder*, then *Maeve* (described by its author as 'A Psychological Drama') begins by resembling *Hedda Gabler*" (2002, 120), and an Ibsen aesthetic was even more pronounced in the ITC plays authored by him and his colleagues. The ITC delivered a healthy dose of Chekhov, Ibsen, and Strindberg, but it also staged several Irish-authored, locally set plays clearly influenced by those dramatists. Of its Dublin plays, Martyn's *The Dream Physician* (1914), *The Privilege Place* (1915), and *Romulus and Remus* (1916), and MacDonagh's *Author! Author!* (1915) and *Pagans* (1920) earned the most attention. These plays do not offer any specific commentary on Dublin life. Rather, the Dublin setting in all except *Pagans* is merely a backdrop to satirize local literary figures, including Yeats, Lady Gregory, and George Moore. Many ITC writers, actors, and supporters were involved in the 1916 Easter Rising. The executions of William and Pádraig Pearse (who wrote, performed, and included their students from St. Enda's School in ITC productions), Joseph Plunkett, and Thomas MacDonagh and the internment of John MacDonagh proved too difficult for the fledging company to overcome. The ITC carried on for a few years, but mostly with Henry O'Hanlon's poor imitations of Ibsen. With the Plunkett family's refusal to renew the building lease and

Martyn facing difficulties during the War of Independence, the company disbanded in 1920.

The plays staged by the Liberty Hall Players for the Irish Workers' Dramatic Club (IWDC) at Liberty Hall tended to reflect that space's home to organized labor. As will be discussed in chapter 6, the IWDC holds the distinction of being the first Dublin theater company to feature a play set in a Dublin tenement. *Victims* (1912), by A. Patrick Wilson, uses its poverty-soaked setting to great effect in delivering a pro-syndicalist message. The IWDC was officially started by Delia Larkin (sister of James Larkin) in June 1912, with Wilson taking charge of most of the directing and some acting. The company faded somewhat after the 1913 Lockout, but James Connolly revived its efforts in the fall of 1915 when he assigned Helena Moloney to head the theater company. There were many personnel overlaps between the IWDC and the Abbey. In addition to Moloney, Wilson and Sean O'Casey were involved with both companies. O'Casey attended shows and ran in the same social circles as the Liberty Hall Players, and as Christopher Murray muses, "it is impossible to believe [O'Casey] was not in some ways involved and a member of audiences" (2004, 94) at Liberty Hall. His Trilogy avoids the agitprop nature of the Liberty Hall plays, but obviously shares a prevalence of working-class characters. This group was as badly hit by the Easter Rising as the ITC and, like them, never quite got back on its feet. The group's troubles were further impacted by the heavy damage done to Liberty Hall by British forces. No official moment when the company disbanded is apparent. They seem to have just drifted away sometime between late 1919 and early 1920, around the same time the ITC closed shop and all Dublin theaters, including the Abbey, faced frequent disruptions, including curfews, because of the escalating War of Independence.

The physical structures where other companies performed certainly factored into their play selections and set designs, but none (except the Gate) lasted long enough for any patterns to be discerned. The Gate, still going strong at Parnell Square, always had ample space (once it left the Peacock) to prevent the size of the stage from having any impact on its repertoire. But the physical shape and size of the original Abbey, with its proscenium measuring 21 feet wide by 14 feet high and a stage only 15 feet deep, imposed constraints on play settings. Its parameters may have also impacted early play selections and influenced creative development of writers who aspired to see their work staged at the Abbey. The stage used by the Irish National Theatre Society (INTS) headquartered on Lower Camden Street from 1902 to 1903 also presented challenges. The INTS stage, described by Willie Fay as "so small that you couldn't swing a kitten, let alone a cat" (Fay and Carswell 1971, 125), was less than six feet deep and contained no backstage space to facilitate set changes. This size is particularly relevant considering the INTS's role in shaping the Abbey's early repertoire. Several plays that went on to become staples at the Abbey and, therefore, contributed to its signature reliance on interior settings premiered here and at other temporary headquarters, including Molesworth Hall, before the Abbey opened in 1904.

When the entirety of the early urban repertoire is laid bare, it reveals a treasure trove of commentary on the state of Ireland. Although in the minority, this repertoire is significant enough that the urban plays are deserving of examination similar to those plays of the peasant oeuvre and provincial plays that have been so often scrutinized. The plays that comprise the Abbey's early urban repertoire demonstrate that the Irish urban experience was far from absent on the Abbey stage and that the O'Casey Trilogy, although artistically and financially significant, is but a fraction of the Abbey's urban story.

As will be discussed in chapter 1, the groundwork of the urban repertoire is found in the ILT's production of Frederick Ryan's *The Laying of the Foundations* (1902). This Dublin-set play espouses some self-sacrificial elements commonplace in the Abbey's first decade. However, the authority figures against which the heroically written protagonist sets to assert himself reflect three characteristics that emerge as recurring qualities of oppression in many of the Dublin plays: they are entirely local, homegrown, and capitalistic. Indeed, the Abbey-staged urban plays steadily evolve toward an increasingly Shavian model and a more clearly recognizable problem play. Although a similar thread is found in some rural and provincially set plays, notably those by William Boyle and Paul Vincent Carroll, it is seldom with the sting expressed in the urban repertoire.

The plays examined here are admittedly a mixed bag; as Walter Macken once said in regard to the Abbey repertoire, "all plays cannot be works of genius" (Mikhail 1988, 203). Although some are more deserving of attention than others, this survey aims to provide the broadest picture possible of the Abbey's urban plays from 1904 through the summer of 1951. In dealing with generic conventions, the plays' metadramatic responses to the Abbey, and the cultural nationalist project simultaneously, a slightly horizontal approach is taken. The major plays are given prominence, but some elements will carry over into other subgeneric conventions. As a result, conversations carry across chapters. The study is segmented, in part, by location, reflecting the position that although it is not the sole generic marker, setting drives genre since the urban-set plays adhere to shared conventions that operate within a dramaturgy largely driven by the tenets of realism. Dominant subgenres, including the tenement and labor plays, operate on a more micro level within the broader urban category. The subgenres serve as gateways toward examination of the period's biographical plays, which offer the most optimistic portrayals of Dublin and celebrate men whose contributions to literature and independence endured to become central to the city's history.

Chapter 1 builds on the work of scholars, including Ben Levitas and Nelson Ritschel, who helped dispel the common misconception that urban Ireland did not appear on the Abbey stage until the emergence of the O'Casey Trilogy, which begins in 1923 with *The Shadow of a Gunman*. There are thirteen plays set in urban Ireland before the launch of the Trilogy, comprising 7 percent of first-time productions. By the summer of 1951, such plays—set in the cities of Dublin, Cork, Galway, and Belfast—represent 15 percent of the repertoire and, with revivals taken into account, 34 percent of all stagings. Although the urban plays are the minority genre, the frequency with which they are staged, particularly those set in Dublin and led by the Trilogy, is substantial.

Chapter 2 explores the ten plays set in the cities of Belfast, Cork, and Galway. Their propensity to address socioeconomic and political concerns is a quality shared with the Dublin plays, and this is a thematic convention of the urban repertoire. Abbey management is also considered as a factor in advancing an urban repertoire, particularly the roles played by managing directors assigned after Willie Fay stepped down in 1908. Lennox Robinson, A. Patrick Wilson, and Frank O'Connor all had stormy tenures in this dual role, but directed—and in some cases authored—many of the more significant urban plays, begging the question as to what extent their championing of the minority genre reflects their complicated relationships with the Abbey.

Attention to the Dublin plays begins in chapter 3 with an examination of the works of W. F. Casey, the first playwright to have a Dublin play premiere at the Abbey. *The Man Who Missed the Tide* and *The Suburban Groove* (both 1908) stand out for their portrayals of a static, provincial city in a Joycean mode. This representation was short-lived, but adopted as farce in some of the tenement plays, most notably M. M. Brennan's *The Young Man from Rathmines* and *A Leprechaun in the Tenement* (both 1922). Many of the Dublin plays contain elements of satire and parody, but chapter 4 considers the possibility that Sean O'Casey's *Kathleen Listens In* (1923) and Paul Vincent Carroll's *Coggerers* (1937) can be read as employing these devices to re-vision *Cathleen ní Houlihan* (1902), the most canonical play of modern Irish drama. It identifies one of the primary methods of the urban plays' dialogue with cultural revivalism as being contained within the metadramatic. This attention to metadrama carries over into chapter 5, which focuses on the cluster of plays set in public arenas. Included are two plays—St. John Ervine's *The Critics, or a New Play at the Abbey* (1913) and Lennox Robinson's modernization of Richard Brinsley Sheridan's *The Critic, or a Tragedy Rehearsed* (1931)—set in the most overtly metadramatic place possible: the Abbey Theatre. Chapter 6 takes a look inside the domestic settings of Dublin's converted Georgian mansions. Two boarding-house plays—Matthew Brennan's *The Big Sweep* (1923) and Brinsley MacNamara's *The Grand House in the City* (1936)—use the Georgian space to problematize shifting socioeconomic relationships between the city and the Ascendancy, a class largely ignored in the tenement plays. A. Patrick Wilson's *The Slough* (1914) was the first to recreate a

Dublin tenement room on the Abbey stage, and eleven others followed over the next three decades. In addition to a cynical tone, the tenement plays share several qualities when examined as a whole, including considerable aggressiveness in challenging urban power brokers, who are consistently identified as constructing an environment to maintain a ghettoized class. Not surprisingly, most of the domestic plays include labor-related issues. However, labor commentary is secondary to the tenement set being used to portray poverty. Chapter 7 discusses those plays in which the issue of organized labor is central, including Edward McNulty's *The Lord Mayor* (1914), Wilson's *The Slough*, and J. A. O'Brennan's *Scrap* (1931). The Wilson and O'Brennan plays are given prominence for their negative portrayals of union organizers and veiled references to the 1913 Lockout. Since labor leaders of this period were aligned with the cultural nationalist project, these plays further challenge the movement. The Dublin section concludes in chapter 8 with consideration of biodramas featuring Robert Emmet, Jonathan Swift, James Clarence Mangan, and Jeremiah O'Donovan Rossa. Historical referencing exists throughout the urban repertoire, but the biodramas are the plays most entrenched with dramatizing history. They are unique in the urban repertoire for their generally optimistic tone and romanticism, and are the urban plays that come closest to reflecting the aesthetic of the early Abbey's dominant canon.

The urban repertoire represents no unified ideology; the plays embrace and transcend the metaphorical impulse of city literature generally and city drama particularly. This repertoire can even be read allegorically, in that it functions on both a local and a national scale. Indeed, a chronological reading of these plays shows a "working through" of modern drama within a uniquely Irish literary tradition. The influences of Wilde and Shaw are apparent, particularly in the targeting of either ill-used or outdated social conventions. The city as catch basin of the masses, resulting in a collision between haves and have-nots, is also on display. Most noteworthy is the extent to which these plays challenge the thematic messaging of the Abbey's dominant repertoire and are, in the end, metonymic of the Abbey's early decades.

# 1 Fifteen Percent

## *The Minority Genre*

RAYMOND WILLIAMS wrote that "the pull of the idea of the country is towards old ways, human ways, natural ways [and] the pull of the idea of the city is towards progress, modernization, development" (1973, 357). During the first decades of the twentieth century, when the political and cultural nationalist movements were influencing, some might say dictating, a significant amount of Anglo-Irish dramatic output, Williams's "idea of the country" was reflected in many works staged at the Abbey. The impulse toward rural settings resulted in detraction from the urban and was predicated upon a goal of reclamation, a "pull" toward that which differentiated Ireland from industrialized England. The strength of the nationalist movement during the Revival was an obstacle to urban-set plays in part because "the identification in the Gaelic revival of Irishness with peasant culture . . . served to confuse attitudes towards the city. Urbanization and urban problems fitted uneasily with the strongly rural ethos" (Daly 1984, 1–2). Although this unease did not prevent the urban setting from finding its way into the Abbey repertoire, it contributes to urban-set drama's minority status within the Abbey canon. Although some plays in the rural canon—most notably those by J. M. Synge—can be read as challenging the shortcomings of the cultural nationalist movement, most support its tenets through adapting the mythological (i.e., *Cathleen ní Houlihan*, Yeats's Cuchullain plays) or dramatizing conflicts, symbolically or otherwise, between an Irish "us" and a colonizing "them." The urban canon, however, consistently rejects or deconstructs the mythological and is predisposed to presenting conflict within Irish society as being between an "us" and a "them" that is two sides of one domestic coin.

One explanation of why urban-set plays are in the minority in the early Abbey repertoire can be found in the writings of the founding directors, and in the tenets of the revivalist movement of which the Abbey was a component. They explain the rural majority and the ironic position of urban centers dictating the rural as the authentic Irish setting.

The Abbey incorporated with a goal that reflected the Irish Literary Theatre's intent to "show that Ireland is not the home of buffoonery and of easy sentiment, as it has been represented, but the home of an ancient idealism. We are confident of the support of all Irish people, who are weary of misrepresentation, in carrying out a work that is outside of all political questions that divide us" (Gregory 1913, 9). This apolitical declaration is actually a political position and, as Lionel Pilkington has argued, the Abbey was deeply influenced by and a conduit of both "constructive unionism . . . and those energies associated with the struggle for Irish political independence" (2001, 2).[1] Pilkington demonstrates that the Abbey directors were adept at modifying personnel and repertoire, particularly in the early decades, in response to and in anticipation of changing political climates. This malleability offers one compelling explanation for the staging of works that highlight internal class divisions rather than a homogeneous Irish society. Such plays, found primarily among the Dublin repertoire, premiere in largest numbers in the 1920s and 1930s, when power was transferred from Sinn Féin to Cumann na nGaedheal and then to Fianna Fáil. This period also coincides with the Abbey's application for, and

1. Constructive unionism is a term for that which "owed nothing to cultural nationalism, nothing to crusades for 'Irish Ireland' and very little even to parliamentary pressures" (Lyons 1971, 198). Rather, proponents felt they could halt the nationalist movement's progression in Ireland by implementing (long overdue) social improvements (i.e., housing). Often summed up by Wyndham's famous quotation as "killing the Home Rule movement with kindness."

eventual receipt of, state subvention, which undoubtedly contributed to the Abbey's decision to stage a wider range of plays. Lauren Arrington takes this a step further, stating that the directors "self-censored plays when they foresaw an opportunity for financial gain" (2010, v). Financial expediency was a factor; the urban plays often served to turn the financial tide.

The notion of an "ancient idealism" is both a deflection of the stage Irishman and a reflection of the cultural nationalist agenda that can be traced to the 1880s. In his study of cultural nationalist ideology, William Thompson outlines the characteristics that defined its foundation. Citing the influence of eighteenth- and nineteenth-century works of Irish history that emphasized reclamation of Celtic mythology, Thompson traces the influence that Sylvester O'Halloran, George Petrie, Standish O'Grady,[2] and other scholars had on literature and drama that emerged during the Revival, as well as its significance within the cultural nationalist movement. Thompson identifies one of the characteristics of the ideology that shaped the Revival and its dramatic component as "the rejection of industrial civilization. The next natural step was to move out from the individual to society, and to present, against the fragmented collective of Ireland's vestigial feudalism and primitive capitalism, an image of the beautiful community of moor and glen" (1972, 42). Rejection of urban representations offers further explanation for its secondary status on the national stage.

As Thompson argues, because of its mythological component, this ideology is based on imagination. With an intrinsic reliance on the imagined, it erases urban realism from literary and dramatic prominence. But the elements of the movement did not emerge from isolation. Rather, they are a culmination of what John Hutchinson identifies as three distinct stages of Irish cultural nationalism: preparation,

2. O'Grady was perhaps most influential on Yeats, Russell, and other young enthusiasts. Ironically, he found their stage adaptations of the heroic legends to which he introduced them to be a mistake. After seeing *Deirdre* and *Cathleen ní Houlihan* at St. Teresa's Hall, O'Grady wrote in the April 12, 1902, *All Ireland Review* that they had best "leave the heroic cycles alone and [not] bring them down to the crowd."

crystallization, and articulation (1987, 50).[3] Hutchinson reminds us that the Literary Revival, of which the Dublin-based Abbey and its predecessors (the ILT and the INTS) were leading institutions, embraced a cultural nationalism that evolved over time, and this cumulative effect reinforced Dublin's centrality to the movement.

In addressing the link between the political and the cultural mandates that existed within the early twentieth-century nationalist movement, and the inconsistencies inherent to both, Declan Kiberd observes, "the fact that some of the fiercest fighting between the rebels and the forces of occupation took place in cities has never much dented the notion of rural Ireland as real Ireland. Like other forms of pastoral, this complex of ideas was a wholly urban creation [that] helped to create the myth of a rural nation" (1996, 481). Kiberd's declaration of a "complex of ideas" being woven to create a synchronistic political and cultural mandate as a form of pastoral reveals several issues that speak to the "myth of a rural nation" as one created by internal, primarily eastward-moving, migrants whose new roots could often be traced back to rural communities. Those who settled in Dublin eventually made an imprint on political and cultural nationalism on a par with that of Ascendancy participants, including some of the Abbey's earliest directors. But their voices remained on the periphery of the national stage. In essence, they were subverted by the imagined. As Fintan O'Toole notes, "The notion of the peasant and of the country which the peasant embodied was not a reflection of Irish reality but an artificial literary creation, largely made in Dublin, for Dubliners. It was a political image of the countryside which helped to create a sense of social cohesion in a country which was trying to define itself over against England. [The] Abbey had to create an imagined country in the heart of the city . . . In presenting revolutionary new plays, the Abbey players were already presenting an image of their own collective past, already in a sense disowning the present" (1985,

3. See also Lyons 1971 (part 2, chap. 5) and Thompson 1972 for examinations of the movement's key historical touchstones.

112). O'Toole's assertion that the rural literary/dramatic creation was a "political image" forged to help define Ireland apart from England squares with the Abbey's earliest years, when Ireland remained colonized by England and the political and cultural nationalist movements were operating synergistically.

Kiberd's use of the term *pastoral* to describe the political and cultural mandate of a newly urbanized leadership speaks directly to the paradox of the rural as "real." The term *pastoral* applies to a variety of literary forms, but its roots (from Theocritus and Virgil) rest in an inherently false representation of country people enjoying an eternal summer, where toil and hardship are romanticized, only marginally represented or absent, in favor of a non-city aesthetic. But the pastoral applications of the early Abbey rural tradition break from these foundations significantly. Although the comedies often embrace Virgilian qualities transplanted to the west of Ireland, the tragedies maintain personal hardship as a dominant force, as do, poignantly, the tragicomedies of Synge, whose characters' hardships are never sentimentalized or rewarded. Indeed, Synge's plays stand out in the rural repertoire as exceptions to the rule. The majority of the rural plays, however, do reflect the Wordsworthian position and rationalization expressed in the *Preface to Lyrical Ballads*. However, a glaring difference between Wordsworth and the Abbey directors appears when the *Preface* is read against the 1906 pamphlet *Irish Plays*, authored by Yeats, Synge, William Boyle, and Lady Gregory:

From the *Preface to Lyrical Ballads*

> Humble and rustic life was generally chosen because, in that condition, the essential passions of the heart find a better soil in which they can attain their maturity, are less under restraint, and *speak a plainer and more emphatic language* [italics mine]. (Wordsworth 1944, 386)

From *Irish Plays*

> The Irish peasantry of the hills and coast *speak an exuberant language*, and have a primitive grace and wildness, due to the wild country

> they live in, which gives their most ordinary life a vividness and colour unknown in more civilised places [italics mine]. (reprinted in Saddlemyer 1982, 317–18)

These tracts offer a similar desire to reflect the pastoral, but the glaring issue of language separates them when the directors decry "more civilised places" as being less worthy of dramatic representation. Wordsworth points toward a desire for simple, organic language that is stripped of artifice, whereas the Abbey directors prioritize the opposite. It is difficult to read the directors' opinion regarding "civilised" locales as anything other than the urban or metropolitan sphere. This deliberate positioning of the urban/metropolitan as being less worthy of representation equates to its being less culturally significant or authentic. It also emphasizes that in staging the earliest urban plays, the directors were willing to stretch the boundaries of dominant revivalist discourse, including that which they articulated themselves.

One explanation for minimizing the urban can be found in Thompson's perception of a Wordsworthian link to the adoption of pastoral motifs. It is a link he makes specific to Ascendancy participants of the Revival when he notes that "writers like Hyde, Yeats, Synge, and Gregory, were people of good family who had stumbled upon difficult times; in the eighteenth century the Anglo-Irish upper classes had known an era of brilliance and prosperity, but with the Act of Union and the Industrial Revolution, feudal Ireland went into eclipse, and Dublin became a provincial city. Born into a world that favored the machine, commerce, and the growth of cities, slums, and empires, a person of imaginative capacity recoiled from a setting that offered no role for his abilities" (1972, 41). In this light, rural settings and motifs seem an appropriate device for urbanized political and cultural leadership that is compelled to build on the mythical or imagined when the present is volatile and the future uncertain, issues that make the urban plays particularly emblematic of Pilkington's assertions. If cultural nationalism is a "*defensive* response by educated elites to the impact of exogenous modernization on existing status orders, which may result . . . in a reassertion of traditionalist values in the community" (Hutchinson 1987, 32), then the urban plays' focus on contemporary issues stood to challenge the "haze of sentiment and nostalgia" (Kiberd 1996, 481) that dominated the Abbey stage until the early 1920s. With very few exceptions, the Abbey playwrights who chose to explore urban themes rejected pastoral sensibilities in a manner that transcends the obvious signifier of location.

Kiberd points out that "Dublin was in 1904 [the year the Abbey opened] a classic example of a periphery-dominated-centre, that is to say, a conurbation dominated by the values and mores of the surrounding countryside" (1996, 484). However, like many other Dublin-based cultural institutions, the Abbey was predisposed to disseminate rural representations to an urban audience. The domestic urban audience was the one common denominator. Consequently, the representation of urban Ireland takes on significance. If a national theater "serves both as a prominent public site associated with the prestige of national self-representation, and as a means of instituting, or attempting to institute, norms of political agency" (Pilkington 2004, 232), then the marginalization of urban productions, with their tradition of challenging the imaginative elements of revivalism, denote the urban as too prominent to be ignored, but too subversive to be championed. It would appear the Abbey walked a line between minimizing representations that were "real" to its predominantly urban audiences and offering representations that were "authentic" to the ideology from which the institution emerged.

Hutchinson argues that within cultural nationalism there are "unique, autonomous and integrated territorial communities . . . with . . . two educated groups . . . fundamental to its emergence: secular intellectuals, who are the formulators of its ideology, and the intelligentsia, who form its first constituency and its political organizers" (1987, 3). Because Yeats and Gregory were significant in defining the dramatic representation of the ideology and to dictating its stage-based articulation, they served a dual function as formulators and intelligentsia in the Abbey's early decades. That Yeats and Gregory favored invocation of the mythological amid nonurban settings is well established. This preference is reflected in the plays they authored and in the vast majority of those they championed. Those managers and directors who challenged the dominant aesthetic—including Patrick Wilson, St. John Ervine, Augustus Keogh, and Frank O'Connor—had volatile tenures with the Abbey. But most notable of the early dissenters was Edward Martyn, a key artistic and financial catalyst in founding the Irish Literary Theatre (ILT).

Realism and an urban aesthetic had a staunch ally in Martyn, first president of Sinn Féin and codirector with Yeats and George Moore (Martyn's cousin) of the ILT. But when he parted company with the ILT in its third season, in part because of its predisposition to the poetic and the peasant, any objective to incorporate an urban aesthetic went with him, leaving preferences for the non-city setting as the foundation on which the Abbey repertoire took root. Martyn's disagreement on what should constitute a national repertoire was a significant factor in his withdrawal from the ILT. He had "no interest whatever in peasant plays [and was] absorbed in the new conception of drama that had been introduced by Ibsen and Strindberg" (Gwynn 1974, 136). An argument is often made that Martyn, who reacted strongly against any play he perceived as anti-Catholic, left on religious grounds. However, as Denis Gwynn (1974) and William Feeney (1984) document, Martyn remained with the ILT during such debates, including the first and most notorious one surrounding Yeats's *The Countess Cathleen* (1899). Produced at the Antient Concert Rooms in conjunction with Martyn's *The Heather Field* as part of the ILT's inaugural efforts, *The Countess Cathleen* was under sharp scrutiny from Cardinal Michael Logue "for its travesty of the Irish peasant, whom it represented as selling their souls to proselytisers" (Gwynn 1974, 128). Martyn sought the opinion of his parish priest, who deemed it acceptable. This approval, along with Cardinal Logue's admission that he had not actually read the play he was publically attacking, put the matter to rest. Martyn did not part ways with Yeats, Moore, and Gregory until nonreligious repertoire issues were his primary motivation. Martyn would go on to cofound the Theatre of Ireland (TOI) and the Irish Theatre Company (ITC), two companies that self-identified as having a nationalist remit and strove to include urban plays in their repertoires.

The issue of language, like setting, is a crucial element in differentiating an urban aesthetic from that of the rural. Speaking of urban playwrights at the ITC, Nelson Ritschel notes that "these writers used their own everyday urban language . . . the speech familiar to urban nationalists was, thus, an integral part of the urban aesthetic, an alternative way to portray dignity in the Irish image" (2000, 20). Although such language was used in the ITC plays, the Abbey founders' intentions to replicate "exuberant" peasant language carried over into much of the urban repertoire, including the Trilogy, at times mitigating any significant elevation of character. Kiberd finds that the Trilogy is "populated with urban leprechauns and sloganeering caricatures, forever jabbering away in an sub-language of their own which owes more to the texts of Synge than to the idiom of the Dublin tenements [with] the rolling cadences of Synge . . . ill-suited to the rhythms of urban life" (1996, 232). According to Francis Bickley, Yeats said "that [Synge] was contemplating a play of Dublin slum life" (Bickley 1968, 48) shortly before his death in 1908, and one cannot help but wonder at how or if Synge would have modified his "rolling cadences" had such a play been realized.

The rural represented a constructed "authentic" Ireland, but population statistics show that cities represented reality to a significant portion of Irish citizens. Beginning in the mid-nineteenth century, Dublin in particular saw a marked increase in population. As Joseph O'Brien notes, "much of this increase doubtless represented the influx of the landless poor, of artisans attracted by speculative building ventures, as well as, in the late 1840s, of those fleeing famine and desolation for the organized philanthropy of the capital" (1982, 7). This "rural exodus was such that the urban population accounted for a steadily growing proportion of the whole, from about one-eighth in 1841 to about one-third in 1911" (Lyons 1971, 90). Urban residents were a combination of people who had lived in cities for several generations and first-generation urbanites. Both groups may have had experiential connections to rural Ireland, but the city was the practical reality for a majority of audience members. In depicting this home, the urban plays cast a fairly wide net for subject matter.

The first use of an urban set in the Abbey repertoire, Frederick Ryan's *The Laying of the Foundation*, actually predates the 1904 opening of the theater. Produced by Willie Fay's Irish National Dramatic Company (INDC), this two-act drama premiered at the Antient Concert Rooms in October 1902 as a fund-raiser for Cumann na nGaedheal, and was staged again in December by the INDC's successor, the Irish National Theatre Society (INTS) at 34 Lower Camden Street. In 1903 it was also part of Dublin and London fund-raising efforts for the INTS, the governing body of the original Abbey Theatre.[4] Yeats was an advocate of the play, and his appreciation did not diminish over time. According to Lennox Robinson, Yeats wanted to revive the play at the Abbey to honor Ryan following his death in 1913, but the script could not be located (Hogan and Kilroy 1970, 11). Yeats's support for this socialist-leaning, somewhat Ibsenite play, might be found in the altruistic determination of its protagonist, Michael O'Loskin. Ritschel argues that the early "urban aesthetic dramatists ultimately owed more to Yeats" than met the eye (2000, 21). Ritschel observes that their plots, although not rurally or mythically based, and their characters, although not mythically developed or lyrically spoken, nonetheless often mirror the model of self-sacrifice personified by Michael Gillane in *Cathleen ní Houlihan*. "There was no room," Ritschel argues, "in early Irish theatre's urban or rural aesthetic plays for Ibsen-type characters suffering with personal dilemmas. It was a theatre that primarily attempted to offer an elevated Irish model rather than to portray people as they were" (ibid.). This attempt especially applies to *The Laying of the Foundations*, a play whose young protagonist becomes a detective of sorts, ultimately revealing slum landlords to be city aldermen and wealthy publicans.

4. The name was changed to the National Theatre Society in 1906 and remained the same through 1951. In August 2005 it became the Abbey Theatre Limited, which it remains.

O'Loskin forsakes his own comfortable job on the city payroll to do his part in building a "city whose foundations are laid in Liberty and Truth" (Ryan 1970, 37). In this regard, the Ryan play might be viewed as a transition drama that transplants a component of the tradition of self-sacrifice for a common good, apotheosized in *Cathleen ní Houlihan*, from a rural to an urban setting. However, in recognizing his own complicity in societal corruption if he remains in his position, and then acting against this, O'Loskin is also a character of the Ibsenite and Shavian traditions, as many protagonists of the early urban repertoire would also be. Functioning both within and apart from the dominant Abbey model, the Ryan play transplants a component of the Yeats-Gregory tradition from a rural to an urban setting, while adhering to a convention of the problem play.

Williams's argument that "rural virtues . . . mean different things at different times" (1973, 22) begs the question: Do urban virtues and representations also mean different things at different times? The Ryan play's focus on a young underdog willing to carve out his own space certainly parallels the INDC's attempt to gain traction. Likewise, an overview of the Abbey's urban repertoire from 1904 through 1951 suggests that this is a legitimate line of inquiry. The plays remain constant in their predisposition toward dramatizing conflicts within Irish society and focusing on those centers that were the most highly industrialized (Belfast and Dublin), but there is a significant increase in urban-set plays post-Treaty and after independence is achieved, coinciding with the fading presence of the Revival.

Approximately 370 plays premiered on the original Abbey stage (exclusive of pantos, Irish-language plays and translations), of which approximately 15 percent are set in urban centers as follows:

| | *No. of Plays* | *% of Total Urban Repertoire* | *% of Total Repertoire* |
|---|---|---|---|
| Dublin | 42 | 82% | 11% |
| Belfast | 5 | 10% | 2% |
| Cork | 3 | 6% | <1% |
| Galway | 1 | 2% | <1% |

Considering the Abbey's role as a conduit of the Dublin-based revivalist movement, it is not surprising that Dublin comprises the largest segment of urban settings. Heinz Kosok also suggests that for many plays, a Dublin-set focus is the result of convenience, and Irish playwrights sometimes chose the city as setting "because it was the milieu of their intended audience" (1984, 27). His assertion bears consideration in light of the many comedies and melodramas—including James Stephens's *The Wooing of Julia Elizabeth* (1920), Lennox Robinson's *Never the Time and Place* (1924), F. R. Higgins's *A Deuce O'Jacks* (1935), T. C. Murray's *A Spot in the Sun* (1938), Bernard McGinn's *Remembered For Ever* (1941), and Anthony Wharton's *The O'Cuddy* (1943)—where Dublin serves no significant purpose apart from anchoring the drama in a location familiar to audience members. Although the same might be said for some of the Belfast plays, the majority, like those set in the cities of Cork and Galway, use their setting to address issues specifically pertinent to events or circumstances reflective of their locations.

With approximately 15 percent of its repertoire depicting the Irish urban experience, that first Abbey building at the corner of Marlborough and Abbey Streets in Dublin's north inner city presented urban Ireland at all points of the compass: the heavily industrialized north of shipyard workers and sectarian conflict, the slum conditions of the west, the labor and political unrest of the south, and the volatile capital city in the east. Overall, there are several constants among the Abbey's urban repertoire. In whichever city the plays are set, they tend to contain references that assume the audience's intimate knowledge of their locales. Even at the turn of the century, Dublin was a city that absorbed internal migration from across the island. The reliance on local specificity suggests that the plays were staged to appeal primarily to a domestic audience.

It is well established that Yeats and his fellow directors were driven to stage works that spoke to a higher aesthetic than was commonly found in Dublin theater houses at the turn of the century. However, Abbey directors were not immune to measuring the political or financial climate of any given season, and to adjusting the repertoire

1. The Abbey Theatre, 1913. Courtesy of the Abbey Theatre Archives.

accordingly. Many scholars have examined the Abbey's early repertoire for political implications, but Pilkington (2001) and Adrian Frazier (1990) provide the most comprehensive analyses of the extent to which it can be read as a simultaneous reflection of and reaction to changing political movements through the 1940s, including constructive unionism, and the political fluctuations of Sinn Féin, Cumann na nGaedheal, and Fianna Fáil. More recently, Arrington (2010) has added to the discussion by arguing that the Abbey's pursuit of state subvention impacted repertoire decisions. What these scholars remind us is that repertoire selection and repertoire-rotation issues are fluid. Examining any theater company's production history and related income is an imperfect forensic practice if one is trying to determine with absolute certainty why decisions were made, but very useful if the goal is to measure a repertoire's popular success. What is clear is that financial concerns and audience reception, as measured by box office receipts, played a large part in the Abbey's evolution, and there appears to be a connection between financial fluctuations and the growth of the urban repertoire.

In 1982 James Flannery analyzed the role that finances played in the creation and subsequent administrative and artistic development of the Abbey. Flannery shows that the Horniman subsidy (see chapter 2) made viable several key foundational elements, all of which contributed to putting the Abbey on the theatrical map:

> Were it not for her gift of a permanent home it is likely that the Irish National Theatre Society would have drifted from hall to hall, as did so many companies of the time, without ever acquiring a focus for its work. [The] subsidy also made possible the development of a company of professional actors . . . it provided the technical resources that enabled the Irish Players to stage over fifty original plays between the opening of the Abbey in 1904 and December 1910; and it enabled the company to make a number of tours to England without which the name of the Abbey Theatre and the work of its dramatists would not have achieved world renown. Perhaps most importantly, the subsidy . . . allowed the Abbey Theatre to present and keep before the public plays which no ordinary commercial theatre would have dared to present. (Flannery 1982, 252–53)

Concentrating on the pre-1920 years, Flannery presents evidence of meager houses and the necessity of the Horniman subsidy to cover production shortfalls. Although a factor, the meager houses in this period were not solely the result of repertoire. There were flu epidemics that forced theaters to close, a fairly rapid turnover of general managers, and indications that, to put it mildly, budgeting was not a strength of the Abbey's administrative team. The 1916 Easter Rising was also a factor. The physical destruction and disruptions it brought to the city, along with curfews and theater closures, resulted in "all the positive gains of the previous months [being] nullified [and] the Abbey entered a period of financial decline" (Arrington 2010, 15) that would prove difficult to recover from in the early years of the next turbulent decade. When the 1920s began, there was no immediate relief. The War of Independence (1919 to 1921) and the Civil War (1922 to 1923) both resulted in prolonged periods of closure and curfews that further impacted box office. It would take the combined impact of the emergence of the O'Casey Trilogy (in 1923) and state subvention (in 1924) to right the Abbey's financial ship.

Examination of the production and performance records from December 27, 1904, through July 17, 1951, as well as existing box office records (partial through 1919; complete thereafter)[5] reveals that there was a steady audience for urban plays. Although they comprised only 15 percent of the repertoire, these urban plays represented, on average, approximately 20 percent of box office receipts. Not surprisingly, this increase is due largely to the O'Casey Trilogy.

The popular reception of the urban plays also impacted the Abbey's rotation schedule. For years, there had been a policy in place that a play not run more than two consecutive weeks no matter how well it was received, a rule that actress Eileen Crowe states, "Yeats was very definite about," but that was altered shortly after *Juno and the Paycock* opened and "the theatre was besieged. They had to keep it on" (Mikhail 1988, 131). With the box office success of *Juno*, three-week runs became acceptable, and this policy remained in force until another Dublin play, Denis Johnston's courtroom drama *Blind Man's Buff* (1936) altered length-of-run policy further. *Blind Man's Buff* ran for an unprecedented five weeks, a record that would not be broken until a six-week revival of *The Plough and the Stars* in 1942. The popular reception of the urban plays demonstrates how audiences drove their success, and how their popularity impacted the evolution of Abbey Theatre policies.

Depictions of urban Ireland and its social distinctions have changed over time, but not nearly as radically as expected considering the significant political and socioeconomic transformations occurring during the first half of the twentieth century. What remains constant

5. All Abbey box office receipts referenced herein are from the Abbey Theatre Archive (ATA), Dublin: ATA/FIN/6 (vol. 1: 1920–1925); ATA ATC/FIN/5 (vol. 2: 1925–1932); and ATC/FIN/34 (vol. 3: 1932–1951).

is a simultaneous working through and resistance to the imagined and fantastic that is analogous to the "ambiguity between representation as both an aesthetic and political process" (Murphy 2008, 5) that Paul Murphy finds in Irish drama of the period. This opposition changes in almost direct correlation to political and cultural forces of power. The urban plays seldom whisper for permission to be noticed. Their messages are largely self-reflective of the city and, like urban actions, hardly ever subtle. Helen Lojek reminds us, "playwrights do not select dramatic sites arbitrarily and . . . stage spaces are not casual backgrounds, but deliberate reinforcements of important themes" (2011, 5). The urban themes the Abbey directors selected for staging are diverse. As varied as the urban repertoire is, aggressiveness is a shared quality, and one reason they appear so deliberately chosen for inclusion in Abbey productions at very specific points in the nation's history. Still, the Abbey's motive for staging them remains open to interpretation. Although the themes of the urban plays remain fairly consistent (societal and economic disenfranchisement dominate), the political targets fluctuate over time in their dominant focus between the very local and the more national in scope. But one must consider the intent of both the playwright and the Abbey in challenging various political and economic power bases, and, as the following chapters will explore, their intentions do not always appear to be one and the same.

# 2 Second Cities

## *The Urban Plays of Belfast, Cork, and Galway*

THE APRIL 26, 2012, edition of the *Irish Times* highlighted the 2011 census results with the headline "Three-fifths live in urban areas," with the five most populated cities listed as Dublin, Cork, Limerick, Galway, and Waterford. This result likely surprised very few. The path to the 2011 census began in 1901, when 31 percent of Irish citizens were living in towns with populations in excess of two thousand people (more than double the amount from 1841, the first year such statistics were compiled) (Vaughan and Fitzpatrick 1978, 27). The numbers were smaller and what is now Northern Ireland was part of the mix, but the 1901 census contained a city ranking not very different from the one conducted in 2011. At the beginning of the twentieth century, the island's most populated cities were Belfast, Dublin, Cork, Derry, Limerick, Waterford, and Galway. In theory then, the inclination would be to consider Dublin a second city of the island, just as it was the "second city in His Majesty's dominions" (O'Brien 1982, 3) with the Act of Union over a century earlier. But population alone does not designate second-city status. Industry, cultural centrality, and political influence are equally relevant (Hodos 2007). Now, as in 1901, "second city identity is constructed in large part via comparisons with other cities. These comparisons position the city above, below, and parallel to other cities" (ibid., 328). With Dublin as the capital remaining constant, it becomes the benchmark, overriding the higher population and stronger industrialization of Belfast.

Belfast, led by its shipyards and linen industry, was "at the height of its commercial and industrial power" (Goldring 1991, 34) in 1901, but Dublin's centrality to cultural and political influence led to Belfast's joining Cork and Galway among the second cities on the island of Ireland. Like most capital cities, Dublin was a magnet that drew anybody looking to make his or her mark in the arts, and the Abbey benefited greatly from the talent pool of such internal migrants. Although Dublin's "international image originated in phantom villages in the west of Ireland, its personnel increasingly came from the Belfast/Dublin/Cork touring axis" (Morash 2002, 147). These personnel contributed on the stage and behind the scenes, leaving an indelible mark on the Abbey's urban repertoire.

The Cork-born Lennox Robinson was the longest-serving manager in the early decades, and, as Christopher Morash notes, along with St. John Ervine, the "most prominent" (2002, 147). Robinson authored only three urban plays: *The Dreamers* and *The Critic*, both set entirely in Dublin, and *The Cross-Roads* (1909), which contains an important Dublin-set prologue. But Robinson directed fifteen, including *The Plough and the Stars* and the second-city plays *Mixed Marriage* and *The Labour Leader*. Although Robinson did not author any of the urban plays set outside of Dublin, he had a hand in all of them finding their way to the Abbey stage. Two—St. John Ervine's *Mixed Marriage* (1911) and Daniel Corkery's *The Labour Leader* (1919)—premiered during his two tenures as artistic director (1910 to 1914 and 1919 to 1921). The rest—Hugh Quinn's *Money* (1931), Frank O'Connor's *Moses' Rock* (1938) and *Time's Pocket* (1938), Nora MacAdam's *Birth of a Giant* (1940), Joseph Tomelty's *The End House* (1944), Walter Macken's *Mungo's Mansion*, and John Coulter's *The Drums Are Out* (1948)—all premiered while he was a member of the Abbey Board, a position he held from 1923 until his death in 1958.

Because Robinson championed so much of the urban repertoire, it is fitting that his first Abbey play, *The Cross-Roads*, contains a city scene and comparative commentary about city versus rural life. The prologue presents Co. Cork native Ellen McCarthy as a scrappy up-and-coming member of Dublin's Erin Debating Society. The men who run the Society are dismayed when she announces her withdrawal in order to return to Co. Cork: "I thought Dublin was the hub of the country; I thought it was the centre of nationalism and that if I wanted to work for Ireland I could do the best work up here—but I've found out my mistake. The few houses that we call Ballygurten . . . is more of a centre of nationalism than Dublin" (Robinson 1911, 14–15). Such a comment, addressing one of the contrasts between the "ideas of the country and the city" that Williams offers—particularly the concepts of mobility and isolation—is rarely spoken in a city setting. Ellen is disillusioned to discover that the city's centrality to ideas takes precedence over the ability to turn those notions into actions. She returns to the country, where action is privileged and where she expects to find greater opportunity to contribute to the nationalist cause. However, her retreat to the country leads her into a life of isolation, in direct contrast to the "idea of the country" that she sought to embrace.

Ellen foregoes romantic love in favor of an arranged marriage, through which she believes she can contribute to Ireland by implementing efficiencies on her new husband's farm and by starting a village cooperative to export fresh farm products to Dublin. When one of her suitors from the Society arrives in Cork some years later, finding her a poor, neglected, beaten wife, he proposes to take her away, and she initially agrees. This acceptance is short-lived. Self-sacrifice wins out in the end, culminating in what Robinson called "peasant tragedy of the most ruthless kind" (1942, 21). Ellen decides to remain in her loveless marriage, even though she knows that her commitment to putting Ireland ahead of her own happiness has resulted only in misery. The play subverts the concept of the city as a place of isolation, while simultaneously targeting the notion of martyrdom celebrated in *Cathleen ní Houlihan*. It calls to mind Synge's *In the Shadow of the Glen* (1903), a play that faced public opposition because of the farmer's wife's eagerness to be free of her loveless marriage. She is ultimately "forced to choose between an unimaginative farmer and a volatile wandering poet [a plot that] would be used again . . . later in *The Playboy of the Western World* (1907)" (Morash 2002, 121). In *The Cross-Roads*, though, the wandering poet is replaced by an idealistic Dubliner who offers security and love. Her rejecting him does not come across in any way as an anti-city position. Instead, it serves to present the rural life as having completely diminished any sense of hope Ellen once held for the nationalist cause. The periphery wins out, but it is a hollow victory and one that deeply criticizes that space.

Robinson was one of two Cork Realists to take a lead artistic role through 1951. The other, Frank O'Connor, had a stormier and more short-lived tenure, serving as managing director from 1935 to 1939, but he also contributed to the second-city repertoire. Of the Cork Realists—including Daniel Corkery, O'Connor, T. C. Murray, and Sean O'Faolain—who wrote plays that premiered at the Abbey, Corkery and O'Connor, whose paths first crossed when O'Connor was a young student of Corkery's, were the only ones to actively address the urban experience. T. C. Murray's *A Spot in the Sun* (1938) is set in Dublin, but the city is an innocuous backdrop to the pressures of young married life. This group, "who rose to prominence in the early 1910s, rebelled against the image of peasant Ireland propagated by the Abbey" (Malone 2010, 4) through "frank tragic and comic approaches to economic and social anxieties" (Trotter 2008, 51). The Cork City plays of these years are Corkery's *The Labour Leader*, O'Connor and Hugh Hunt's *Moses' Rock*, and O'Connor's *Time's Pocket*. Those authored and coauthored by O'Connor represent two-thirds of his Fenian trilogy, which examines major events during Ireland's struggle for independence. The two that include Cork City address the Parnell split (*Moses' Rock*) and the Civil War (*Time's Pocket*).[1] The Corkery play focuses on labor unrest on the Cork quays.

*The Labour Leader* is the least compelling and appears to be an attempt by the Abbey to perhaps capitalize on the success of A. Patrick Wilson's *The Slough* that was staged five years earlier and also featured a worker's strike and a Larkinesque figure as protagonist. But the

1. The third, the Dublin-set *The Invincibles* (about the Phoenix Park murders), was coauthored and directed by Hunt in 1937 and staged at the Abbey. It is discussed in chapter 5.

didactic Corkery fell far short of Wilson, and *The Labour Leader* did not appeal to critics or audiences. Several critics of the day pointed to its being entirely set in a union committee room as a major fault. Cork City is alternately praised and condemned, but its presence is entirely offstage, and the characters are so unsympathetic that it is difficult to feel support for their efforts to improve working conditions. Davna, the labor leader, is written so sanctimoniously that the character borders on parody. He sees himself as divinely inspired—"Fate speaks through me" (Corkery 1920, 35)—but has no time for the nuts-and-bolts union work of accounting and setting agendas. Though drawn as a sanctimonious character, his passionate speeches succeed in growing membership, while those who focus on details do so to their detriment. The bureaucrats ultimately fail in their power-struggle with Davna, who succeeds in retaining union leadership. Rhetoric winning out over labor would also, as discussed in chapter 7, be a recurring motif in the Dublin labor plays.

This play provides no sense of the city because the city never actually permeates the stage. Slum tenements are referred to as worker housing, but no set brings them to audience view. *The Slough* succeeded in part on a familial subplot that brought Dublin slum conditions to life (the acts alternate between committee room and a worker's tenement home), but *The Labour Leader* may have failed, in part, because "critics found a naturalistic portrayal of a committee meeting as boring as a real committee meeting" (Maume 1993, 64).

Unlike Corkery, O'Connor (both alone and with Hunt) favors an intimacy of character interactions within inner worlds. This quality served him well in his celebrated short stories and novels, but it often posed a stumbling block in his stage plays. O'Connor biographer James Matthews observes, "Place is never the primary dimension in an O'Connor story; setting for him is atmosphere, emerging as a complement to the voice of the story. Thus most of the stories are wrapped in darkness, casting the disarray and desolation in silhouetted relief" (1983, 68). As a result, his stage efforts often rely on melodramatic moments, in an attempt to portray characters' inner conflicts and to fortify interactions with characters that carry emotional burdens.

*Moses' Rock* premiered in 1938 and marked the third collaboration between O'Connor and Hunt. As is often the case when the Parnell split serves as a dramatic backdrop, this play is essentially a critique of Ireland's Catholic middle classes. The Cork City of this play is home to the fine house of Cady O'Leary, whose early life as "a bare-footed boy from Carrignagoshil" (Hunt and O'Connor 1983, 48) has been reduced to cliché in his never-ending pursuit of ever-upward mobility. His immediate family serves as a microcosm of Irish society's shift from authentic to constructed experiences, with church politics often the catalyst for bitter cynicism. Authenticity fades from one generation to the next. Grannie O'Leary still speaks Irish and laments the famine; O'Leary is a successful merchant who begins as a Parnell supporter but adjusts his opinions to fit the prevailing clerical winds; his daughter, Joan, just wants out of the hypocrisy, leaving the play at its conclusion on a train bound for Dublin and the arms of a British soldier. The shifting political allegiances of O'Leary's Cork community show financial opportunity replacing any sense of loyalty as the plot progresses. As the character of Dr. Corney Jackson states, "the priests always have the last word" (ibid., 81). The new "realist philosophy" (ibid., 85) of capital and opportunity embraced by O'Leary and Coughlan (the now anti-Parnellite suitor of Joan's hand) near the play's conclusion ultimately disgusts Joan to the point of her abandoning Cork city entirely. The character of Joan might be read as an urbanized female Ireland. The young woman moves from a sweet-natured convent girl to a cynical woman who runs off the night before her wedding to an anti-Parnellite to marry a British soldier in order to escape local politics and insincerity.

*Time's Pocket* portrays more than a decade in the life of Nance, a young woman whose high spirits and passion are a threat to local clergy and conservative members of her community. Against the backdrop of the Civil War, she falls in love with a young republican, Dargan, who is eventually imprisoned. Left alone and pregnant, she is forced to marry Sullivan, a man who feels that because he "saved" her from disgrace, she is his possession to abuse as he wishes. When Dargan is released from prison, he returns to Cork to find Nance a beaten woman, old before her time. Upon learning about the existence of his son, he takes them both from the abusive home to live with him. Dargan's return gives Nance back some of her spirit, and she stands up to the priest, husband, and community members who "are turning the whole city against" them (O'Connor 1938, 63). The priest and Sullivan lead the charge in threatening to destroy her for living outside the norms of society. When the community, led by the parish priest, imposes its will again, it appears the couple will finally succumb to the city's imposed conservatism. But Dargan's former allies come to his aid, and the commitment he showed to his nation is rewarded with the promise that he can continue to lead a quiet life with Nance and their son on the edge of the city. Placing them on the city's edge is an obvious analogy to their status on the margins of respectability. This placement is unusual in the urban repertoire, where Dublin in particular tends to provide room for those who do not acquiesce to society's demands (the "spoiled priest" of *The Man Who Missed the Tide* comes to mind). The play's critique of conservative Catholicism is so muted by its assault and attention to Nance's victimization that it gets lost. When it does emerge, it is unexplained and confusing. This repeated disruption, as well as an anticlerical message during the conservative 1930s, likely contributed to the play's lack of success.

Like the Cork Realists, those involved with the Belfast-based Ulster Literary Theatre (ULT) impacted the Abbey administratively and artistically. In some respects, the ULT's social realism plays out-Abbeyed the Abbey in their proliferation of western settings (in the ULT's case, Co. Down) and adoption of Irish myth. Many of its plays assert "a rejection of the North as simply the land of shipyards, factories and mills" (McNulty 2008, 124) that is very much aligned with the early Abbey's reclamations. As in Dublin, Belfast had its share of the "periphery-dominated-centre" to which Kiberd alludes. Although the ULT's repertoire included some Belfast-set works (several of which played at the Abbey), many of the best known, including *Mixed Marriage*, were offered to the Abbey by writers perhaps looking to maximize the odds that their plays would make it to the stage.

The plays set in the city of Belfast—St. John Ervine's *Mixed Marriage*, Hugh P. Quinn's *Money*,[2] Nora MacAdam's *Birth of a Giant*, Joseph Tomelty's *The End House*, and John Coulter's *The Drums Are Out*—are primarily sectarian-related melodramas, with west Belfast serving as the prevailing setting. Only *Money* breaks from this dominant theme and locale. The *Irish Times* reviewer found *Money* essentially a "Belfast version of the Boyle family." Ellen McConaghy, married to a blustery mess who prefers time with his pal Ducksy to work, makes ends meet by renting her front room out for wakes and tapping into the deceased's insurance money. The plot concerns Ellen's failed attempts to marry her daughter to Blaney, the grocer who, although considerably older and dealing with a serious drinking problem, is her idea of a good match because his shop does a steady trade. St. John Ervine acknowledged the character and language parallels between *Juno and the Paycock* and *Money*, but championed *Money* with the distinction that *Juno*'s Boyle and Joxer "have the tongues of men in whom romance has become rancid: theirs is the speech of decay. But Mickey McConaghy and 'Ducksy' Dugan . . . have the tongues of people to whom reality is more than romance" (Quinn 1932, ix). That is a fair assessment, but one that means Abbey audiences preferred the more romantic "decay" that *Juno and the Paycock* offered. In 1931 the five-day run of *Money* (on a shared bill with Shaw's *Blanco Posnet*) earned about £81; the three nights *Juno* played grossed over £229.

The one quality all the Belfast plays share is the attempt to reconcile generational division. Ervine, MacAdam, Tomelty, and Coulter present the issue of sectarianism in Belfast from a familial point of view. For the most part, they offer fairly one-dimensional portrayals, presenting Catholic families as victims of oppression who react to their condition with drink and violence, and Protestants as oppressors who are cavalier in their positions of power. Within several of the plays, however,

2. Published as *Mrs. McConaghy's Money* to avoid confusion with an older play of the same title.

such stereotypes are tempered with subtleties that provide deeper commentary on the social conditions of west Belfast, and present attempts by younger generations to question the reasons beyond religion in the sectarian world they stand to inherit. This is most notable in *Mixed Marriage* and *Birth of a Giant*, when younger men contemplate the unrest at their workplaces. Both plays embrace realism and draw on historical events. As Lauren Arrington notes, Emmet Larkin and Frances Sheehy-Skeffington recognized the 1907 Belfast dockers' strike as the source material for *Mixed Marriage* (2011, 61) and, more directly, *Birth of a Giant* is set in 1855, when sectarian unrest among shipyard workers was simmering. In both plays, unrest is dramatized through younger workers considering that management is pitting Catholic and Protestant workers against each other as a ploy to hide the real issue of poor working conditions. But their efforts to encourage older men to see that working together across religious divides can improve the community as a whole are unsuccessful. Both plays end with the death of a young optimist and the impression that nothing is likely to change. However, as Ben Levitas points out, in voicing opposition, "the challenge itself was a sign of change" (2003, 140).

The Belfast play that provides the most multidimensional portrayal of both sides of the equation is John Coulter's *The Drums Are Out*. Set in the Shankhill–Falls Road district during the early 1920s, this community-focused play is based partly on the author's own experiences of growing up Protestant in the Catholic community of west Belfast. Its Abbey run began on July 12, 1948. This was a symbolic opening, with July 12 marking the anniversary of the Battle of the Boyne and the height of the North's "marching season" by the Orange Order. *The Drums Are Out* proved a critical and popular success, with the scheduled one-week run extended to five weeks. The plot centers on the Sheridan family and the roles that father and daughter play in the Troubles. The police sergeant father is a loyalist; his daughter, Jean, a teacher, is a republican. Her parents know of her republican position and agree to disagree on the issue. It is not a point of contention within the family. However, neither of Jean's parents is aware that she is secretly married to Denis, an IRA man on the run, and is pregnant with his child. When street fighting breaks out (offstage), Denis arrives at the Sheridan home to seek shelter because he has been shot and, with Jean, tells her parents about their marriage and her pregnancy. Sheridan keeps his son-in-law hidden until his fellow IRA men (disguised as policemen) arrive to take him out of Belfast, where he is being hunted by the police. Sheridan feels guilty for assisting Denis and for allowing his duty as a father to override his duty as a policeman. To save his neighbors the indignity of house-to-house searches, Sheridan decides to report harboring Denis. The play ends with Jean exclaiming, "we should pray our babies never would be born into a mess like this, except to change it" (Coulter 1971, 77).

What is noteworthy about *The Drums Are Out* is that this melodrama is the Belfast-set play concentrating on the Troubles to most transcend stereotypes. With the exception of one officer, none of the principal characters is one-dimensional. Denis is committed to his republican activities, but not at the expense of the family's safety. Jean is committed to her support of republican causes, but is neither a strident activist nor interested in pushing her beliefs onto her loyalist parents. Finally, Sheridan struggles with his responsibilities to job, family, and neighbors. When he ultimately decides to be true to his job, he risks losing the pension that he is only one year from receiving, in order to be able to live with himself. This representation of decent humanity and cooperation across the Belfast divide, although glimpsed in *Mixed Marriage*, had not previously been central to a play on the Abbey stage. The issue of job security permeates this play and, like the labor issues at the forefront of *Mixed Marriage* and *Birth of a Giant*, becomes one component shared with many of the plays set in Dublin.

The countryside of Co. Galway is a dominant location in the Abbey's rural plays, but the city of Galway appears only once through 1951, in Walter Macken's *Mungo's Mansion*. A novelist, playwright, and actor, Macken was no stranger to Ireland's theatrical communities. In Galway, he was a leading force behind Irish-language theater and an active member of Taibhdhearc na Gaillimhe. But he was also well known in Dublin, where he performed in many productions, including several at the Abbey. His later relationship with the Abbey included serving as artistic advisor/assistant manager as the company was preparing for the July 1966 reopening. Macken's son cites "the stress of coping with the workload in the Abbey Theatre and his dislocation from the west of Ireland" (Macken 2009, 425) as the reasons for his resigning within a year.

Set in the Galway slums, *Mungo's Mansion* is "both a strong evocation of slum life and a strong condemnation of it" (Hogan 1967, 66). It represents a somewhat gender-based generational divide between the romanticism of the father and the practical realism of his wife and children (most vocally by eldest daughter, Nellie). Mungo King is, as his surname suggests, very much the king of his castle. His castle, however, is a derelict tenement on Buttermilk Lane in Galway's inner city, where he was born and raised, and "all the divils in hell wouldn't drag" him away (Macken 1964, 8). He is initially presented as an indifferent father, husband, friend, and neighbor; but as events unfold, it becomes clear that he is simply afraid to leave the Lane for a promised new council house. His identity is deeply entrenched in his home, and to leave it would mean relinquishing the status that his familiarity in the Lane provides. But following a string of unfortunate events—including his son's being diagnosed with diphtheria and an upstairs neighbor's going mad and committing murder—he begins to agree with his wife and Nellie about leaving the Lane. When the horse upon which he placed a bet leads to Mungo's winning a sweepstakes fortune of £2000, the decision is settled.

Paul Murphy notes the parallels between *Mungo's Mansion* and *Juno and the Paycock*, both in how Mungo banters with neighbors and in the setting, where "the Dublin slum-dweller reappears in a Galway tenement" (2008, 109). Such transplantation of the poor is one example of fluidity among locations in the urban plays. The plays tend to contain local references depending upon location, but associations between poverty and urban settings remain constant. However, it appears that the Galway slum location, although popular with Abbey audiences, provoked some degree of protest. Macken felt compelled to address this protest in a note he wrote in the 1948 publication of *Vacant Possession* (a play that was rejected by the Abbey for "being too similar to *Mungo's Mansion*" [Macken 2009, 207]): "Lest readers of this play and *Mungo's Mansion* should visualise the city of Galway as a town of tenements and condemned houses, I hasten to make it clear that Galway Corporation is one of the most efficient bodies in the land, that they have eradicated slums and have almost abolished tenements, and that it would be virtually impossible to find the 'Ganthry'[3] in the up-to-date city of to-day [*sic*]" (Macken 1948, v). Noble as this defense of his home city is, *Mungo's Mansion* is set in 1946, and the slums were still very much in evidence when Macken wrote his comments in 1948. Also prevalent were the childhood illnesses and high unemployment that the play explores. However, on the early Abbey stage, Dublin was the dominant home for dramatizing these ills and conflicts within Irish urban society.

Popular reaction to plays set in Cork, Belfast, and Galway was uneven, and only *Mixed Marriage* had longevity on the Abbey stage. It was revived as late as 1940, a notable four-decade presence in the repertoire. *The End House* and *The Drums Are Out* were both enormously successful at the box office when they premiered (ATC/FIN/34, vol. 3), but neither remained in the rotation. John Coulter wrote that the Abbey intended to revive his play in 1951, but the fire derailed those plans. Manager Ernest Blythe, though still interested in a revival after the fire, according to Coulter, felt the company's temporary home, the Queen's Theatre, "was not the theatre for it" (Coulter 1971, 4). As will be discussed in the remaining chapters, the Dublin plays were also inconsistent in their ability to find traction, but, unlike the second-city plays, these were given more opportunities to be heard, and, as a result, there is a tendency for them to endure in the Abbey repertoire.

3. Ganthry is the name of the crumbling house that is home to the primary characters in *Vacant Possession*.

# 3 W. F. Casey

## *A Joycean Dublin*

IN ONE RESPECT, the early Abbey was like any new theatrical enterprise: it required a financial base to survive at least long enough to find its footing. Subscribers provided the initial financial resources to launch the ILT, and the combination of inexpensive rentals and short seasons kept things afloat when, in 1902, the ILT merged with Willie Fay's INDC. But the desire to secure a permanent home with full seasons required a source with capital reserves that could be relied upon to build the company. The Abbey's angel came in the person of Annie Horniman, whose promise of an annual subsidy to begin in 1904 secured the Abbey's lease on Dublin's north side. From the start, however, the relationship was "enormously complicated by Annie Horniman's facile belief that it was possible to omit politics altogether [and she] interfered constantly in [the Abbey's] management" (Murray 1997, 4). Such interference came to a climax in 1910, when she finally revoked the subsidy. Its termination was, on the surface, abruptly dramatic, but circumstances leading to the decision can be traced back to at least 1906. In February of that year, Lady Gregory alerted Synge that Horniman had made a particularly "exasperating move": she "demands to see a list of all plays proposed to be played in the Theatre, and will refuse its use if she disapproves of plays, that is, if there are propagandist ones" (Hogan and Kilroy 1978, 62). Her overarching imposition on the broad issue of repertoire proved a gateway to increasingly specific demands and disruptions, all of which helped open the door for the plays of W. F. Casey.

Two of her earliest targets were Willie Fay and Synge, with whom she initially found fault personally. A few months after her demand to review new plays, their relationships with Abbey actresses Brigid O'Dempsey and Molly Allgood sent her "on the warpath" against Fay and, in September, she fired off a letter to Yeats complaining that Synge "has proved himself to be no good" (Frazier 1990, 157). On a professional level, she complained constantly about Fay's competency as stage manager, taking exception to what she perceived as his unwillingness to acquiesce to her authority. "She settled on putting Fay in his place," Adrian Frazier summarizes; "he was just a paid actor, open to dismissal, nothing more than that, but Fay insisted on acting as though he was her equal, even in theatrical matters her superior" (1990, 179). Her relationship with Synge endured on tenuous lines, but the mutual animosity between her and Fay never subsided. Both Willie and Frank Fay, who were instrumental in bringing the naturalistic style of acting to the Abbey players, would leave the company in 1908.

Horniman wrote Synge that she found *The Playboy of the Western World* "splendid" (Hogan and Kilroy 1978, 161), and her initial reaction to the public uproar when the play premiered on January 26, 1907, bordered on glee. But the play provided her simmering dislike of Synge a convenient outlet nonetheless. When she learned "that during performance some actors had hissed the behavior of the drunken students from Trinity College who had come to defend King, Empire and the Rights of Artists, Horniman scolded those involved" (Frazier 1990, 218). She deemed the hissing by the actors political expression. Such behavior, she asserted, was "low political spite [and] the directors should do their best to prevent conduct in the actors which would justify my closing the theatre. From the very first and ceaselessly I have held firm to the position that *I will have no politics*" (Hogan and Kilroy 1978, 161). With Willie Fay in the title role as Christy Mahon, Horniman's wrath satisfied her disdain for both the actor and the playwright/Abbey director in one fell swoop.

The well-documented outcry against *The Playboy of the Western World* resulted in 1907 beginning on a financially ominous note that Yeats's public response did little to alleviate: "Yeats issued a statement declaring that *The Playboy* would be kept on stage for its entire run of a week . . . and notified the police to be on hand in case of disturbances" (Frazier 1990, 215). The directors defended the play and Synge, but criticized audiences, press attacks, and those nationalist organizations, including Sinn Féin, that called for a boycott. But as Ben Levitas argues, "the directors, following their defiant rhetoric, had to quickly alter their ground. Principles of 'art for art's sake' could not be followed indiscriminately while the Sinn Féin boycott had decimated attendance" (2002a, 38). This, combined with Horniman's escalating complaints and intrusions, put the company on notice that her subsidy would likely not be renewed when its terms expired at the end of 1910.[1]

Conversations between the Fay brothers and Abbey architect-diarist Joseph Holloway indicate that the Fays viewed this as a need, as much as an opportunity, to bring more commercially popular plays to the Abbey stage:

> [the Fay brothers] had put up with much that was really at variance with their basic concepts of theatre. Yeats' mysticism, the obscurity of some of his dramatic verse, and experiments such as pitched verse speaking had little appeal to them. Nor did they enjoy facing a howling mob night after night in order to keep *The Playboy of the Western World* on the boards. When Yeats insisted on challenging that mob, and when attendance figures began to drop drastically as a result, a spirit of rebellion began to set in. Disheartening as it was to play to empty seats, the Fays were bothered even more by the thought that no money was coming into the box office . . . to them the principal significance of the [probable] loss of Miss Horniman's subsidy was that salaries were going to have to be paid through ticket sales. It was obviously going to be necessary to win back the "man in the street."

1. This ending proved true when, in May 1910, the Abbey did not close in respect for the death of King Edward VII. In a May 11, 1910, letter to the editor of the *Freeman's Journal*, she announced that "unless proper regret is shown in the Press by the directors, my subsidy to the National Theatre Society will cease immediately." Finding their explanations and response wanting, the subsidy ended.

> And the only way that could be accomplished was by performing "popular" plays. (Flannery 1976, 226–27)

By August, Holloway reports, the Abbey was "anxious to get [William] Boyle's plays back into their repertoire" (1967, 93), a desire certainly based on the need to establish a solid rotation that would increase ticket sales in preparation for the loss of the subsidy. Boyle's *The Building Fund* (1905) and *The Eloquent Dempsey* (1906) were very popular with audiences, and when he pulled his plays in protest against *The Playboy of the Western World*, there was a visible gap left in the repertoire. Holloway reprints a letter Boyle wrote to his friend, the literary historian D. J. O'Donoghue, in which it is clear that Boyle was as concerned with his personal income as the Abbey was with its box office and that he took some delight in refusing the directors' request that he reconsider allowing them to stage his works: "the Abbey folks are amusing. Of course, I won't have any more to do with them under any condition. But the suggested payment! . . . They must be fools pure and simple to take me for a fool of such magnitude. Still I'm glad you didn't give them a direct answer, as I'd like to have the pleasure of giving a direct refusal" (Holloway 1967, 93). With Boyle refusing their request and ticket sales in a lull, it became clear that "it would be necessary to produce more deliberately popular work" (Flannery 1982, 257).

Enter William Francis Casey. He wrote the first two Dublin plays to premiere on the Abbey stage and was responsible for improving the theater's finances (however temporarily). Although identified by numerous critics and Abbey stalwarts as one of the most promising Abbey dramatists of the time, Casey wrote only two plays. Both plays foreground and then suppress the dreamer, and, in doing so, subvert the imaginative. Casey's protagonists take ownership of their ambitions, but in juxtaposing their dreams against an urban landscape, the author presents dreaming as an attempt to survive in a city that demands conformity. As Casey's plays sometimes shared double bills with Yeats and Gregory plays, including *Cathleen ní Houlihan*, it is an arresting contrast to say the least, as though audiences were put in a position of choosing between an ideal and the mundane.

The Casey plays were among the most popular to premiere in the first decade. *The Man Who Missed the Tide*, the first Abbey play to be identified by Abbey publicity and critics as "urban" or "metropolitan," was revived six times within a year of its February 1908 premiere and an additional sixteen times through 1923. Its success led to the Abbey's requesting a second play, and *The Suburban Groove* premiered on October 1. Subsequently, Casey revised the first two acts of *The Man Who Missed the Tide*, and the new version was staged at the Abbey shortly thereafter. Like *The Man Who Missed the Tide*, *The Suburban Groove* enjoyed numerous revivals. It was staged twenty-six times through 1932. Both plays deal with middle-class suburban Dublin, a "phase of Irish life," Lennox Robinson observed, "which had not hitherto been touched on" (1951, 59) at the Abbey. The sociopolitical climate may have contributed to their popularity. As Ben Levitas notes, this post-*Playboy* period was marked by an "expansion in confidence of middle-class ideology at the expense of dispirited marginal movements" (2002b, 42). Perhaps such emerging middle-class confidence was recognized by both the keenly observant Casey and the financially concerned Abbey directors as timely subjects to interrogate on the stage.

Casey was an unlikely candidate to resuscitate the Abbey coffers. By the time his plays premiered in 1908, he had spent his early adulthood at Trinity College, studying medicine for two years before transferring to law, the school from which he graduated in 1906. His legal career was short-lived. He is quoted in his *Times* obituary of April 22, 1957, as once distilling it to "one year, one brief, one guinea." In 1913 he left Dublin for London, where he enjoyed a long and celebrated career at the *Times* that culminated in his serving as editor (1948 to 1952). *Times* chronicles are peppered with colleagues' memories of Casey as a low-key, personable journalist who, although respected for the quality of his work, possessed a healthy ambivalence about his profession and his own ascent through the ranks. These traits appear to have been long-standing: "even [during his time at the Abbey, he] had an attitude very different from that of most proud young dramatists towards their masterpieces. During a rehearsal of one of Casey's plays an actor stumbled several times over two quite important lines. 'Oh well, if they trouble you, let's leave them out,' said Casey. 'I don't suppose they really matter'" (McDonald 1984, 165). His easygoing attitude must have been welcomed by Abbey principals at a time when the company was under financial and political pressure. In addition to his contributions as a playwright, Casey also briefly served as the Abbey secretary. Frank Fay's son, Gerald, recounts that Casey had "good stories to tell of the ingenious way the theatre was run even four years after it opened. One of his best illustrates the alleged unworldliness of Yeats, for when Casey presented at the bank certain cheques for salaries and other expenses the cashier brought them back, puzzled, to enquire 'Mr. Casey: why does your director sign his cheques 'yours sincerely, W. B. Yeats'?" (Fay 1958, 138). Gregory, in particular, seems to have taken to the young writer, inviting him to her Galway home, Coole Park, and encouraging his efforts. She wrote to Synge in August 1908 that Casey was there getting *The Suburban Groove* "into final shape" and sharing her optimism that it would "be popular" with audiences (Saddlemyer 1982, 289). Her instincts were good: Casey's plays were a primary reason that 1908 was the first year that "box office receipts [began] to cover expenses" (Flannery 1982, 257).

However, Casey's work would likely "not have even been considered" (ibid.) had the Abbey not been facing a box office drought and the likely revocation of the Horniman subsidy. As James Flannery notes, "In order to survive, starting with the 1908–1909 season the Abbey began to produce on a regular basis the very kind of stage Irish parodies of life in Ireland that the whole movement was originally designed to combat . . . Ironically, such bastions of high culture as *The Irish Times* applauded this new departure. In an editorial published in August 1910, the *Times* declared that the middle class comedies . . . of writers like W. F. Casey . . . were 'of greater educational value than whole Iliads of prehistoric Irish myth, or entire worlds of Irish fancy'" (1982, 262). Although the *Times* editorial referenced by Flannery also mentions the popular success of provincial satires by William Boyle, which were rivaled only by Casey's plays in terms of financial success during this time period, the negative commentary on "prehistoric Irish myth" bears consideration. The *Times* is clearly questioning the relevance of this element in the Abbey's repertoire, and box office receipts suggest that audiences were questioning it as well. As Holloway noted some years later (April 25, 1912), the plays of both Boyle and Casey were looked down upon by a certain type of drama critic, but the public disagreed:

> That [a play] is literary does not matter a straw if the dramatic instinct is absent. Most of those who judge the plays at the Abbey are literary critics pure and simple, and have little sense of the theatre—hence the puffery of literary craftsmanship and the belittling of true dramatic work. To be successful as a dramatist on the Abbey stage is to be despised by the highbrows. Boyle and Casey, who know well how to write successful plays and draw audiences as well, are no class with the high and mighty type of non-theatrical critic brought into being by the production of undramatic literary plays. They can only see merit in the unactable. If the turn of phrase pleases, then its dramatic worth may go hang. (Holloway 1967, 153)

What Casey's plays contained to bring forth such notice was a stagnant and provincial Dublin society determined to suppress change or outside influence. But his plays also showed young people trying to make their way, dealing with local pressures that would have been readily recognizable to any Dublin audience. These plays provide insight into the evolution of Dublin portrayals in the Abbey repertoire as well as into audience reception in the Abbey's first decade.

*The Man Who Missed the Tide* is the more satirical of Casey's plays.[2] Set amid provincial life, it spans four years and focuses on three men: the pompous Dr. Quinn; the "spoiled priest" James Walsh, "whose

2. Script and promptbook of *The Man Who Missed the Tide* remain missing (possibly destroyed in the 1951 Abbey fire). Summary notes of the play are taken from the *Irish News* review of February 14, 1908 (NLI MS. 25, 489) and the *Freemans Journal* review of February 14, 1908 (Hogan and Kilroy 1978, 213–15).

hesitancy at the beginning of his career proves his ruin"; and the practical Martin Kelly. The lives of the three young men intersect when Quinn moves from Dublin to a northern town to set up his medical practice. The first two acts take place in the Quinn home and the third is set in the bar of a Dublin hotel. Quinn is described in the *Irish News* review as a man who, because he spent years in Dublin, can "look down with fine contempt on the futilities of provincial life, though he is provincial to the backbone." The man referred to in the title as having "missed the tide" is James Walsh. He begins the play described as a spoiled priest, denoting his status as a failed clerical student, and is considered something of a dreamer by his surrounding community. He is a dreamer because he wishes to work in a profession for which he is passionate. This desire is impractical by community standards: one should do what one sets out for initially (not change paths) or what has been preordained by birth order or other familial plans. His hometown rejects him for turning his back on the priesthood, and he spends the rest of the play facing similar rejections, personally and professionally, as societal retribution for not doing what he was supposed to do. As the February 14, 1908, *Irish News* review put it, "He never recovers lost ground, and progressing from one failure to another, winds up a wreck of humanity in a Dublin hotel bar." His dreams of a journalism career have been replaced by dreams of a big win at the race track. In this play, Dublin represents the last chance of opportunity for a young man who has spent four years being told there is no place for him. His ambition remains unrealized; societal pressure to conform has killed it. He missed his one opportunity and another will not be offered.

Navigation between professional aspirations and domestic expectations are also at the heart of *The Suburban Groove. The Suburban Groove* was billed as a "mild satire" (Casey [1908], n.p.). On the surface, this three-act comedy is a light glimpse into the conventions of marriage as viewed by James O'Connor, a middle-class civil servant. O'Connor encourages a young family friend, Dick Dalton, to avoid romantic entanglements, because marriage would kill Dalton's plan to quit his drab (but secure) insurance job in Dublin to pursue a journalism career in London. O'Connor warns Dalton that if he marries he will end up like O'Connor: a middle-aged man full of regret for giving up his own ambitions, leaving him unfulfilled and sleepwalking through a safe suburban routine (the "groove" of the play's title). The family is composed of a practical father, a silly wife, and an insightful daughter, Una. Una sees through her mother's upwardly mobile illusions and those of Claude, the man her mother would like her to marry. Una is drawn to Dalton's ambition not to settle for the mundane simply because it is safe. But on the night before Dalton is to depart for London, he professes his love for her. She reciprocates, and they resolve to stay in Dublin. The closing scene suggests Casey's intended satire of middle-class marriage conventions to be more an observation of men who dream big but live small. The play, however, stalls in its satirical intent by not criticizing this social stratum. It merely observes it with ironic detachment.

What this play brought to the Abbey, apart from a Dublin setting, was a twist on the mythological. When mythological tales are evoked in the rural plays, it is primarily to elevate nation or community, and the result is, to varying degrees, palliative. The myth of *The Suburban Groove* is that women pressure men into giving up dreams in exchange for marriage and stability, but the underlying message is that men are searching for an excuse not to take risks, and women conveniently serve that end. The *Sinn Féin* review of October 10, 1908, found the "commercial undertaking" a "trifling attempt at drama" and suggested that if the Abbey directors have nothing better to offer, "it would be much more dignified and whole-some to keep their theatre shut" (Hogan and Kilroy 1978, 224). *Sinn Féin* was, however, the dissenting opinion. Joseph Holloway was in attendance when *Groove* premiered on October 1, 1908, and recorded that "Casey scored another bull's eye" and that *Groove* was enthusiastically received by a full house: "There was a splendid audience, and they took kindly to the comedy almost from the first, hearty applause following each act, and loud and prolonged calls for author at the end" (1967, 115). Its popular reception appears to have reminded Yeats of the Abbey's ongoing stalemate with William Boyle. Yeats summoned Holloway to a chat after the opening night performance where "Boyle was the subject of our conversation, and his plays and the recent unsuccessful negotiations of the theatre with his agent to secure them was [*sic*] gone over by Yeats. I could learn from all he said that he was in fear and trembling that the Theatre of Ireland would secure them, and the Abbey wanted them solely to prevent that happening" (ibid.). Holloway told Yeats that he recently had a discussion with Boyle about this and that Boyle claimed to have already signed a ten-year contract with his new agent "to place his plays at a certain percentage" and "the opportunity of [the Abbey] securing them on reasonable terms had slipped by forever" (ibid.). "Forever" in Abbey and Boyle time turned out to be roughly five years. In 1912, the Abbey staged Boyle's *Family Failing*, and revivals of this play as well as *The Building Fund*, *The Eloquent Dempsey*, and *Mineral Workers* were staged at the Abbey through the 1920s.

Casey's *Groove* initiates two qualities of early Abbey drama that span its introduction of a middle-class urban setting: paralysis and urban myth. The October 23, 1908, *Irish Times* review observed that although the laughs were many, "there was much in the dialogue as well as in the characters and situation, which is as painful as it is true, for Mr. Casey's tale spares none of those classes to whom the paralysis of ideal and of anything beautiful in life is due." The notion of Dublin as a city of paralysis is one most readily identified with James Joyce, but one that Casey explored six years before the full publication of *Dubliners*.[3] However, where Joyce overtly identified the external forces of nation, Church, and family as pressures that imposed paralysis, Casey keeps the paralysis either internal (*Groove*) or nonspecifically societal (*Tide*) and does not venture deeply into its contributing factors. Because Casey did not "name names," we are left to interpret O'Connor's and Dalton's fears of risk as isolated inertia on the part of Dublin men both old and young. The script revisions suggest that Casey's original intent

3. Serialization of some of the stories that comprised *Dubliners* began in 1904; however, the full collection was not published until 1914. The story most aligned with Casey's plays is "A Little Cloud," which was completed in 1906, but not published until 1914.

was slightly more somber. He wrote O'Connor as a representative of a risk-free generation that recognizes the frustration that can emerge from safety, but is incapable of imparting this wisdom to the next generation. Such gloominess was noted in the October 2, 1908, *Irish Mail* review, which described O'Connor as "an old and disillusioned civil servant with a plentiful harvest of regrets," and by a second *Irish Mail* critic as a man who "has fought his battle and lost," the "battle" being one waged by the individual against society.

Although *Tide* is set primarily in a small town rather than in the city, the source of the town's provincialism is identified as containing urban roots (in the character of Dr. Quinn). James Walsh is forced toward Dublin in an effort to find a home where his ambitions can be realized. But even in Dublin he is forced to revert to a type that society permits. Only relegated to the margins, he is permitted to exist as a man with a drink in one hand and the racing sheets in the other. A vehicle of unrealized ambition, Walsh has been silenced and is safely out of mainstream society's path. In the end, the capital city is just as provincial as the small northern town from which Walsh has fled.

The popularity of the Dublin plays may rest on a rejection of the backward glance and rural community structures that were cornerstones of the dominant repertoire. Although many rural plays were heartily received by Abbey audiences, copious volumes of critical analysis document a resistance as well. Some plays, including Synge's *The Well of the Saints* (1905) and *The Playboy of the Western World*, were famously met with outrage as an affront to sacred national ideologies. Others, including Yeats's *The Countess Cathleen*, were challenged for their disregard for the power of the Catholic Church. As will be discussed in remaining chapters, many of the Abbey plays set in urban Ireland touch on controversial subject matter including clerical and nationalist subjects, but for the most part they avoid any mass outcry. The notable exceptions—M. M. Brennan's *A Leprechaun in the Tenement* (1922), *The Plough and the Stars*, and Seamus Byrne's *Design for a Headstone* (1950)—faced public opposition because of issues that had nothing to do with specifically urban concerns. As reviews discussed in chapter 6 attest, *Leprechaun* was opposed for its representation of the mentally handicapped; *The Plough and the Stars* for challenging nationalist symbols, icons, and events; and *Design for a Headstone* for "communist sentiments expressed by one of the characters" (MacAnna 1971, 99). Interestingly, such controversies became less detrimental to the Abbey box office as the decades passed. Tomás MacAnna observed that *Design for a Headstone* "had a longer run than intended; whereas earlier audiences had stayed away following alleged outrage, the tendency now [1950] was to throng in to find out what it was all about" (1971, 99). There has never been an urban play, let alone a Dublin play, that was challenged in the press simply for how it portrayed the city, or, as in the case of Lennox Robinson's *The Cross-Roads*, for how it juxtaposed rural Ireland with urban Ireland. Overall, the city setting was welcomed.

This reception might be reflective of a desire to see Ireland in the present, and for Dublin audiences to see themselves and their city as it is, whether good or bad, tragic or humorous. It is as though the rural plays piqued audiences more than the urban plays, because the rural challenged cultural nationalist tenets with an imposed notion of what constituted "real" Ireland. Dublin audiences found opportunities to reject the setting by objecting to the messaging. In fact, many urban plays challenged nationalist and clerical doctrine, but remained popular enough with audiences for those issues to be tolerated with considerably less protest than rural-set plays with similar themes. Dublin audiences found these issues acceptable if presented in an urban setting.

This acceptance may be partly attributable to an urban audience's desire to see its history or contemporary life portrayed as it is, not as how architects of cultural revivalism wish it to be. G. J. Watson argues that there was a deep ambivalence among urban Irish citizens about the concept of the Irish peasant, and that this carried over into their reception of dramas presented at the Abbey: "many natives did not like being reminded that Ireland was an overwhelmingly rural or peasant society . . . The point was that the natural audience for this drama was urban, Dublin-dwellers who felt they had made good by leaving the land, as many of them had in the recent past. The Famine had produced not merely a tradition of emigration, but an inexorable drift to the town" (1979, 25–26). Casey's plays lack any rural backstory and focus on characters who are controlled by Dublin's expectations. But even in such a stifling city as the one presented, there is room for characters to be absorbed. It is a dubious reality that even "no place" is a place for urbanites whose dreams are thwarted.

# 4 Confronting a Rural Icon

## *The Urbanization of Cathleen ní Houlihan*

ON JULY 22, 1929, several hundred people gathered in Co. Clare to watch President William T. Cosgrave throw the switch officially opening the first stages of Ireland's national electric grid. The Shannon hydroelectric scheme had been in planning and debate since shortly after the end of the Civil War, when the new Free State faced significant infrastructural challenges after the border "cut it off from the heavily industrialised areas around Belfast; [leaving] industrial skills and training . . . scarce" (Moody and Martin 1984, 334). The Shannon Scheme created more than two thousand jobs and marked the first significant effort toward the self-sufficiency mandate that was a hallmark of the early Free State government. On the same day that Cosgrave ceremoniously opened the Shannon Scheme, rehearsals were under way at the Abbey for W. B. Yeats's *Fighting the Waves* (1929). This "play for dancers" was an adaptation of Yeats's Noh-modeled *The Only Jealousy of Emer* (1919), part of his Cuchullain cycle of plays based on the Ulster sagas that gained prominence during the first peak of cultural revivalism. As the young nation was taking a major step toward modernization in the rural west, the national theater was experiencing a similar paradox in Dublin: modernist form enveloping ancient narrative.

This contrast between the Free State's emerging modernity and the Abbey's continued reexamination of ancient myth was a fitting conclusion to a decade during which Abbey productions set in urban Ireland more than doubled, but the city remained a minority setting.

This dance between the urban and the rural had been under way at the Abbey since it opened, but took on speed in the 1920s. The 1920s saw the most significant increase in urban-set additions to the repertoire, as well as the use of parody and satire targeting nationalist sensibilities, two literary devices that would become established conventions of the Abbey urban genre. The most robust examples are found in the O'Casey Trilogy, with all three plays challenging nationalist discourse and containing elements of parody or satire to highlight discontent. Within the O'Casey years, Denis Johnston was developing his own response to "Dublin and her damned politics" (Henderson 1973, 33) in the form of *The Old Lady Says "No!"* Famously rejected by the Abbey, this play featured its own unique re-visioning of Cathleen ní Houlihan, the most iconic characterization of Irish nationalism.

Johnston's Cathleen appears in the character of the Flower Woman, and the rhetoric of the play *Cathleen ní Houlihan* is echoed in *The Old Lady*'s play-within-the-play. Johnston's Flower Woman hawks the produce of her "four beautiful gre-in fields" (Johnston 1992, 71), but these flowers and apples come cheaply, hardly a celebrated output of Ireland's fertile fields. The Poor Old Woman devised by Yeats and Gregory rejected an offer of currency from the Gillanes, but Johnston's Dublin street peddler is eager to have "lovely gentlemen spare a copper for a cuppa tea" (ibid., 72), only to realize they have nothing for her. She ultimately finds the men of Ireland, including the Emmet actor, a "brood of sorry scuts" (ibid., 115), but, ever the optimist, is still willing to offer "a bit of sport" (ibid., 113) if it will bring in a bit of income. She is the ultimate opportunist and willing to use her own body for gain while Cathleen ní Houlihan uses the bodies of others. Such a cynical Cathleen did make its way to the Abbey's main stage before and after *The Old Lady* was produced by the Gate, but never with quite so much humor or bite.

The roots of Cathleen ní Houlihan are found in very early traditional Irish social order, which was "dominated by [the] image of the *puella senilis*, the woman who is literally as old as the hills yet endlessly restored to youth through union with her rightful mate" (MacCana 1982, 520). This union served both parties: the old woman regained youthful beauty, and the man gained the promise that his descendants would rule the land. As a "goddess of sovereignty" (Ní Bhrolecháin 1982, 525), the old woman had significant power. The trope evolved as oral tales converged to written literature. Initially, her sexual powers remained in the foreground; but by the time Yeats and Gregory constructed their version, the trope, although still representative of land, increasingly represented the concept of nation. Within literature of the Revival, this was the dominant conceptual usage. Concurrent with this shift to nation was the elimination of sovereign reciprocity. It was replaced by the promise of immortality for those who sacrificed themselves in order to fulfill the old woman's desire to reclaim her nation.

No use of the trope has solidified its dramatic endurance as much as *Cathleen ní Houlihan*. Its first staging, starring Maude Gonne, was produced in Dublin by Willie Fay's INDC in 1902 at St. Teresa's Hall on Clarendon Street. This initial production converted the mythical Cathleen into a stage-based nationalist symbol and icon. The setting, Killala, Co. Mayo, in 1798, embeds *Cathleen ní Houlihan* in the memory of Wolfe Tone and the failed Rebellion by the United Irishmen. Killala was the landing point for the French forces that arrived in August 1798 to assist the United Irishmen in their liberation effort, and it is the arrival of these forces that is alluded to in the opening of the play when Peter and Patrick Gillane question the noise they hear in the distance. It is toward the fighting, and away from the domestic cottage and his imminent marriage, that Michael Gillane is lured by The Poor Old Woman.

When the Abbey opened on December 27, 1904, *Cathleen ní Houlihan* (with Maire Nic Shiubhlaigh, who played Delia in the 1902 production, starring in the title role) was the centerpiece of the opening night bill. This Poor Old Woman requires the sacrifice of young men in order to reclaim her land and, consequently, to reclaim her youth. She does not need immediate bodies; the promise alone of a blood sacrifice is enough to transform her into "a young girl" with "the walk of a queen" (Yeats and Gregory 2001, 93). She wanders the countryside in search of recruits, establishing the character in a specifically nonurban space that stresses the national image as a rural female. When this icon is moved toward the city and ultimately placed within it, she is open to harsher criticism than those meek voices of protest offered by the Gillanes, and she simultaneously becomes a critical voice herself.

When Seumas Shields remarks in *The Shadow of a Gunman* that her "way's a thorny way," he speaks well to the prickly path that marks Cathleen's transformation from a rural setting to one that is increasingly urbanized. O'Casey's *Kathleen Listens In: A Political Phantasy in One Act* and Paul Vincent Carroll's *Coggerers* borrow so much from the structure and plot of the Yeats-Gregory play that they beg consideration as parody. All three one-acts rely on: a spatial tension poised between a domestic (or domesticated) interior and a nationally tumultuous exterior; use of patriotic ballads to reinforce the historical references of the times in which they are set; and take place against a violent backdrop of Irish history, with the representation of the nation as C/Kathleen a pivotal component. However, the female nation takes on decidedly different characteristics depending on the plays' degree of urbanization.

In the simplest terms, parody involves the imitation and transformation of another author's text. Of particular interest here are its cultural ramifications from an intertextual position. The urbanized plays against which *Cathleen ní Houlihan* serves as precursor text blur the lines between specific and general parody. This hybridity is achieved by strictly adhering to the format of only one specific dramatic work, but in selecting an iconic hallmark of nationalist drama, *Kathleen Listens In* and *Coggerers* transcend parody of *Cathleen ní Houlihan* to parody the movement it represents.

In a Bakhtinian theory of parody, specific texts stand in opposition to their targeted work. Bakhtin acknowledges that unity exists between the works, but views this as unity in opposition and sees parodic discourse as containing "two 'languages' (both intra-lingual) [that] come together and to a certain extent are crossed with each other: the language being parodied . . . and the language that parodies. This second parodying language, against whose background the parody is constructed and perceived, does not—if it is strict parody—enter as such into the parody itself, but is invisibly present in it" (Bakhtin

1981, 75). What is invisible in *Kathleen Listens In* and *Coggerers* is the cultural nationalist movement. The elements of "unity in opposition" that require specific address to read the parodic elements of *Kathleen Listens In* and *Coggerers* are the trope of Cathleen ní Houlihan, the plays' historical backdrops, and their use of political ballads.

O'Casey and Carroll move Cathleen away from the rural sphere, but retain the Yeats-Gregory construct by linking her presence with a historical battle and juxtaposing her presence with a domestic (*Kathleen Listens In*) or domesticated (*Coggerers*) interior. However, the benchmark work makes Cathleen an inspirational contributor to a historic battle and an intrusive presence in the domestic sphere, while *Kathleen Listens In* and *Coggerers* question her intentions and the gullibility of those who enter battle on her behalf, while enclosing her in domesticated spaces and challenging nationalist ideology. In doing so, these plays take the first step toward challenging the trope. They place Cathleen among the masses (population shifts had already skewed east by the turn of the century) and amid battles that were witnessed in their lifetimes. Most notably, they demonstrate the aftermath of her presence, all of which lessen the romanticism and call-to-arms entrenched in *Cathleen ní Houlihan*, creating a duality in the plays' Cathleen figures (Kathleen in the O'Casey play; Brigid Galgoogley in *Coggerers*), allowing them to exist concurrently as both national figure and national critic.

*Kathleen Listens In* premiered the first week of October 1923 and is set in "the present," establishing the action in the wake of the Civil War. The war had lasted for twelve months and greatly divided the citizens of Dublin, where some of the fiercest fighting took place. Although many Dubliners were breathing a collective sigh of relief that the war was over and enjoying a degree of pragmatic optimism that such a moment would naturally elicit, there were still factions competing for representation. Unlike the protagonist of *Cathleen ní Houlihan*, who is a nomadic outsider to a domestic interior, O'Casey's Kathleen O'Houlihan is safely protected within the family home and doted upon by her parents. With the fighting over and recruits no longer needed, she excludes the citizens from a safe hearth and prefers to keep them outdoors to fend for themselves, as she is "not mysteriously transformed by independence but positively oppressed by liberation and the contending suitors for her hand" (Grene 1999, 137). If one accepts the O'Houlihan home as the Free State house, then there are dual metaphors at play: the O'Houlihan house maps against the new national boundaries, and Kathleen is a national image confined by various opposing factions.

Unlike the time period, the setting is slightly ambiguous. The action occurs in the garden beside the damaged home of the O'Houlihan family. Although the setting is no more specific than that, Bray is referred to as being nearby, suggesting that our Kathleen has moved toward the urbanized east, if not directly within the confines of Dublin. This step toward the city and modernity is reinforced by Kathleen's preoccupation with listening to broadcasts from London. Her namesake transmitted ancient tales to inspire; this Kathleen is inspired by jazz music and stories from the British capital. This transformation implies a cynical shift of power to those who construct narratives. The implication is that those ancient stories were/are commodities no less commercial than London's broadcast output of popular culture. The trope's eastward movement reflects the nation's population shift and the city of Dublin's centrality to the nation. Kathleen is placed in the most densely populated region and within earshot of the seats of government. As a result, she is stripped of any rural fantasy.

Part of the emotional impact of *Cathleen ní Houlihan* rested with its reliance on a failed battle from the significant past as backdrop: the mythological Poor Old Woman can weave her spell most effectively on an audience when there is no tangible collective memory to disrupt the play's message. Such Brechtian historicization was not afforded to the audience of *Coggerers*. The play premiered in 1937 when Dublin streets and public buildings were still being rehabilitated from the destruction caused from the Easter Rising through the Civil War.[1]

1. For an overview of the city's rebuilding, see Yvonne Whelan's *Reinventing Modern Dublin* (2003).

Memories of these events would still be fresh in the minds of Dubliners. The action occurs on the first day of the Easter Rising, the most romanticized event in the city's history. Carroll arrived in Dublin in 1916 and was equally romantic in his memories of both the Rising and the Abbey, "I saw in this theatre the spiritual rebirth of the Irish race, and in 1916, one day as I was leaning against Nelson's Pillar, I saw the stern realization of these Abbey stage dreams, when Pearse seized the G.P.O." (Carroll 1938, 10:1). His idealistic view changed when he returned to his hometown in 1920 to find "the family grocers, the publicans and the clergy richer than ever as a result of the war. There was no learning or culture of any kind in the town" (ibid.). This duality of romantic and pragmatic memory is reflected in the setting of *Coggerers*, with the Easter Rising backdrop evoking the romantic possibility and the library of the action adding a dose of intellectual domesticity.

Carroll's modification of the trope takes the form of urbanized fusion. The play's central character, Brigid Galgoogley, is a charwoman who works at a Dublin city library near St. Stephen's Green and dotes on the statues of Robert Emmet, John Mitchel, Lord Edward Fitzgerald, Wolfe Tone, and Charles Stewart Parnell that adorn the library's entrance hall. Her care and attention to the fallen patriots, interspersed with her stories of her son, Oweneen, make her a mother figure paralleling Bridget Gillane, but her age and status mirror that of the Yeats-Gregory Poor Old Woman.

The songs in *Cathleen ní Houlihan* are sung only by the Poor Old Woman and rely heavily on two recurring "themes of rebel balladry: the cult of the dead hero and the glorification of martyrdom" (Zimmerman 1967, 69). When she is inside the cottage, she sings of a man who died in her name, drawing the interest of Michael. This first song marks the beginning of her seduction of the young man, and from it emerges stories of men from Ireland's historical past. Michael's mother, Bridget, observes the interaction and does her best to break the Old Woman's spell by suggesting she be given some food and "a few pence or a shilling" (Yeats and Gregory 2001, 90) and sent on her way. But Michael continues to engage the Old Woman and ultimately offers to go with her to serve her cause. With the seduction achieved, the Old Woman's songs change from tales of others to celebrations of herself. She moves to the doorway, luring Michael outward. Finally, outside of the cottage and heading toward the fighting, she sings about the promise of immortality for those who follow her cause. At this point, the Poor Old Woman gives Michael no way out of his commitment to her: she is singing orders. Without exception, music is used to facilitate the Poor Old Woman's seduction, as well as to establish a connection to her power as a national metaphor and to justify the actions of young men who sacrifice themselves in her name.

In contrast, O'Casey's Kathleen is resident in a family home and has men singing their causes to her. The songs of *Kathleen Listens In* belong to the men Kathleen refuses to see as they plead for her attention and try to draw her outside. Unlike the Yeats-Gregory Cathleen, this Kathleen is not a pursuer. The nation is now established as the Irish Free State and has no use for the favors of men. Kathleen is "a modern young woman" (O'Casey 1963, 274) devoting her energies to practicing fine manners and listening to jazz broadcasts from England "so as to be . . . lady-like when [making her] deboo into the League o'Nations" (ibid., 282). The men may have earned her a new status, but London will now serve as model for the finishing touches required for an international presence.

Those wooing her are identified by their special interests and include The Free Stater; The Republican; The Business Man, who could be said to be representing urban interests; The Farmer, representing rural interests; and The Man with a Big Drum, representing the Orange Order. O'Casey's use of the definite article in these character names identifies the characters as archetypes rather than stereotypes. O'Casey would famously employ the same technique three years later in *The Plough and the Stars*, with the naming of The Figure in the Window. The reliance on archetype taps into the Jungian collective unconscious that was used to great effect in *Cathleen ní Houlihan*. But by applying it to elements that emerged from cultural revivalism (most notably The Man in the Kilts/Gaelic Leaguer), it serves as an additional layer of parody.

O'Casey is drawing on the historical past and evoking the resonance of both the mythological trope and her characterization in *Cathleen ní Houlihan.* However, the original work used archetype to inspire citizens to follow, and here it draws attention to nameless faces that reinvent the nation for modern consumption only to be later dismissed. This exposes the revivalist predisposition for creating modernized ancient authenticities. The only two male pursuers who are worthy of names in the cast list are Joey and Johnny, identified as members of the Nationalist Party,[2] but even they are reduced to 1st Man and 2nd Man within the text.

Singing is plentiful throughout the play and encompasses a broad range of traditional Irish ballads, including "Wrap the Green Flag Round Me, Boys," "A Soldier's Song," "The Harp That Once Through Tara's Halls," "Kathleen Mavourneen," and "There's a Dear Little Colleen (The Dear Little Shamrock)." However, O'Casey makes several of the songs uniquely his own, altering key lyrics to emphasize a parodic point. For example, to draw attention to the imposed idleness of Joey and Johnny, their chorus of "Wrap the Green Flag Round Me, Boys" changes from "Wrap the green flag round me, boys, to die were far more sweet / With Ireland's noble emblem boys, to be my winding sheet," to "Wrap the green flag round me, Joe, to die 'twere far more sweet / Than to be sacked out o' me job, An' sent to walk th' street" (O'Casey 1963, 280). This bit of song from Joey and Johnny suggests that fighting in battle would be preferred to idleness, and that the idleness has been imposed on them by the establishment of the Irish Free State. The song reinforces their abandonment by Kathleen now that their service is over, and suggests that they have been "sacked" by her.

2. Since 1st Man states, "the pair of us went to school with Kathleen; we learned our first lesson together in Easter Week" (281), the term "Nationalist Party" appears to be a name for the unified forces (Citizens Army and Volunteers) that fought during the Easter Rising.

Perhaps the sharpest cut is found in The Gaelic Leaguer's (The Man in the Kilts) song, "Ce Chuirfidh Tu Liom?" (phonetically spelled in the text, as is often the case in O'Casey plays where Irish is used, "Key Kirheh Thoo Lyume").[3] Loosely translated, its title is "Who Will You Send with Me to Herd the Cows?" Its origin was a traditional song sung by girls spinning at the wheel. Each girl would sing a verse, asking another the question, and the respondent would reply with the name of a favorite boy, and so on. This choice of song suggests childish stubbornness on the part of the Irish language movement and a sarcastic jab at those Civil War leaders who embraced it. As John MacNamara notes, "the political movement [that] led to the establishment of the Irish Free State, in 1922, was closely associated in fact and in men's minds with the movement to restore Irish. Both Michael Collins and his adversary in the Civil War, Eamon de Valera, stated that to them the restoration of Irish was at least as important as political independence" (1982, 124). When the curtain falls amid the men invading the house to reach Kathleen, the songs become an overture that might remind the audience of their ongoing internal bickering. Any potential for noble narrative is lost in the cacophony.

The use of songs suggests that O'Casey reinforced his exposure of divided national interests by deliberately trying to divide the audience, a somewhat inverted metadramatic element that further enhances the play's parodic efforts. Gabriel Fallon, who played The Man in the Kilts in the original production, recalled the opening night: "Throughout the performance of *Kathleen* there was much sectional laughter. Hardly more than ten percent of the audience laughed together. The effect on the stage was slightly unnerving. In a flash it became clear what was happening. You laughed when my party fell under O'Casey's lash; I laughed when your party caught it. Both of us tried to laugh when the other fellow's party was made to squirm. And then slowly

3. O'Casey critiqued the Gaelic League on numerous occasions, as Declan Kiberd observes, sometimes targeting League president Douglas Hyde directly. See the chapter "Deanglicization" in Kiberd 1996.

but surely all the laughing died away" (Fallon 1965, 14). The laughing that diminished as the play progressed on opening night was only part of the stunned audience's reaction. O'Casey claimed to be the only playwright to have an Abbey opening that met with absolutely no applause: "after curtain-fall, every mother's son and daughter in the theater kept a dead silence, got up from their seats, and filed out of the theater without a single handclap or a word" (O'Casey 1989, 380). The sharp dialogue certainly contributed to the sectarianism alluded to by Fallon, but the music must have maximized the impact of the dialogue. A domestic audience would have been intimately familiar with the powerful tradition of political ballads and the ability to sing up one party as a way of singing down another.

In *Coggerers*, the singing belongs primarily to Brigid. Dublin engulfs her, and she becomes as much the spirit of the city as the spirit of the nation. Although the statue of Wolf Tone sings a few lines of "My Dark Rosaleen" (echoing another version of the female trope), he does so only to encourage Brigid to sing herself. Tone's invocation of the Dark Rosaleen frames Brigid as a worthy treasure in her own right. But she also represents mothers of the nation's fighting men and serves as critic of the mythical, rural-based Cathleen ní Houlihan. Her main function, though, is as the capital city's conscience. This function is reinforced in her song, where Dublin is a mother itself, although not the sort likely to be celebrated in traditional ballads embraced by nationalists:

> Oh, Dublin is a frowsy dame, 'Tis her's the brazen Tartar,
> Her petticoats are Saxon lace, her perfume's Guinness's porter.
> To see her kneelin' at the Mass, you'd swear she was a martyr,
> 'Til Parnell in O'Connell Street[4] stares cock-eyed down at her garter.
> She'll sit on Dan O'Connell's[5] steps, And froth at Anna Liffey,

4. The statue of Charles Stewart Parnell (unveiled 1911) is located on the north end of O'Connell Street.

5. The pedestal steps at the statue of Daniel O'Connell (unveiled 1882), located on the south end of O'Connell Street.

She'll coort a bit with Dick Muldoon, and cod little Father Fiffey.
Oh, Jerry Mooney is her boy, and Father Matt's[6] her other,
And damn the knowing either knows such caperin' in a mother.
She'll take a sup with Jer O'Brien, and say an Av' [Ave Maria] with
Father Fiffey,
Fill up with spleen in College Green, and empty all into the Liffey.
(Carroll 1939, 179–80)[7]

This song inverts the nobility of the songs of *Cathleen ní Houlihan* and, in doing so, satirizes the trope and begins a more forceful parody of the Yeats-Gregory play.

*Kathleen Listens In* finds Kathleen ensconced in the Free State house and curious enough about the men who have come calling for her to stick her head out of the window. But on hearing their pleas for her time and criticism of her attention to England, she tells them to stop annoying her and quickly retreats back inside. Their relentless outbursts ultimately lead her to being overcome by the attention. Feeling faint, she takes to her bed with the attending doctor proclaiming silence as her only chance for recovery. The doctor informs all that "a whisper may prove fatal—she'll need perfect peace and quietness for the rest of her National life" (O'Casey 1963, 295). Predictably, this advice goes unheeded. The play that opened with a curious Kathleen concludes with her unable to bear any more intrusions from her citizenry. She is exhausted by their insistence that she recognize them and by their interruptions as she attempts to learn about the outside world

6. Father Theobald Mathew (1790–1856) was founder of the Catholic temperance organization Pioneer Total Abstinence Association.

7. Efforts to locate the origins of this song have been unsuccessful. I am uncertain if it is an original by Carroll, a variation on a standard, or an old Dublin ballad. Unlike O'Casey, Carroll was not prone to foregrounding song in his plays and it is unlikely that he wrote this. A survey of Dublin street ballads reveals this song to be similar in meter and subject to "Dublin Jack of All Trades," which is included in the Joyce Collection of 1873 (a definitive text on Irish ballads), so it was composed in the nineteenth century or earlier. Like "Dublin Jack of All Trades," Brigid's song of Dublin takes in the streets of the inner city.

via her radio. Meanwhile, the men continue to fight. Their songs carrying beyond the curtain suggest that disorder will continue among the public and fall on the new government's deaf ears.

*Kathleen Listens In* is a satire in its own right, but it is also a parody. The Juvenalian element is expressed best by O'Casey himself, who wrote in 1961, "it was written specifically to show what fools these mortals were in the quarrelling factions soaking Ireland in anxiety and irritation after the Civil War" (O'Casey 1992, 191). This statement documents the various political factions as his satirical targets, but, closely paralleling the construction of *Cathleen ní Houlihan* also reveals a parodic target to be the Yeats-Gregory play itself. One might read the targets as Yeats and Gregory, who were, by 1922, no strangers to having their work parodied. Although Yeats was the recognized author, O'Casey was aware that Gregory, "foster-mother to some plays of Yeats, [wove] in dialogue for *Cathleen ní Houlihan*" (O'Casey 1992, 122). But when *Kathleen Listens In* premiered, O'Casey was on good terms with the Abbey directors and fresh off the success of *The Shadow of a Gunman*. It is, therefore, reasonable to conclude that O'Casey was responding to the cultural messages of *Cathleen ní Houlihan* rather than to its authors.

In parodying *Cathleen ní Houlihan*, O'Casey targets both the political and the cultural branches of the nationalist movement. As has been laboriously documented, many republicans viewed *Cathleen ní Houlihan* as a call to action. However, the original text frames the rhetoric of nationalism by placing Cathleen in a past rebellion that had been widely co-opted by republican parties,[8] while O'Casey places the trope in contemporary, post–Civil War Dublin, where republican parties were split. O'Casey relies on historical framing of his female protagonist to characterize the nation of Ireland. His characterization of

8. The co-opted figurehead is Wolfe Tone. See the chapter "The Cult of Tone" in Elliott's *Wolfe Tone* (1989) for a concise summary of widespread embracement of Tone by republican factions, traceable, primarily, to Davis and the Young Irelanders movement of the 1840s.

Kathleen shows a self-absorbed nation that is experiencing the growing pains of rebellious adolescence.

Kathleen's father, Miceawl, is the nation-builder. His plans to improve the O'Houlihan house serve as metaphors to the modernization Ireland itself was undergoing at the time. When the men interrupt his work, he tells them he's "busy now with th' plans for the electhrification of the Shannon an' Suck, th' Lee an' th' Liffey, th' Bann an' th' Boyne an' th' Tolka" (O'Casey 1963, 279). The rivers he catalogues cross the entire island, running through the cities of Cork, Dublin, Belfast, and Limerick. His borderless Ireland stands in stark contrast to the reality of the times and the more practical side of the nation-building being undertaken. His reference to electrification via hydropower speaks to the very real infrastructural challenges facing the new Free State government and the debates that ensued regarding the location of the power station. Before the Shannon Electricity Bill became law in June 1925, numerous proposals were made (as early as 1922) regarding which river should be tapped first and which city should be home to the grid's first power station.

Miceawl is looking forward, away from the icons of Emmet and Tone that once held his interest. The men he hired to adorn his walls with images of those figures, whom he describes as citizens who performed "th' hardest [work] an' [were] th' worst fed" (O'Casey 1963, 280), now stand in the way of progress. It is Miceawl's indifference to them that causes the men to pursue Kathleen; but her father attempts to warn them off, telling them they cannot call on her because "it's young men she's lookin' for, not oul' fossils like [them]" (ibid., 281). Like her namesake, this Kathleen wants her men young. Unlike Yeats and Gregory's Cathleen, she is not embodying the past; she is looking toward the future. In the words of one of the play's theme songs, she is forsaking the life of Tone and the poetry of Davis to "read th' hymnbook o' Churchill" (ibid., 282),[9] a reference to England that is reinforced by the London broadcasts she listens to at home. The dou-

9. From the song "Kathleen Mavourneen."

bling of the English focus adds irony to the play's title: it is not the new nation of Ireland Kathleen is listening to, but rather its prior oppressor. She is looking outward toward England in preparation for her debut, rather than looking for inspiration at home.

O'Casey's satirization of "the silliness and danger of the then divided Ireland—Free State [vs.] Republican, Labour [vs. private enterprise], Northern Catholic [vs.] Northern Protestant" (O'Casey 1989, 194) suggests that his intent is one of reform. By transforming them from orators in hallowed halls to bullies shouting in the garden of a house in disrepair, they are stripped of any dignity. We are left with street fighters interested solely in their own positions rather than in reform for the nation's common good. They all claim to love Kathleen and to be acting in her best interests, but their aggressive courtship is for their own self-preservation at her expense. Their posturing and inability to compromise make the image of Ireland (Kathleen) physically ill. In essence, they destroy the national image they elevated to iconic status and, as a result, perpetuate a nation of division.

O'Casey's Kathleen is not transformed into a woman "with the walk of a queen," but one could certainly make the case that she is a bit precious. Her parents work tirelessly fixing and cleaning their house, but the most effort Kathleen exerts is rearranging the ornaments on the mantle over the fireplace. Her father does not know "what's comin' over her—she won't do a [hand's] turn" (O'Casey 1963, 288) since she started listening to English broadcasts. She is also deaf to all attempts by those eager for her attention, if they do not have the degree of sophistication she hears from the wireless. When her mother implores her to give the men a bit of time, she makes it clear that she has heard enough from them all: "Oh, I've heard this too often, ma; I'm getting' sick of it . . . it's all codology!" (ibid., 292). The only transformation is the memory of a noble, female national spirit/image into the reality of a self-absorbed, female national spirit/image that (ironically) cannot listen to her own people, but only looks afar for inspiration.

The male citizenry seeking attention from Kathleen are not, like Michael Gillane, selfless young men willing to sacrifice themselves in order to help her recapture her home. Rather, they are young and old men who want recognition and gratitude for their labors on her behalf. Once again, nobility is absent. Kathleen's inability to receive them results in their rushing the house and undoing the progress that Miceawl and his wife made restoring it. In O'Casey's vision, the Civil War continues beyond the control of official truces. Both the builder and the image of the nation are housed together, but the citizenry is intent on preventing them from repairing windows shattered by their outrage. At the street level, no armistice exists.

O'Casey's construct of *Cathleen ní Houlihan* provides critical commentary on divisiveness within political and cultural nationalism, and Carroll uses it to reexamine the Easter Rising and its legacy. He witnessed the Rising as a young man and it deeply moved him. But the "heroic idealism Carroll observed in the Rising was juxtaposed with the . . . general sense of conservatism, complacency and philistinism" (Murphy 2008, 195) that rose in its aftermath. That critical stance clearly informs his questioning the legacy of earlier nationalist icons while, like O'Casey, re-visioning the title trope of *Cathleen ní Houlihan*.

*Coggerers* was Carroll's third play for the Abbey and his only Abbey play to be set in Dublin. Its cynicism was probably not surprising to those familiar with his earlier works. Both *Things That Are Caesar's* (1932) and *Shadow and Substance* (1937) received criticism for portrayals of the Catholic clergy. But broaching the sacred event of the Easter Rising was a rather radical act even more than a decade after independence and the outcry over O'Casey's *The Plough and the Stars*, which, like *Coggerers*, presented the Rising in an unromantic light. In *Coggerers*, the Rising is used to question the icons of Parnell, Tone, Emmet, Mitchel, Fitzgerald, and (in absentia) O'Connell. These legendary figures in Ireland's struggle for independence serve to question those who keep their memories alive without considering the consequences of such reverence. Rather than being portrayed as active, Parnell, Tone, Emmet, Mitchel, and Fitzgerald are presented in the form of statues. Gracing the hall of a Dublin library, they are situated on the stage in rank of age, with those that died youngest the farthest from the audience. The slab reserved for the senior member of the group, Daniel O'Connell, ultimately serves to receive the body of Brigid's son, Oweneen, who dies during the Rising. The figures are elevated on pedestals and set in places of prominence in a public building, but their marble forms reinforce the concept that they belong to the past. It is more the idea of these men and their deeds that permeate the memory of the nation and Dublin as the Rising begins. O'Connell's empty pedestal in the stage's most dominant location foregrounds the absence of leaders who favor progress by legislative means, a circumstance echoed by the Parnell statue, which is present but damaged/incomplete.

Like *Cathleen ní Houlihan*, *Coggerers* reveals a son joining the nation's fight for independence and employs the rhetoric of nationalism. However, the 1916 urban setting contributes a heightened cynicism toward the harsh realities of domestic warfare. Carroll himself witnessed the 1913 Lockout and was a "liaison man" in the War of Independence, "carry[ing] guns from one flying squad to another" (O'Donovan 1972, 11) while only a teenager. The pressure of it all led him to ask his "commandent [*sic*] for three months leave because my hands were absolutely shaking. I was on the edge of a nervous breakdown" (ibid.). He spent those three months in a Glasgow hospital. The cynicism of *Coggerers* is in stark contrast to *Cathleen ní Houlihan*, which leaves the audience unaware of whether Michael has reached the battle. Like *Plough* and *Juno*, *Coggerers* shines a light on the rhetoric of nationalism within the harsh realities of the impact of urban warfare on a Dublin family. If *Cathleen ní Houlihan* "marks the demand for commitment by the sons of Ireland" (Innes 1993, 27) and insists that the mothers of those sons honor their sacrifice, then *Coggerers* makes the demand that previously fallen leaders be held accountable for the sacrifices made in their names. Like the suitors of *Kathleen Listens In*, *Coggerers* insists that those left behind question the ramifications of following fallen leaders.

As in *Cathleen ní Houlihan*, *Coggerers* is set in an interior that outside noises penetrate from a distance. But here the interior is a domesticated public space and the intruding sounds are innocuous (a ship's siren call from the Liffey, the call of a newsboy) rather than military. Into this space enters the head librarian, O'Curry, and the charwoman, Brigid, each respectively representing Dublin's educated and poor working classes. They revere the icons in their own way: O'Curry with solemnity, Brigid with motherly concern and a bit of cheek. The library is closed to the public for the Easter holiday weekend, but O'Curry has come to change into the uniform of the Volunteer Army before joining the efforts on St. Stephen's Green, and Brigid to tend to the cleaning. Both talk to the statues, but the statues hold the humans in very different levels of esteem. They view the educated O'Curry with contempt: Mitchel refers to him as "a puzzling old fool" and Tone calls him a "stupid old classical bookworm" (Carroll 1939, 169–70). Even when O'Curry removes his coat, revealing a Volunteer uniform beneath, the man going out to fight earns no respect. Unlike O'Curry, Brigid is held in high regard by the statues, all of whom are grateful for her care and attention to their upkeep.

The play opens with O'Curry going off to fight (unknown to Brigid) and Brigid dusting Parnell's face with reverence, but this opening is not without its light moments. O'Connor is absent because he is out for repairs to replace two of his toes, a finger, and the curls from one side of his head broken off by American tourists, whom Tone identifies as "the new Barbarians" (ibid., 167). The smell Edward and Emmet believe is gunpowder is identified by Parnell as being the stench of the Liffey. When O'Curry asks Brigid how Dublin looked to her on her way in that morning, she provides the play's primary description of the city: "Sure jist as it always looks—like a woman paradin' in all her finery, but a dirty house at home" (ibid., 173). After telling Brigid to go home for the day, O'Curry leaves and the statues come back to life. They believe "the moment" has finally arrived and fall silent in the presence of the cleaning woman, who is the mother figure of the nation-to-be. The death of her son brings a further deconstructive element to the use of the trope. In *Cathleen ní Houlihan*, the Poor Old Woman stands only to gain by the sacrifice of Michael; in *Coggerers*, the Poor Old Woman will lose her "one little bit of riches that [she] was hiding" (ibid., 185) from the marble icons.

Emmet tells Brigid that her son is not at home, and she becomes alarmed, especially when gunfire is heard from outside in the street.

The statues become "a chorus for the big drama outside and for its microcosm inside, the death of the charwoman's son" (Hogan 1967, 58). Lord Edward tells Brigid to be brave, and Emmet tells her that Oweneen is behind the barricades in St. Stephen's Green. Renowned for his verbal obstructionist tactics at Westminster, Parnell claims to have "no words. I have cast them all to the winds." As a sudden rapid volley of shots is heard, Parnell continues, "That, that you hear is the words of the new generation, and I am too old to read them" (Carroll 1939, 183). But Brigid neither lets Parnell off the hook for not warning her, nor faces the unfolding events with stoicism. To her, the nation is an "oul bitch" (the ultimate reduction of Cathleen ní Houlihan), the marbled icons are ungrateful for her service to them, and, most important, her son is not to be sacrificed to meet their unfulfilled dreams:

> Yous knew this was comin' and yous wouldn't tell me! Yous villains and cut-throats and stinkin' coggerers! I that always had the wee word for yous and the wipe of me duster. And did I not sing for yous the song of the greedy oul bitch that yous all died for. (*volley of shots*) I know what it is that's up with yous! Yous are jealous of Oweneen and the way his strong arms can fling a hundred o' coal on his shoulder—jealous of the pant of his breath, the cry of his blood and the ring of his heart beats. My Oweneen has warm blood that he will give not to yous, nor to that oul' bitch that wanders O'Connell Street (*volley of shots*). My seven curses on yous and my seven curses on the oul' bitch yous died the death for! (Carroll 1939, 184)

In the end, Brigid acquiesces to the statues' request for her son's body, as though her own fire has gone out with the death of her son. When Emmet tells her that he tips his hat to the spirit of her son for his sacrifice for Ireland, she responds with "pathetic eagerness" (ibid., 189) and guides Oweneen's body to O'Connell's vacant pedestal. Her action is met with solemnity by the fallen leaders, but after Brigid leaves the building, they return to the empty rhetoric that Brigid accused them of earlier. The play closes with Emmet celebrating the gunfire on the Green as a symphony of freedom, the loss of Brigid's son quickly forgotten.

Although Emmet and the others do not observe Oweneen's dead body lying on O'Connell's pedestal, the audience would not have been able to overlook the juxtaposition of the body (in the most prominent place on stage) against Emmet's bliss at the "spitting of Thompson guns" (ibid., 189). The closing image reinforces Brigid's message throughout the play and completes it when she no longer has a voice. The contrast between the closing of this play and that of *Cathleen ní Houlihan* is striking. In both plays, men deliver the closing lines in an air of enchantment. But the young Patrick Gillane of *Cathleen ní Houlihan*, clearly taken by the transformed old woman, has been replaced by Emmet's euphoric reaction to the sound of gunfire on the streets of Dublin. Mythical enchantment is replaced by the reality of urban warfare.

When comparing these three plays, what emerges is how the Cathleen ní Houlihan trope undergoes dramatic alterations as she travels toward Dublin, the center of the revivalist movement. The closer Cathleen gets to the environment that elevated her to a stage-based, tangible figure, the more she implodes. It is as though the very weight of her status makes it impossible to make the transition from countryside to city streets. The rural icon of Cathleen ní Houlihan, created before Ireland's independence, is an outsider viewed with skepticism by the domesticated Gillane family intent on upwardly mobile conformity. She spends more of her time outside of the cottage or in its doorway than she does within its confines. Nonetheless, it is her physical presence that takes the son away from his family—she with her noble cause and he to noble service. The suburban Kathleen we meet, as the Irish Free State is about to join the League of Nations, is a thoroughly domesticated product of an upwardly mobile family. She is so far removed from the rural that she never actually sets foot outside her house. No longer a Poor Old Woman calling on men for service, she is a daughter relegated to swooning melodrama as her father takes the dominant role in building the nation beyond the mythical dreams she once represented. Finally, in the Dublin version, Cathleen ní Houlihan is consigned to fragmentation; she is part of Brigid and Brigid is part of her until Brigid loses her son. Once she is childless, Brigid uses all of her energy to condemn that "oul' bitch that wanders O'Connell Street" (ibid., 184).

Just as Cathleen ní Houlihan is a metaphor for Ireland, *Cathleen ní Houlihan* is a metaphor for cultural nationalist drama. By parodying this work, O'Casey and Carroll parody the movement it represents, drawing attention to the fundamental irony of how an urban creation dictates rural ideals. This parody questions the movement's predisposition toward "invocation of the past . . . to inspire [the] community to ever higher stages of development . . . with the goal of providing 'authentic' national models of progress" (Hutchinson 1987, 9). The "higher stage of development" implied by *Cathleen ní Houlihan* is independence, via sacrifices of young men. O'Casey and Carroll deconstruct the trope and, through their parody of it, offer alternate endings to the work. Their alternate endings are the result of attempting to authenticate something that is constructed.

These plays challenged the doctrine upon which the dominant rural repertoire was based. Much of the rural-based repertoire was, like the medieval literature referenced by Bakhtin, based in "memory [and it served] as the source and power for the creative impulse" (Bakhtin 1981, 15), a description that mirrors cultural revivalism quite well. Like many of the other playwrights who contributed to the Abbey's urban canon, O'Casey and Carroll crafted plays that challenged a memory constructed by the cultural nationalist movement. In doing so, they suggest that the mythological has little to offer once it is confronted with the reality of an emerging nation.

# 5 Public Spaces

## *Metatheatricality in the Dublin Plays*

ALL OF THE DUBLIN PLAYS share a tendency to highlight internal class divisions. When set in public places, however, the Dublin plays open a particularly volatile (and sometimes humorous) dialogue between institutions and the public. They also dramatize the impact class divisions have on the outcome of the public events or institutions being scrutinized. The Dublin plays are the component of the repertoire to most often feature institutional settings, paralleling the city's centrality to the movement and the institutions that gave shape to its articulation. The public plays address a broad range of social topics and events, but they are predisposed to exploring a mediation between institutional leadership and the public's relationship with that leadership. In doing so, they reveal tension between those who lead or create doctrines and the urban communities who are expected to acquiesce.

The primary settings of these plays house the arts and political or judicial bodies, but that most social of Dublin institutions—the pub—also makes a strong showing. Metadramatic plays such as St. John Ervine's *The Critics, or a New Play at the Abbey* and Lennox Robinson's *The Critic, or a Tragedy Rehearsed* demonstrate that the nationalist project falls short of its agenda while simultaneously parodying the public pressure under which the national theater operated. The prison and courtroom dramas, Roger McHugh's *Trial at Green Street Courthouse* (1941) and Hugh Hunt and Frank O'Connor's *The Invincibles* (1937), dramatize historical events to provide examples of how the political end of the project "got away from itself" and resulted in public behavior that stood to undermine any notions of justice. The public house not only reflects these communicational disconnects, but reinforces the public's own plotting to undermine notions of societal harmony inherent to the nationalist project. In all of the public plays, the settings draw attention to the role these places perform in Dublin, if not Irish, society. They all reflect some component of the nationalist project and critique its relationship with the public. The plays set in the Abbey are the most overt examples of this phenomenon. Rather than focus on drama as a literary form, they specifically address drama staged by the Abbey and humorously address a disconnect between the national theater's delivery and audience reception.

On November 26, 1909, the Abbey curtain opened on its first production of Gerald MacNamara's *The Mist That Does Be on the Bog*. It is set in a Connemara cottage rather than in Dublin, but its parody of the Abbey peasant play aesthetic, which results in "a distanced scepticism regarding the geopolitics of a Dublin-centric cultural movement and its fetishisation of a mythic West" (McNulty 2008, 168), would be echoed by Ervine and Robinson. Although the works of Synge and Gregory are the Abbey plays most readily recognized in this one-act comedy, its parody of these leading Abbey dramatists' plays (most notably *The Playboy of the Western World* and *A Pot of Broth*) suggests a wider meta-implication that could apply to the entire body of Abbey plays that feature a constructed rural Ireland. The "meta" of this play operates on several levels: it contains a play within a play, it portrays Dublin actors striving for a rural authenticity, and it problematizes the actor-audience relationship by making these roles interchangeable. As a result, *The Mist That Does Be on the Bog* is "not simply an imitative parody of revivalist aesthetics but also a parody of the process of imitation and translation" (ibid., 178). As Mark Phelan notes, "the very concept of 'authenticity' is consistently ironized and undermined . . . as a rhetorical strategy to critique . . . the hegemonic ideologies of cultural nationalism" (2009, 236). Within the Dublin-set meta-plays, parody turns to satire as the movement is replaced for criticism of and by very specific Abbey producers and consumers.

Richard Hornby homes in on metadrama as an experience rather than a technique. It is that experience that is of interest here. Relying on Brecht's foundational alienation theory, Hornby argues for the metadramatic experience being one of "unease" for the audience and creating "a dislocation of perception. It is thus possible to talk about the degree of intensity of metadrama, which varies from very mild to an extreme disruption. At times, metadrama can yield the most exquisite of aesthetic insights, which theorists have spoken of as 'estrangement' or 'alienation.' This 'seeing double' is the true source of the significance of metadrama" (1986, 32). The notion of an audience's "seeing double" is derived from the impact that metadramatic elements can have upon the cultural dynamics contained in a play. These elements can estrange the audience from a production in such a way that they see themselves seeing the work being staged (as was done to great effect in *The Mist That Does Be on the Bog*). As a result, they stand to observe themselves contained within the cultural artifact, and to interrogate their own roles within the culture being documented.

The metadramatic elements of the rural repertoire, like those in the urban plays, transcend the play-within-the-play and are found primarily in the use of literary reference and the ceremony-within-the-play, often weddings and funerals. Literary references appear often in the works of Yeats and Gregory, whose joint efforts to incorporate Celtic mythology and to reclaim oral tales from the west of Ireland were cornerstones for many of the rural and peasant plays they authored for the Abbey. However, it could be argued that Yeats's literary references were either unrecognizable or too familiar to create an impact on the audience. Certainly some theatergoers were familiar with the Ulster sagas and Ossianic legends upon which Yeats often based his plays, but it is equally likely that a percentage was not. If these sagas were too familiar to the audience, the literary references may have been too well known to have a metadramatic impact. The same holds true for the religious allegories and folk stories re-visioned by Gregory. As Hornby states, "The references to well-known Bible stories and characters, standard mythology, and popular folk tales . . .

are no more disruptive than a description of a tree or a rock" (ibid., 89). The manner in which ceremonies are employed can determine the extent to which an audience experiences metadramatic estrangement. If the ceremony is fulfilled/completed as prescribed, as it is in many of the rural plays that incorporate this element, the underlying message is of continuity and tradition. As a salve to a dominant cultural nationalist ideology, it is apt that this model is most commonly found in the nonurban repertoire.

A notable exception to this pattern is Synge. He famously claimed to base the language and plots of his plays on how he heard real people speak and behave. But he repeatedly uses marriage and death ceremonies to challenge the early dramatic tenets of revivalism that relied heavily upon presenting a community where conflicts are resolved for the good of the majority and to maintain continuity. Synge's weddings (and attempted weddings) are always problematic, and are used to expose fractures or hypocrisy rather than unity. For example, the keening in *Riders to the Sea* (1904) can be read as a lament for the death of a way of life, as much as to a son lost at sea. The works of Synge are an exception to the early rural repertoire's use of metadramatic elements to reinforce cultural continuity or tradition.

St. John Ervine's *The Critics, or a New Play at the Abbey* and Lennox Robinson's modernization of Richard Brinsley Sheridan's *The Critic, or a Tragedy Rehearsed* are both set at the Abbey. Plays set in a theatrical space and featuring Abbeyesque characters were critical and popular successes for the Theatre of Ireland. However, although the Abbey (and its directors, actors, and peasant repertoire) were clearly satirical targets of John MacDonagh's *Author! Author!*, Edward Martyn's *The Dream Physician*, and *Romulus and Remus, or the Makers of Delights*, these TOI plays did not name names to the extent of the Ervine and Robinson Abbey plays. The humor of *The Critics* and *The Critic* relies in great part on references to real persons, places, and events and requires a knowledge of the Abbey's history as well as the city of Dublin during the times in which the plays premiered. Both plays were very topical in their day and retain a great deal of their humor, particularly to *devotées* of Abbey history.

2. The lobby of the Abbey Theatre, setting for St. John Ervine's *The Critics, or a New Play at the Abbey* (1913). Courtesy of the Abbey Theatre Archives.

*The Critics, or a New Play at the Abbey* is the first Dublin play set entirely in the public sphere. With its Abbey lobby setting during a production of *Hamlet*, *The Critics* is among the most self-reflective, both of an Abbey author and of the critical climate in which the Abbey was operating in the early part of the twentieth century. Its setting draws attention to the audience's immediate environment. But the real-life references of *The Critics* go further. Its set features lobby portraits of Lady Gregory and George Russell, and contains pointed barbs against Abbey management by the drama critic character. *The Critics* also employs the play-within-the-play (even though the inner play occurs offstage), the role-within-the-role, and self-reference. The only meta variety omitted is the ceremony-within-the-play, the variety most often employed in the rural plays of the period.

*The Critics* premiered on November 20, 1913, under the subtitle "Being a Little Morality for the Press." It is Ervine's payback to the city's drama critics for their negative reviews of his *The Magnanimous Lover* (1912) that had premiered at the Abbey in the previous October. *The Critics* was a well-timed return volley since it preceded the premiere of *Mixed Marriage*, Ervine's first full-length play since *The Magnanimous Lover*, on the evening's double bill. *The Critics* indicts drama critics and the theatergoing public, who are portrayed as being equally overzealous in attacking the actual plays being staged. The newspaper critic, Barbary, is unable to comprehend either the Abbey's intent or its productions. The public is represented by three Dubliners, Quacks, Quartz, and Bawlawney, all of whom walk out of *Hamlet* midway through the production. When not on guard for how the Irish are portrayed on the national stage, they are blissfully ignorant of the play they have come to see.

His newspaper has reassigned Barbary from the City Desk to fill in for an ailing drama critic. His contempt for the dramatic literati and the theater is apparent from the start when he suggests that the Abbey building's prior use was more auspicious than its current incarnation: "That's a bad end for a Morgue—bein' turned into a theatre" (Ervine 1914, 81). He spends the entire play in the lobby, never witnessing the performance he is there to review, and encounters the three Dubliners leaving the performance in disgust. They tell him a summary of the plot points and express their mutual disgust at such a "disgraceful" play being staged by the national theater. Quacks calls it "the worst outrage that has ever been perpetrated on the Irish people [and an affront to] the purity of the Irish women" (ibid., 86–87). This echo of the protests against Synge's *The Playboy of the Western World* is the first of many self-reflective references to the Abbey's relationship with the public that permeate *The Critics.*

Abbey management is criticized for staging such an affront. Yeats is certainly at fault because "all he cares about is fairies and leprechauns" (ibid., 89), which is Bawlawney's explanation for the presence of the ghost of Hamlet's father. Lennox Robinson, who directed the play, is to blame for the bad language, after all "he reads Strindberg" (ibid., 90). Lady Gregory certainly contributed to the dialogue because Quacks is sure Polonius's "That he is mad, 'tis true: 'tis true, 'tis pity, and pity 'tis 'tis true . . . came straight out of Kiltartan" (ibid., 91). Quacks calls for "a crusade in Ireland against this piece and all the Abbey plays" and insists that they "demand the immediate institution of a censorship" (ibid., 93).

In contemplating what his review will say, Barbary is criticized by the Dubliners for intending to publish a review of a play he has not seen. When the men point out that it cannot, as a result, be factual, Barbary exclaims, "if we started printin' facts, the public would go out of its mind. If we were to tell the truth about Dublin, they'd burn the city down" (ibid., 95). This comment brings into question exactly which and whose "truth" is being critiqued in *The Critics.* The primary target is the Dublin drama critic, but Barbary's use of the collective "we" (in reference to the city's journalists) targets the intelligentsia who propagate cultural political agendas as well. In this play, Dublin is a city where truth is expendable if it does not fit the revivalist agenda or, more specifically, the agenda as represented by the Abbey itself.

Ervine's representation of audiences, however, is painted with a broad stroke. Although drama critics are the play's primary target, the audience members serve as conduits for criticizing the public's myopic vision of drama, and for opening dialogue on a humorous aspect of what was a long-standing obsession regarding analysis of Ireland's national theater: whose Irishness does it represent? The theatergoers' comments pertaining to this issue are numerous, but Quacks sums it up succinctly in his attempt to align *Hamlet* with Irish society: "You may marry your deceased wife's sister, but you may not marry your deceased brother's wife; and, therefore, I say that this play is a horrible outrage on the instinctive purity of the Irish people" (ibid., 92). This echoing of the biblical injunction against marrying a deceased spouse's sibling reflects both a prudish sensibility and an adherence to British law: in both cases, a citizenry of conformity.[1] Since *Hamlet* did not conform to Irish values in Quack's view, it had no place on the stage of the national theater. Furthermore, his use of the word "instinctive" links cultural nationalism to Ervine's targets by reinforcing the concept of an innate purity by birthright or lineage.

Ervine is clearly challenging both the audience and the critics to like his new play, *Mixed Marriage*, which followed *The Critics* on the double bill. This is primarily achieved through the use of role-playing-within-the-role and the real-life references alluded to earlier. The role-playing-within-the-role is employed twice: Dubliners are audience members playing critics, and the critic is a city hall reporter playing a drama critic. In both cases, the roles are essentially false, but "the dual device still sets up a feeling of ambiguity and complexity with regard to the character[s]" (Hornby 1986, 67). In doing so, it challenges the audience to be more receptive to the drama onstage by questioning their own notions of what is or is not "good" theater. As such, *The Critics* presents a parody of the Abbey's defensive position against public and critical onslaught, or, as Robert Welch puts it, "the level of uncomprehending stupidity which the Abbey had often to deal with" (1999, 65). It stands out as one of the strongest examples of the

1. The biblical injunction (Leviticus 20:21) was codified in the Marriage Act of 1835. Although it was modified in 1907 to allow men to marry their sister-in-law, it remained illegal to marry one's brother-in-law until 1921.

Abbey's willingness to stage plays that directly address its role within revivalist drama.

Robinson also turned to the Abbey as setting for his modernization of Sheridan's *The Critic, or a Tragedy Rehearsed.* When *The Critic* opened at the Abbey in January 1931, audience members found a prologue by Robinson in their programs that drew attention to some of the play's metadramatic elements (the author also appeared onstage to shake hands with an actor portraying Sheridan): "When it was written, its first act was very topical and much of its humour in that act is derived from the fact that it mentioned by name contemporary persons, newspapers and events" (Robinson [1931], n.p.). All of these elements were updated to contain Dublin references. He goes on to inform the audience that "the ridiculous inner play, *The Spanish Armada*, is left unaltered" because "the 'yon battlements' style of drama is still being written, worse luck; it is my misfortune [Robinson was an Abbey director in 1931] to have read many such plays each twelve months" (ibid.). This defensiveness is short lived, however; *The Critic* sends up its own with abandon.

Although act 1 is the only one not set in the Abbey (it is set in the Dublin home of Mr. and Mrs. Dangle), it is worth noting for its introduction to the real-life references that abound. The play opens with the couple having breakfast and reading the morning newspapers. Mr. Dangle is reading aloud headlines from the *Irish Times*:

> Adverse Balance Rising, Stormy Scenes in the Dublin Corporation, The Scandal of Compulsory Irish, Foot and Mouth Disease Suspected in Kerry, Mr. Blythe's Budget—psha! Nothing in the whole paper but Ireland and politics, and I hate all politics except theatrical politics. Where's the *Daily Express*? *[his wife hands him the* Daily Express]. Ah, here we are! Irish Theatrical news . . ."I am told that a new play has just been put into rehearsal at the Abbey Theatre. It is called 'The Spanish Armada' and . . . it is written in romantic blank verse. We are all very glad to see that the Abbey Theatre is breaking away from peasant plays. Only four new plays have appeared this season and it seemed as if the Abbey's best days were over and that . . ."—Oh, then he goes on with the usual old thing. (ibid., 1.1)

Dangle is a takeoff on Joseph Holloway, whom Dangle's wife mentions as a bad influence on her husband. It is not long before their breakfast is interrupted by an assortment of theater practitioners, including the playwrights Plagiary, Sneer, and Puff (author of *The Spanish Armada*). When talk turns to Puff's new Abbey play, Plagiary (a perfect name for a man obsessed with plagiarism because he himself does it so often) comments that he will "never send another play there," as he sent them a five-act Elizabethan tragedy once, "and it was returned. Within six months, it appeared on the Abbey stage as a one-act Kiltartan comedy!" (ibid., 1.9–10). This reference to Lady Gregory's putting her stamp on submitted works foreshadows the editing that *The Spanish Armada* will undergo at the hands of Abbey players and other interested parties.

Act 2 and act 3 are set at the Abbey, where Dangle attends a dress rehearsal of *The Spanish Armada* at Puff's invitation. Shortly into the rehearsal, it becomes clear to Puff that a substantial amount of cutting has been done to his script. When he protests, the stage manager explains that the players have taken Puff's advice and cut anything they found "dull or unnecessary," and that the play is so short now that he thinks it might be necessary "to begin the evening with *The Workhouse Ward*" (ibid., 2.3), an ironic line because the Gregory play was the one-act that preceded *The Critic* throughout its two-week run. It is then left to the stage manager to explain other changes as the rehearsal progresses:

STAGE MANAGER: There's been a little trouble in the Company, Maureen Delany was cast for the part of Britannia but either for patriotic reasons or because she was afraid of being lowered from the flies . . . she refused to play the part and we can't get another woman in the company to take it on. [Furthermore,] the Thames felt the same way but as he's only from the School of Ballet so he didn't dare to object, but he was heard to say, in his dressing room, that he'd rather be the river Lee—he's a Corkman—and that his father would beat the life out of him if he knew his son was going about impersonating an English river. [And] about the fight—well the Dublin branch of the League of Nations got to hear of it and made strong representations. Said it was a bad example to children and would make them bloodthirsty, and then there's a certain political set in the city who mightn't like to see a Spaniard beaten—might think we meant something political by it—so for all those reasons, we've cut the fight out.

PUFF: But the ballet?

STAGE MANAGER: Well of course we couldn't give in to the Lee—you know what Corkmen are—we're having the Shannon and its tributaries instead. (ibid., 3.16–17)

In the end, Puff's epic with ballet has been turned into a one-act about the Shannon Hydroelectric Scheme. Puff capitulates, pronounces the play wonderful with its changes, and *The Critic* ends. The integration of the inner and outer plays rests upon the modus operandi of the Abbey and its place within the cultural orbit of Dublin. If we read a play-within-a-play as a reflection of "a given dramatist's controlling conception of the theatre" (Nelson 1971, x), then Robinson's "conception" of the Abbey is that its productions are reduced to the lowest common denominator. This reduction no doubt occurs in response to the nationalist impulses that encircle the Abbey both externally and internally. In the end, this play presents the Abbey as an institution where artistic output can be diluted by the nationalist project to the point where plays breed banality, if it acquiesces.

The Mansion House is the primary setting for Edward McNulty's *The Lord Mayor*. Denis Johnston's adaptation of Ernst Toller's *Blind Man's Buff*[2] and Roger McHugh's *Trial at Green Street Courthouse* (1941) make use of the inner city's criminal court building. Issues of justice

2. Toller approached Johnston to write an adaptation of his *The Blind Goddess* (1932), but Johnston ultimately made so many changes to Toller's structure and plot that Johnston's *Blind Man's Buff* can hardly be deemed an adaptation. However, because of legal restraints based on their initial meeting, it remains listed as such. Johnston's 1956 *Strange Occurrence on Ireland's Eye* (1977) is a reworking of *Blind Man's Buff* and a much more compelling treatment of the actual case on which it was based.

are also explored in the Kilmainham Gaol scenes in Hugh Hunt and Frank O'Connor's *The Invincibles* (1937), and in Seamus Byrne's semi-autobiographical *Design for a Headstone* (1950), set in Mountjoy Prison.

*The Lord Mayor* features O'Brien, an ironmonger and city council member who is forced into the position of Lord Mayor by Gaffney, a solicitor who needs a puppet in the ceremonial high office to appease London while he controls the Dublin chamber. Set partly in the Mansion House, the plot relies on the degree to which O'Brien succeeds as an ironmonger playing the role of politician. Gaffney presents himself to the public as a republican, but he uses O'Brien to placate London so that he can play both sides of the political fence to his own benefit. The underlying message of Gaffney's duplicity is that the old political guard may well be placating the public in 1914, but the public should question the guard's intent and perhaps look to a new generation to sincerely represent the undercurrent of republicanism percolating in contemporary Dublin. This message is reinforced by the younger characters of Moira and Kelly, whose commitments to their beliefs contrast the old guard's pliability-for-personal-gain. When their example inspires O'Brien to stop being Gaffney's puppet, the play delivers on its metadramatic promise.

Although a courtroom setting is partly used in *Blind Man's Buff* and McHugh's *Rossa* (1945),[3] *Trial at Green Street Courthouse* is the first Dublin play that can legitimately be deemed a courtroom drama. McHugh noted that some critics in the 1950s coupled this play with *The Invincibles* as dual "attempts to romanticise political murder" (McHugh [1945], 78), but the historical context in which they premiered indicates that both actually obliterate any romantic notions of violence. These historical plays oppose the notion of martyrdom celebrated in the Abbey's earliest overtly nationalist play, *Cathleen ní*

3. The Dublin courtroom scene of *Rossa* serves no purpose except to demonstrate the plot point that Rossa was found guilty. It is the shortest and least significant scene in the play and, therefore, is omitted from courtroom analysis here. Furthermore, the prison scene is set in England and is, therefore, not included.

*Houlihan*, and stand in opposition to violence by any means, be it in the name of nationalism or not.

*Trial at Green Street Courthouse* is a dramatization of the 1871 trial of Robert Kelly, a Dublin carpenter tried for the murder of Thomas Talbot, a former head constable of the Royal Irish Constabulary (RIC). Talbot was rewarded with early retirement and a double pension for his undercover work in Carrick-on-Suir, which led to the arrest of more than fifty Fenians. He eventually relocated to Dublin, where the Fenian rising had essentially been crushed by the time he arrived, but where underground support remained. Talbot was quickly recognized by those sympathetic to the Fenian cause and harassed on a regular basis. He was shot while walking home from a pub one night, and on the way to the hospital named Robert Kelly as the man who shot him. Talbot survived for a short while, but died in the hospital after being operated on for his bullet wounds. Kelly went on trial for the murder in November in what became one of the most sensational trials of nineteenth-century Ireland. Domestic and international newspapers ran extensive, detailed reports; street vendors along the Dublin quays sold souvenir pictures of Kelly and Talbot; and ballads were written about the trial and its assorted characters. Celebrated barrister Isaac Butt defended Kelly, who was acquitted of the crime. Butt successfully argued that the direct cause of Talbot's death was the treatment he received in the hospital, not the bullet.

McHugh wrote *Trial at Green Street Courthouse* from detailed trial reports. One key part of the record that he captured well was the Dublin public's disdain for informers and police spies. This is a critical element of the play's composition, almost overshadowing the trial, which one might expect to dominate the play. The trial was controversial and unique in its day, but the passage of time would likely have kept Kelly from being memorable to the audience. Fresher in the minds of the audience would be the role that police spies played in the city's history and their suppression of the republican movement. Public interest in the trial was directly related to disdain for police spies, but also for the RIC, which had attacked an Amnesty gathering in Phoenix Park only weeks before the trial, fueling the lack of trust the public already had in the RIC. Crowds surrounded the courthouse every day of the trial and taunted RIC members who escorted Kelly between Kilmainham Gaol and Green Street. By the time *Trial at Green Street Courthouse* premiered in 1941, the Irish Free State had been established, but the memory of police infiltrating the community and conspiring against the public endured.

Neither the victim nor the accused is portrayed in the play. Their omission facilitates the prominence of Isaac Butt, who, in the end, was the most memorable character at the trial and who remained a Dublin icon long after his death.[4] All ancillary characters serve as a Greek chorus, echoing the public mood and adding to the play's effectiveness in characterizing the Fenian movement that was struggling to regain momentum at the time. The play's ten scenes devote meticulous attention to the alternating sets of pub (to be discussed later) and courtroom. Each set was constructed to make the audience as much a part of the proceedings as possible. Positioning the audience in this way reinforces the fact that public pressure influenced the trial's outcome. Although the Abbey alternated which set was to be foregrounded in various productions, its first staging had the pub set on a raised platform behind the courtroom. In all productions both sets remain on stage throughout; there were no set changes. McHugh notes that "in the court scenes, the proper placing of the witness-box is important. If it is placed at the back it should project, so that counsel need not speak to the back, but can examine the witness from the side and thus speak partly in the direction of the audience. This has further advantages; the expression of the witness can be seen clearly and the audience is in the natural position of the jury" ([1945], xiv). Staging the courtroom set so that the audience is in the "natural position of the jury" gives them the experience of being part of the cultural process they entered the theater to witness in dramatic form. They would, in a sense, be playing the roles of jurists.

4. Butt's legacy among nationalists was related to his defense of IRB leaders in 1865–67.

Role-playing-within-the-role occurs whenever "a character for some reason takes on a role that is different from his usual self" and "shows not only who the character is, but what he wants to be" (Hornby 1986, 67). Making the audience the role players is a metadramatic indicator. If, as Hornby suggests, this "dualistic device . . . sets up a feeling of ambiguity and complexity with regard to the character" (ibid.), then it infuses the audience with a self-ambiguity and complexity that heightens how they see themselves in the courtroom scene. It forces them to hear the "evidence" as those who will eventually pass judgment. The audience hears final arguments in pinnacle scene 7 when Armstrong sums up his case for the Crown and Butt does so for the defense against a backdrop of public support for Kelly largely based upon public resentment against the informer Talbot.

Public resentment of an informer is also foundational in Hugh Hunt and Frank O'Connor's *The Invincibles*, which premiered at the Abbey on October 18, 1937.[5] Its title refers to the secret society that gained notoriety for its 1882 Phoenix Park murders of Chief Secretary Lord Cavendish and Under Secretary Burke. The group planned to assassinate Chief Secretary Forster, but failed in several attempts. By the time they planned the Phoenix Park murder, Forster had resigned in protest over the Treaty of Kilmainham and the release of Parnell from jail. But the Invincibles went ahead with their plan, changing the target to Burke and inadvertently killing Cavendish. Unlike Forster, Cavendish was openly sympathetic to the Home Rule movement. Parnell supporters and republicans viewed the Phoenix Park murders as impeding the progress that had been made to date. The public locales used as various sets include pubs and Kilmainham Gaol. The prison does not appear until the last two scenes, but it is here that a key Invincible member, the group's de facto leader Carey, turns informer to

5. Text quoted herein, published in 1980, is that used for the September 4, 1967, revival at the Abbey (containing minor revisions of the 1937 script by Hunt). The 1937 script remains missing, as far as I can determine.

3. *The Invincibles* (1937) by Hugh Hunt and Frank O'Connor. Courtesy of the Abbey Theatre Archives.

save himself, and even the officer to whom he divulges information is repulsed by his lack of solidarity.

In scene 6, Carey is in his cell refusing to say who committed the murder or to confirm the names of the organization's membership. Inspector Mallon enters to offer Carey a deal if he talks, but Carey refuses. Mallon lists what he believes to be facts of Carey's involvement, but Carey does not verify any of it and comments that listening to the scenario Mallon outlines is "as good as a play" (Hunt and O'Connor 1980, 60). The fake civility of the scene takes an abrupt turn when Mallon tricks Carey into believing that another member of the group is about to inform on him. Losing his composure and discarding his mask as a respectable man of the city—a mask Mallon has seen through all along—Carey confesses that he was "the ringleader

. . . that plotted everything, but not guilty, not guilty of the murder!" (ibid., 65).

As was the case in the real Phoenix Park events, after Carey names names, all members of the Invincibles—with the exception of Brady and Kelly, who actually committed the murders—inform on each other. The inspector keeps his word and agrees to Carey's release in exchange for his testimony. For the final scene, the stage is split to show the cells of Carey and Brady. Carey is awaiting release, and Brady is preparing to be executed. A light comes up and fades down to indicate the action alternating between each cell. The first focus is on Brady and a warder, who witnessed the final visit of Brady's mother. He tells Brady he admires the woman's strength as she told her son to take his secrets to the grave. Brady replies, "That's the one thing I spared her—to see her son an informer" (ibid., 66). Brady asks the warder if there are crowds gathering in support of the Invincibles, only to be told that "everyone—the priests, the bishops and even Mr. Parnell" (ibid., 68) are against them. Carey is also obsessed with the public mood and with the public shame of being an informer. He momentarily regains his mask of being a community power player and argues that his former status can continue, as Mallon confronts him for not implicating all of the Invincibles:

MALLON: Have you any explanation?

CAREY: Here's my explanation. I have to live in Dublin and I have to leave some of them off or the people would get to distrust me. I was only writing to the Corporation to say 'twould be another couple of weeks before I could go back.

MALLON: Are you mad? Go back to the Corporation? Do you think you can ever live in Dublin again?

CAREY: And where else? Do you think I could live out of it? Dublin is the breath of my body, man. I'm known here, thirty years, man and boy; I know every jackstraw here.

MALLON: (*Lays revolver on table*): Here! Better take that!

CAREY: What's that for?

MALLON: You think there's one human being in Dublin that would be seen talking to you? Let me tell you, I don't trust my own policemen not to kill you in the van. I'll consider myself a lucky man if I can get you to South Africa alive. You can consider yourself a lucky man if you're alive two days after you get there. (ibid., 70)

Back in his cell, Brady sits with a nun, sharing his final thoughts as he contemplates the execution he is to face in the morning.[6] The spotlight remains on Brady's cell as another comes up on Carey's. Kelly, another prisoner to be executed, begins singing a Marian Hymn from offstage and is soon joined by the voices of other prisoners throughout the jail. The sound of this church hymn breaks Carey down, wailing that he "didn't betray them! I'm no Judas Iscariot!" (ibid., 74). The hymn has no impact on Brady, who remains unrepentant. His final lines, "I'm ashamed of nothing . . . Poor Ireland" (ibid.), close the play, with Kelly's praying heard in the background.

These final scenes undermine the notion that this play in any way romanticizes political murder. Rather, as Lionel Pilkington asserts, it is a "robust opposition to nationalist orthodoxies" (2001, 132). The one character who romanticizes political murder, Brady, is left a cynical, unrepentant man who will die shortly. With him will go all romantic notions of death or murder in the name of country. The crowds who gathered did so out of curiosity, as though to view an oddity. Brady's way of life is over. The final religious overtones—Carey's invoking the biblical traitor Judas and Kelly's song, the Marian Hymn "Hail, Queen of Heaven"—suggest that the presence of the Church in the early decades of the Free State overpowered the secret societies to which it was so opposed. However, this conclusion does not overshadow the play's recurring theme of the republican and Home Rule movements'

6. Brady, Kelly, and three others were executed. Eight others were sentenced to long prison terms. Because his testimony indicted all thirteen, Carey was the only one released. Carey was executed by a fellow passenger while traveling to South Africa.

refusals to accept responsibility for creating the climate that led to the formation of this fringe group. When the play premiered, Hunt and O'Connor were compelled to address that situation in a cynical program note:

> The absolute unanimity of opinion, Irish and English, on the Phoenix Park assassinations, makes it obvious that the last word has not yet been said.
>
> English defamation of Brady and his friends is largely propaganda, as is shown by its frequent contradictions and the flat and positive denial given by a prosecuting judge who was compelled to admit that his victims were all men of high character. The propaganda went to insensate lengths; Kelly was accused by rumour of sexual crimes; Brady's head was chopped off and wise men of the College of Surgeons gravely declared that his brain showed a complete incapacity for pity or remorse, while a Trinity College Professor kept a class of students convulsed by an imaginary analysis of the dead man's mental processes.
>
> The Irish calumnies, on the other hand, seem to have been inspired by a very bad conscience. No such monsters ever existed as are pictured by Nationalist and Catholic historians—the "butchers" of Canon Sheehan, the "Ferocius cut-throats" of Parnell's biographers—while the libelling of Carey, a simple, vain, weak man who had given years of his life to the service of Ireland and failed only when tricked by Mallon, passes the bounds of all decency. It is intelligible at all only if one assumes that *Nationalist Ireland blackguarded these brave and decent men in order to conceal from itself the fact that it had betrayed them* [italics mine]. (ATA ATC/MPC/1937)

The betrayal commented on by the authors is one of nationalist organizations refusing to consider their complicity. This situation began immediately upon the murders, and, it could be argued, was an effort to conceal the fact that the nationalist leadership was, at this time, neither in control of the citizens it professed to represent nor willing to accept responsibility for the ramifications of its actions when events did not play out as planned.

The cynical tone of *The Invincibles* highlights the prisoners' complete isolation from the public, republican leadership, and the jailers. The Dublin plays' propensities for highlighting internal divisions usually offer at least one character, however flawed, for the audience to consider as possessing a degree of honor. But in *The Invincibles*, there is none. The result is a lingering sense that leaderships' ambition is measured by the court of public opinion, their actions modified accordingly, and the recruits who respond to their rhetoric become expendable, collateral damage. A degree of this cynicism carries over into Seamus Byrne's *Design for a Headstone*, the definitive prison drama of the period.

The Dublin-born Byrne was a solicitor whose legal practice was interrupted for several years, first by political activism and later by playwriting. In 1940 he was sentenced to two years in Dublin's Mountjoy Prison for illegal radio transmissions on behalf of the IRA. While serving his sentence, he went on hunger strike and was released, having served less than ten months. The autobiographical elements in *Design* are self-evident. It premiered on April 8, 1950, and takes place in the 1940s. Although it never claims the location as Mountjoy, references to Dublin landmarks place it within the city proper, and the names and layouts of the cell blocks correspond to those of the legendary Dublin jail. All of the action occurs within the prison during the course of thirty days, the length of Conor Egan's hunger strike for recognition of his political status.[7]

The prisoners are a mix of political and criminal, and the play contains several overlapping story lines, with Egan's hunger strike and the

7. This is not the first Abbey play to include the hunger strike as a political weapon. That distinction belongs to Yeats's *The King's Threshold*. Although the original production in 1903 by the INTS (and subsequent productions through 1920 at the Abbey) did not include this plot point, Yeats revised the play to have Seanchan use this method to shame the king for heeding the request of "Bishops, Soldiers and Makers of the Law" to have the poet (Seanchan) banished from the court. Critics argue strongly that this revision was made after Terence MacSwiney died on hunger strike in 1920.

antics of recidivist criminal prisoner Jakey at the fore. The political and the criminal prisoners are presented as leading distinctly different lives under incarceration. The political prisoners are a mix of the "twenty-two crowd" (Byrne 1956, 89) and some who were incarcerated at a later point. It is this "twenty-two crowd," veterans of the War of Independence and the Civil War, whose activities confront what has been described as the "sanitized nationalist sentiment" (Welch 1990, 150) of mid-century Ireland, a position applicable to *The Invincibles*' program note by O'Connor and Hunt. The political prisoners meet regularly to study Irish, devise escape methods, and share information about what is happening within the republican movement. Meanwhile, the criminal prisoners focus on angling for favored work assignments and view prison as an escape from the harsher realities of economic survival and family commitments that face them outside of the prison walls.

The size of the cast is one noteworthy aspect of the production (there were more than twenty speaking parts and at least nine non-speaking), but so is the subject matter. Luke Gibbons notes that Byrne was one of the few playwrights of the period to "introduce more controversial subjects into the dramatic canon" (Gibbons 1996, 47). Although the play enjoyed a successful six-week run, it was not without controversy. As Gabriel Fallon recalled, "On the sixth night of the play's presentation a group of people in the audience gave vent to shouts of protest which resolved themselves into charges that the author was (a) using his play 'as a vehicle for Marxian philosophy'; (b) attempting to 'smear the Catholic priesthood'; (c) insulting Ireland, Irishmen, and a Temperance Association. At one point in the play (when Aidan O'Leary mentions Jacques Maritain) a number of young men rushed towards the stage shouting 'Maritain was wrong!' The incident would not be worth mentioning did it not reflect a line of thought and action which is consistent with certain attitudes in Irish Catholicism" (foreword to Byrne 1956, 4). The attack on Byrne for "insulting Ireland [and] Irishmen" echoes the attacks of prior decades, revealing that the Abbey remained a lightning rod for protest. The Irishness under attack is the legacy of the men of '22. Micheál Ó hAodha argues that the combination of the political prisoner characters demonstrates the author's intent to "stress the point of the continuity of the I.R.A. [and that Byrne's] argument would appear to be that Egan, O'Leary, McGowan and the rest are carrying on the unfinished business of 1922 and 1916 and as far back as you wish to go" (1961, 42). There is no denying that the three primary political prisoners are collectively true to a stereotype of an IRA man that has been constructed for cinematic and dramatic consumption over the years. Egan is a "die-hard" and a Catholic, selective of which church doctrines fit his political beliefs; O'Leary is an idealist who "believes in a purely Irish culture and an uncompromising national outlook" (ibid., 41); and McGowan appears modeled loosely on Connolly, a man for whom Marxism and other leftist political doctrines must be intertwined with nationalism for the movement to be freed from cultural trappings. Although the men maintain their positions while incarcerated, their rationales for sticking to them are all proven to be false.

The play opens and concludes with a game of chess, which serves as a metaphor for the posturing of the political prisoners and their perceived relationship to authority, real and symbolic. During the matches, the prisoners reveal their strategies for dealing with incarceration and for obtaining release. As a man set apart and living in the past, Egan is the only one who never participates. Nonetheless, he is an unwitting pawn in a power play led by the State. The jailers intended to provide Egan with political status all along, and he would not have to die for it. McGowan is the most thoughtful player, but when he makes a move, it is a bold one with the greatest risk of capture. But in the reality of the prison escape, he hesitates and it costs him his life. The most ardent and aggressive chess player, O'Leary, is the only survivor of the trio. In shock at the loss of his comrades, he forces another political prisoner to play chess with him, goading him on and, as he ponders his next move, vowing to "play this out to a finish" (Byrne 1956, 119).

Were it not for the play's setting, one might argue that the survival of O'Leary, its one prototypical republican idealist, supports the notion that the drama in some way romanticizes political murder. After all, a character who endures is often used to symbolize an implied theme of continuity. But O'Leary remains trapped in prison and his ideals are trapped with him. He and his ideals are separated from society and, once the authorities learn of his participation in the attempted escape, unlikely ever to rejoin it. The play can be read as the death of two branches of republican ideology (as characterized by Egan and McGowan) and the isolation of the third, most mainstream, as characterized by O'Leary. As Ó hAodha suggests, if O'Leary "represents the popular idea of what an IRA man was and still is" (1961, 42) and his popular idea remains behind bars, then the "unfinished business" is not to be played out in society. In other words, society is fine with the "uncompromising" IRA man remaining true to his ideals as long as he remains true to them under lock and key. Locks and keys are more figurative when the Dublin setting moves from the big house to the public house.

The pub first appeared on the Abbey stage in Synge's *The Playboy of the Western World*, where it challenged a rural ideal. The first Dublin pub arrived the following year in W. F. Casey's *The Man Who Missed the Tide*. In Casey's plays, the barroom is the setting for James Walsh's final failure, but also retains its primary social function as a place of rest. Contrarily, in later plays of the period the pub is a place of action. Although pub scenes often begin innocuously, they soon give way to external pressures or are used as settings for plotting and intrigue. Each of the plays with significant pub scenes incorporates historical events, including *The Dreamers* by Lennox Robinson (1915), *The Plough and the Stars*, *The Invincibles*, and *Trial at Green Street Courthouse*. There is also a compelling pub scene in act 2 of Louis D'Alton's Mangan biodrama, *The Man in the Cloak* (1937), but here the historical event is replaced by a historical figure and the setting is backdrop for group pressure imposed on an individual.

*The Dreamers* and *The Plough and the Stars* both reference Dublin risings; the former deals with Emmet's failed attempt to take hold of Dublin Castle in 1803, and the latter focuses on the Easter Rising. Act 2 of *The Dreamers* contains two scenes set in The White Bull Inn on Thomas Street. In the first, Emmet learns that his message to the Wicklow leadership has failed to be delivered. He realizes the effort will certainly be futile, but nonetheless decides to proceed with the plan. The pub here is a setting of intrigue and political uprising that ultimately transforms into a scene of impending doom. The second scene occurs while the Rising is under way and shows a group of Emmet supporters who have backed out of the plan in favor of several pints. This convivial, raucous gathering is one of the few pub scenes in a Dublin play to reflect the "realistic" mood of a pub setting, but the audience knows that outside its doors Emmett is about to fail. This knowledge undermines the scene's otherwise jovial tone.

History intrudes more directly in act 2 of *The Plough and the Stars*, in a scene labeled the "most severe critique of Irish nationalism," in part because it "juxtaposes the Pearse quotations [through the Voice of the Man] and the public house discourse" (Mustafa 2000, 108). The presence of the Voice of the Man citing Pearse has an impact on the audience, but it is lost on those gathered in the pub. This dramatic irony is only broken when Clitheroe, Brennan, and Langon enter with the tricolor. At this point, the rally outside establishes a presence inside the pub. The three men react to the Voice while having their drinks, but the rest of the crowd remains unmoved. As with *The Dreamers*, the pub serves a dual function as setting for rebellion and traditional location of respite.

Three of the ten scenes in *Trial* are set in Barney Kiernan's pub on Little Britain Street. In the year the play was set, it was one of the busiest pubs in Dublin. Because of its proximity to the criminal court on Green Street, it was frequented by "barristers, solicitors, policemen, jurymen, informers, and all those associated in any way with the law" (McHugh [1945], xii). The pub serves as the conduit through which the Dublin citizenry voice their sympathy for the accused Robert Kelly solely through condemning the actions of the murdered RIC Head Constable Talbot. The songs and chants of the crowds that gather outside the courthouse are heard through the pub's open doors. This public support is echoed by the men who gather inside contemplating the trial's outcome (scene 1), awaiting the verdict (scene 8), and, ultimately, celebrating Kelly's acquittal (scene 10). The pub set opens and closes the play and serves as more than a place of reprieve from the trial being dramatized. The pub conversations reference the public mood, which is more against Talbot's status as police spy than it is in support of Kelly for possibly being wrongly accused. This mood is most clearly stated in the opening scene between two local Dubliners awaiting the trial's start, who comment on the players involved and the climate of the city while Fenian tunes can be heard from out on the street:

RYAN: Poor old Butt! Champion of lost causes. The '48 men, the Fenians, and now Robert Kelly.
OLD MAN: Many's the time I saw the same Talbot himself staggering round the city spending the double pension he got for informing and babbling with his boozy tongue about his dirty deeds. God forgive me, it's often I wished I could shoot him myself. . . .
RYAN: Oh, it looks simple enough. Talbot dies. Kelly swings. And the circulation of the *Freeman* goes down until another peeler is shot. No doubt the Lord will provide. (ibid., 5–6)

Even this scene's conversation between Butt and O'Leary, the expert witness Butt hopes to call to support his claim that Talbot's operation is what actually killed him, focuses on the public mood. The two men spend more time discussing the status of the Fenian movement than they do the trial itself. In the end, the scenes in the pub serve as an expression of trial by public opinion that parallel and impact the "trial by jury" that is occurring in the courtroom on stage.

The action returns to the pub for the final scene, where crowds are celebrating outside with bonfires and song even though Kelly is not free. He has been remanded for shooting one of the policemen who arrested him. Three locals contemplate his fate:

RYAN: When the excitement has died down and Dublin has forgotten him, Robert Kelly will be quietly given about fifteen years.
JERRY: Still and all, he has his life, hasn't he?
RYAN: What sort of life? He'll come out of gaol an old man at fifty. There'll be no torches and cheers for him then.

JERRY: Ah, you have me heart scalded!

RYAN: Dublin, my dear Jerry, spends its time celebrating causes and forgetting men.

OLD MAN: He'll be remembered all right.

RYAN: What makes you so sure? The crowd outside will forget him tomorrow . . . They'll cheer as long as their torches flare; they'll cheer for a while and forget their slums and their hunger. (ibid., 69–70)

This passage nullifies any possibility of long-term public support for the underdog. The Old Man clings to romantic notions, but the younger Ryan is more pragmatic and acknowledges that the trial has been merely a diversion for residents of the inner city.

The pub is also used to house public reaction to a historical murder case in *The Invincibles*. In this play, the promise of public support is a tactic to recruit (scene 1); public outrage is a measure of failure (scene 3); and, finally, it parallels the realization by the Invincibles that they stand to be ostracized by other republican factions and will likely not survive the manhunt currently under way (scene 4).

The play opens in a pub in the autumn of 1881, with Kelly being recruited into the Invincibles by Tynan, Carey, and Brady. In this and the two subsequent scenes, the pub is a setting for secrecy, plotting, and manipulation. Playing on the reluctant Kelly's republican passions, Tynan assures him that joining the group will offer him the opportunity to "strike such a blow for Ireland that your name will be written forever in the hearts of all *true* Irishmen" (Hunt and O'Connor 1980, 13). Kelly takes the oath, and he and Brady are assigned to carry out the murders in Phoenix Park.

Scene 3 opens in a pub on the edge of Phoenix Park, with the publican and a visiting angler lightheartedly discussing Parnell and the appointment of Lord Cavendish as the new chief secretary. The Invincibles enter to review the murder they have just committed and to discuss how best to leave the area undetected. Initially they are full of themselves for a job well done, but the mood quickly changes when they realize they have murdered the populist Lord Cavendish in addition to their intended target, Burke. As the men leave the pub, others enter, share rumor of the murders, and agree that it was a horrible injustice to kill Cavendish, "a friend of the people" (ibid., 37).

Scene 4 returns to the pub of scene 1. Kelly and Brady are sharing news of public reactions: an opera at the Gaiety was cut short, with the audience leaving "in a fright," and local clergy are condemning the murderers as "low breed assassins not worthy of the name of Irishmen" (ibid., 41). Public fear and pulpit pronouncements do not concern them, though. It is only when Fenians enter the pub condemning the murders and carrying official proclamations signed by various Fenian groups throughout the city as well as by Parnell himself that they start to worry. Carey enters as they are reading Parnell's proclamation, but he is unfazed by it. He calms Kelly and Brady, sends them away with instructions to "lie low," and resumes his pint. But Carey's respite is interrupted by two policemen who briefly question him about the events in Phoenix Park before dragging him away for questioning.

As with the previous plays, the pub setting of *The Invincibles* is used to house figures of insurrection and to give voice to public opinion. It is also the only place apart from the prison where Carey maintains his dual faces as a pillar of the community playing the part of leader of an assassination squad, and leader of an assassination squad playing the part of community leader. As a result, he is both a man with evil inside wearing the mask of an honorable man and an honorable man wearing the mask of an evil one. The blurred line between private (the snug) and public space that is inherent to pubs parallels the ambiguity created by Carey's duality. It is not until the previously mentioned prison scenes, when he ultimately becomes a much-abhorred informer, that the "real" Carey is revealed to be the assassination squad leader, not a man of civic service. Like most public officials in public, tenement, and labor plays, Carey has his own secret agenda. Perhaps the preponderance of this sort of characterization is one explanation for why so many of the Dublin plays contain a cynical tone.

Such character duality and cynicism are emblematic of the times in which these plays were staged. When *The Critics* appeared in 1913, the Lockout was under way, the Irish Citizens' Army was active, and heightened social divisions undoubtedly led to suspicion of (and necessity for) disguised agendas. Between the premiere of *The Critic* in 1931 and *Trial at Green Street Courthouse* in 1941, unemployment was high, Dublin housing problems were ongoing, and the "economic war" with Britain continued to foster a sense of isolation. These situations showed no signs of abating when the new constitution was enacted in July 1937 (just a few months before the premiere of *The Invincibles*). Not coincidentally, outlawed republican groups increased activity significantly during the mid 1930s. This political faction of the nationalist project is criticized in *The Invincibles* and *Trial at Green Street Court House*, in a manner that is as overt as the cultural side is lampooned in *The Critics* and *The Critic*. The metadramatic plays use the theatrical experience to explore fissures in cultural revivalism, but those set in the courtroom and prison rely on the dramatization of historical events to suggest that fueling the flames of heightened nationalism carries consequences that undermine the movement's objectives. Even the public house offers no break from the pressures. Rather, its use is as a site of intrigue where citizens gather to question issues of nationalism and, more often than not, serve up evidence of its shortcomings.

# 6 Domestic Settings

## *Dubliners at Home*

ON SEPTEMBER 2, 1913, tenements located at 66 and 67 Church Street on Dublin's north side collapsed, killing seven people and injuring eight others. Citing the fact that both properties had passed city inspection less than three weeks earlier, many journalists "began to focus blame on the government itself for neglect of duty" (Kearns 1996, 18). The middle-class readership quickly supported that position, marking a shift in public opinion toward addressing the long-standing problem of safety and disease affecting the Dublin tenements. Church Street had been a problem as far back as 1818 when it was one of two streets (Barrack Street being the other) generating the most patients in that year's fever epidemic. It would go on to be cited in virtually every city report on poverty, crime, and illness issued in the years leading up to 1913. Although various organizations, including the Sisters of Charity and the Catholic Ragged Schools, served the Church Street community, nothing appears to have improved conditions. Slum landlords served as housing commissioners and civic leaders spoke of environmental determinism while the general mood remained largely one of apathy. Public outcry over the Church Street collapse led to Dublin's first comprehensive housing report (begun in 1913 and released in 1914), an overhaul of housing code protocols, the city's first significant slum clearance, and, not long after, the emergence of the tenement set on the Abbey stage.

More than 25 percent of the Dublin plays, including several that were staged before the Trilogy, are set in a tenement. Although tenement life is central to the second-city play *Mungo's Mansions*, the tenements of converted Georgian homes in Dublin dominate the urban repertoire's domestic settings. The Dublin tenement set is used so often in the Abbey's first half-century that it came to be the most symbolic setting of Irish urban drama on the national stage. As Sean O'Casey's Trilogy famously demonstrates, a play set in a Dublin tenement proved an ideal vehicle for drawing attention to class divisions in the city.

The Dublin plays' propensity for interior sets reflected the limitations of the Abbey stage, and appears to have been born of practicality. In her benchmark analysis of the Abbey's peasant plays, Brenna Clarke observes that the stage accommodated a "stage cottage [that] was perfectly scaled to the exact dimensions of an Irish cottage one would find in the West: 12 feet high in front, sloping down to 8 feet at the back wall, 20 feet long and 12 feet wide" (Clarke 1982, 57). These physical limitations provide one explanation for why cottage kitchens appear so often in the rural-set plays. The limitations also approximate the typical tenement room found in a converted Georgian townhouse: fifteen feet square. This size would prove to be a blessing in disguise. The history of converted Georgian homes was rife with drama to be exploited by playwrights creating works set in such spaces.

After the Acts of Union went into effect in 1801, the Ascendancy left Dublin in mass numbers, but many retained ownership of their homes. Agents responsible for supervision of properties often allowed them to fall into disrepair. This process was aided by the complicity of the Dublin Corporation, which had control over building codes and ignored safety violations in order to maximize occupancy rates. The Georgian mansions became tenements owned either by the Corporation as a governing body or by individuals who replaced the Ascendancy as power brokers in the housing market. Kevin Kearns notes that the values of these houses "plummeted to unimaginable levels. Georgian houses, which had been purchased for £8,000 in 1791, sold for only £2,500 a mere decade later. And by 1849 the same houses commanded a paltry £500" (1983, 41). The initial property slump of the early nineteenth century could have been a temporary, albeit protracted, issue of supply and demand that would go on to correct itself, had it not been for deliberate intervention. Agents who allowed the homes to deteriorate stood to profit either by purchasing the properties at low prices and becoming profiteering landlords themselves, or by purchasing them to resell to the city at a profit.

Dublin faced a severe working-class housing shortage for most of the second half of the nineteenth century, particularly during the Famine years, when it "became the principal catchbasin for the rural masses fleeing hardship elsewhere in the country" (ibid., 45). Profiteering landlords found willing tenants, no matter how bad the conditions. They also found ready buyers in local businessmen willing to be slumlords themselves, or in the Dublin Corporation. Quite often the roles of landlord, slumlord, and city bureaucrat merged. The city government, many of its Corporation members, and the wealthy who had vacated the city all played a part in the transformation of stately homes into tenement slums and appear, to varying degrees, in all the tenement plays.

*The Slough*, which premiered in November 1914, was the first play to recreate a tenement room on the Abbey stage. Eleven others followed over the next three decades: *Blight*; M. M. Brennan's *The Young Man from Rathmines* and *A Leprechaun in the Tenement* (both 1922); *The Shadow of a Gunman*; *Juno and the Paycock*; Kenneth Reddin's *The Passing* (under the pseudonym Kenneth Sarr) (1924); *The Plough and the Stars*; Arthur Power's *The Drapier Letters* (1927); Louis D'Alton's *The Man in the Cloak* (1937); E. F. Carey's *Caesar's Image* (1939), and Bernard McGinn's *Remembered For Ever* (1941). During this four-decade span, the tenement was also present in numerous revivals, including more than eighty of the Trilogy plays alone.

One convention of the tenement plays is the use of overcrowding as a plot catalyst, a portrayal that reflected the very real housing conditions of the Dublin poor and was used to memorable effect in *The Plough and the Stars*. Perhaps the clearest picture of how tenement living created a world devoid of privacy lies in the statistics of occupation. The 1901 census disclosed that the twentieth century began with "over 72,000 people (one quarter of the population) living in 21,747 single rooms, of which 12,925 were occupied by three or more persons" (quoted in O'Brien 1982, 130). By 1913, less than a year before the premiere of *The Slough*, conditions had hardly improved. The 1913 Housing Inquiry, instigated in part by public outrage over the Church Street incident, released findings that verified the dangerous structural conditions that existed in housing of the poor and warned of the dangerous overcrowding experienced by most tenement dwellers.[1]

The first and third acts of *The Slough*, a critical look at organized labor (see chapter 7), are set in a tenement. The union leadership plans to forgive the arrears of men who acquiesce to union authority and to expel those who challenge it. They are intent on building power by sheer numbers; financial responsibility and the welfare of labor are secondary to that objective. When the play moves to the tenement, money and work become tangible issues by their absence. *The Slough* alludes to organized labor and to rigid class structures as factors that collude to perpetuate poverty. The second tenement play in the Dublin repertoire is *Blight*, which premiered December 11, 1917, and holds the distinction of being the first Abbey play that Sean O'Casey claims to have attended (Murray 2004, 112). *Blight* takes this notion of outside forces' complicity and moves it to the fore, blurring the lines of division between the public and private spheres that were rigidly demarcated in *The Slough*.

*Blight*'s tenement setting accentuates the harsh living conditions of Dublin's poor, but it also serves as a space to aggressively challenge the urban power brokers, as it did in *The Slough*. Taking a page from *The Laying of the Foundations*, the slum landlords of *Blight* are all members of the city hierarchy, a characterization that dominates the tenement plays. The slumlord protagonist, Tully, is a former tenement-dweller who becomes as unconcerned with the welfare of his former neighbors as the landlords he once rallied against. A wealthy member of the Corporation, Tumulty is a self-sacrificing man who grows so disillusioned

1. See Ruth McManus, *Dublin, 1910–1940: Shaping the City and Suburbs* (2002) for a thorough examination of this subject.

by the turn Tully has taken and by the Corporation's focus on perpetuating a ghettoized class that he resigns, vowing to champion the housing plight of the poor. Although Tully's often comic antics risk the character's fulfilling what Declan Kiberd identifies in Trilogy comic figures as an invitation to "the literate, theatrical audience to patronize rather than understand" (1996, 232) the working class, Tumulty's actions prevent *Blight* from falling into sentimentality. *The Laying of the Foundations* ends on a note of youthful optimism, but Tumulty's parting comment as he departs the stage in *Blight* is more cynical: "this city will continue to be the breeding ground of disease, vice, hypocrisy and discontent" (Gogarty 2001, 544). The cynical tone is shared by so many tenement plays that one can point to it as a convention of the genre.

The power brokers of *The Slough* are working-class members of the community whose obsession with union solidarity ironically compels them to turn their backs on one of their own. By offering a mob mentality as the chief way to explain why these men forsake a member of their own community, *The Slough* represents the alienation of the poor as an internal force. One might argue that the poor adopt a hierarchal model based on the business construct created by the rich. *Blight* also questions the morality of workingmen when influenced by outside forces. It expands its condemnation of urban power brokers to include the upper- and middle-class leadership of the medical community, the Church, and Church-related charities. In doing so, it suggests that the social and government order in Dublin is not only complicit in perpetuating tenement poverty, but also active in maintaining a ghettoized class. Tully gives voice to this concept when he rallies his neighbors to take part in a rent strike until repairs are made. But it is also an idea acknowledged by the powers-that-be. One young doctor admits he is part of a system of "hypocrisy" that lacks "courage to face facts; because we won't realize that prevention is better than the cure, because charity must prey on suffering" (Gogarty 2001, 530). It is implied that if the committee members fix the problems of the slums, they will put themselves out of work. The class distinctions of *Blight* reflect one outcome of the 1913 Lockout and its aftermath, "growing class-conflict in Dublin . . . which not only focused attention on the social questions neglected by cultural nationalism but also polarized the revival itself" (Hutchinson 1987, 184). Hutchinson traces this class conflict back to the Gaelic League's declining influence that began in 1908, but the Lockout also certainly drew attention to the movement's insufficient attention to the poor. All of the Dublin tenement plays bring class distinctions into focus, a further convention of the tenement genre.

Anticipating the *Report on Dublin Housing* that would be published the following year, *Blight* suggests that in the Dublin slums, environmental determinism "prevails for the average person . . . and just because some certain individuals rise above their appalling surroundings . . . it does not negate [the] central reality" that most cannot escape that environment (Prunty 2000, 3). *Blight* echoes this determinism and accuses the ruling class of creating an environment that perpetuates poverty. It is also the first of the Abbey tenement plays to oppose any "cultural distinction between what is urban and what is Irish" (O'Toole 1985, 115). In *The Slough*, union committee members lament the inability to face the reality of harsh city living among "labouring men from the country" (Wilson 1914, 41). *Blight*, however, omits any mention of the rural. The city is presented as an Irish reality; the playwrights make no attempt to consider the ideal of a constructed notion of authenticity to be found in rural Ireland.

*Blight*'s urban focus was underscored by a journalistic note in the program of its first production: "Of the 25,822 families inhabiting the tenement houses, 78% or 21,000 families, consisting of about 90,000 persons, occupy each only one room. No description can adequately convey to the mind the extreme wretchedness of such homes as these, where there can be no effectual separation of the sexes, where the parents, the adolescent, and the child must live, sleep, dress, cook, eat, wash body and clothes, read and study in one apartment. —*The Evening Herald*, November 3rd" (ATC/MPC/1917). In addition to preparing the audience for the setting they are about to witness, the use of a press account to document tenement living conditions reflects the role journalists played to bring Dublin's tenement problems to the public consciousness.

In the first two acts, set in a tenement, Tully is all bravado and optimism, seemingly bigger than his surroundings and ready to confront the city's complicity in the circumstances of his family and neighbors. But the third act, set in an elegant boardroom, finds him absorbed by the setting. He has become "one of the Corporation star turns" (Gogarty 2001, 529) and is focused on his chance to profit as the new owner of his tenement building. His earlier passion against hypocrisy is taken over by fellow board member Tumulty, who observes that "in no town is charity vainer or more misplaced . . . vast, useless sums are spent yearly in the name of charity and nothing comes of them, but misery continues unabated" (ibid., 539). Rather than Tully, it is Tumulty who takes a stand to champion the plight of Tully's own family and neighbors, but he is overruled and silenced by all fellow board members, including Tully himself.

The fictional board of *Blight* provocatively mirrors the social standing of the Abbey's own opening-night audience as well as its directors and shareholders. The full list of directors is not available because records from the 1911 filing by the National Theatre Society Limited were destroyed during the Civil War.[2] But share distribution was stable during the Abbey's early decades. The 1921 records, which survived, can be presumed to reflect the year when *Blight* premiered. The 1921 shareholders were Gregory, Yeats, Udolpho Wright, Sara Allgood, Edmund Bourke, the Rt. Hon. William F. Bailey, Philip Hanson, and Lennox Robinson. Gregory, Yeats, Wright, Allgood, and Robinson enjoyed prominent social standing in the community. Other, less well-known shareholders also held high-status positions including: estates commissioner (Bailey), a commissioner of public works (Hanson), and the inspector of the local government board for Ireland (Bourke).

2. These papers were destroyed when the Four Courts burned at the start of the Civil War. See Kavanagh 1950, *The Story of the Abbey Theatre*, for details on the Articles of Association for the NTSL.

Joseph Holloway found the group assembled for the opening night performance as noteworthy as the play itself:

> Not for years has such an audience been inside the Abbey as assembled tonight to see the first performance of *Blight*, a play of Dublin slum life by A. and O. (Dr. Oliver Gogarty and Joseph O'Connor, Heblon of *Studies in Blue* fame). To me the audience was quite as interesting as the play. In the vestibule before eight were grouped together Con Curran, Conroy (the Gaelic writer), Susan Mitchell and her sister, George Russell, Mr. and Mrs. Darrell Figgis, Mrs. Stopford Green, Seumas O'Sullivan, Estelle Solomons, Lady Gregory, Mr. and Mrs. James Stephens, George Roberts and Mrs. [George Roberts] (*nee* Maire Garvey), and crowds of other well-known figures. (Holloway 1967, 194)

There are no accounts of Yeats's or Gregory's reactions to the play, but Holloway claimed that after speaking with a member of Gregory's party, "the general opinion was that the piece was more a discussion than a play, and that the characters argued more than conversed" (Holloway 1967, 195). This defensive reaction suggests that the authors' targets recognized the accusations launched in their direction, but chose not to take the bait.

The message did not go unnoticed by members of the press, however, including one *Irish Times* critic who wrote on December 12, 1917, "the moral is skilfully pointed. The authors send their shafts accurately home, and no one is spared. The Corporation, the Health Committee, the slum landlord, the agent, and the hypocritical philanthropists are unmercifully and justifiably laid under the lash." This direct attack was met with mixed results. Holloway notes that on the opening night "the theatre was abuzz with excitement before the play began; it had got about that the play might be suppressed after the first performance due to its condemnation of city power brokers—that, in fact, it was very 'hot stuff'" (ibid., 194). The play ran its scheduled ten-day run, playing to full houses. It was revived a month later, and at least two additional times in 1918, to repeated financial success. Nonetheless, the assertion that it was perhaps too "hot" for the Abbey board is plausible. Three revivals of a box office hit were fewer than the norm during this time period, and *Blight* was never again staged at the Abbey.

*Blight*'s limited longevity on the Abbey stage might also be the result of its limited comic relief. The other tenement tragedies did not fare much better with audiences: *Caesar's Image* and *The Man in the Cloak* were each staged only once, and *The Drapier Letters* and *The Passing* had only two productions. Each of these tragedies is more depressing than the next. *Caesar's Image* is set in a rat-infested tenement room where women face unwanted pregnancies and the men—when they are not avoiding the responsibility of parenthood—are getting drunk or dying of pneumonia brought on by their poor living conditions. In the end, all characters are dead, arrested for murder, forced to emigrate, or left alone to fend for themselves. D'Alton's *The Man in the Cloak* is a dramatization of the last hours of James Clarence Mangan, featuring the poet in an opium-induced state of regret as cholera sweeps through the Bride Street dosshouse in which he resides. The author's direction for the set insists that "there should be nothing missing that will convey the aspect of utter poverty, neglect and desolation" (D'Alton 1971, 4). The plot and dialogue are similarly grim. Arthur Power's *The Drapier Letters* is set in the slums near St. Patrick's Cathedral. In its attempt to identify the individual who inspired Swift to write *The Drapier's Letters*, the play focuses on a young woman living in abject poverty who is accidentally killed by police as they search the tenement looking for the provocative author. *The Passing*, by Kenneth (Reddin) Sarr, is a one-act play, set in an attic tenement on the Dublin quays. It dramatizes the final hour of a streetwalker who, as she lies dying, laments over the son she will leave behind: a mentally handicapped young man who stands over his mother's bed unable to comprehend her condition. Although it was not a particular success with Abbey audiences or contemporary critics, *The Passing* was awarded the Best Play prize at the 1924 Tailteann Games, suggesting at least a pocket of critical support.

Within the tradition of the tenement plays, tragicomedies tended to have the greatest longevity on the Abbey stage, although Bernard

McGinn's *Remembered For Ever*, in which the first act is set in a Dublin tenement, was only staged once. Tomás MacAnna describes the McGinn play as one of "frustration at a lost idealism" (1971, 98). That thwarted idealism is only a small part of a crowded storyline that includes racketeering slumlords, corrupt politicians, and disingenuous republicans, as well as the ghosts of Parnell, Emmet, Pearse, and Mitchel. They haunt Cassidy, a celebrated veteran of the War of Independence torn between his desire to be anonymous and his desire to be venerated. In the foreword to the published play, Lennox Robinson attributes the first act's shortcomings in part to its imitation of O'Casey: "the first ten minutes . . . might be a transcript from the first ten minutes of Sean O'Casey's *The Plough and the Stars*. Fluther Good mends a lock, Cassidy mends a window. They talk alike, they are alike, they are twins . . . but it is very difficult to write a play about a tenement in Dublin without falling under O'Casey's terrific genius" (McGinn 1943, 5).

Abbey audiences' preference for tragicomedy is not limited to the Dublin tenement plays. One can easily find examples not set in a tenement, ranging from *The Playboy of the Western World* to the rural and provincial plays of Louis D'Alton, William Boyle, and George Shiels. Lighter works—even when they contained some dark elements—often had the greatest longevity. What distinguishes the urban plays that successfully bridged tragedy and comedy from plays that took place in rural settings is a propensity to use key political events as either catalysts of, or intrusions upon, the domestic setting. The plays of O'Casey's Trilogy are the only tenement plays to employ this plot strategy. Notably, they are also the plays in this group that enjoyed the greatest popular and critical success.

The conclusions of *The Shadow of a Gunman*, *Juno and the Paycock*, and *The Plough and the Stars* are tragic, but these plays all contain moments of great comic relief. O'Casey's comedic elements are most often found in the form of characters who "fight against all forms of authority and respectability—Irish as well as British, religious as well as nationalistic" (Krause 1982, 98–99). When Donal Davoren reminds Seumas Shields in *The Shadow of a Gunman* that he once "believed in nothing but the gun," the comic foil Shields resists being drawn into Davoren's romantic notions of Irish nationalism's violent side. Shields's moment of resistance becomes an opportunity to critique the origins of that fallacy: "I've a different opinion now when there's nothin' but guns in the country . . . An' you daren't open your mouth, for Kathleen ni Houlihan is very different now to the woman who used to play the harp an' sing 'Weep on, weep on, your hour is past', for she's a ragin' divil now, an' if you only look crooked at her you're sure of a punch in th' eye" (O'Casey 1998, 39). In *Juno*, the comedic antics of Joxer and the Captain are based solely on their efforts to avoid all forms of respectable work or sobriety. As numerous critics have observed, *The Plough* abounds with examples of comic relief that rely on the juxtaposition of opposing ideologies, including those of the Covey and Uncle Peter, Fluther and Mrs. Grogan, and Bessie Burgess and Rosie Redmond. In each instance, the comedy is at its highest pitch when the character who takes comfort in the path of least resistance foils the one who believes in taking the higher road.

The 1922 comedies of Matthew Brennan—*The Young Man from Rathmines* and *A Leprechaun in the Tenement*—offer different examples of juxtaposition, and fall horribly flat by exemplifying "the problems with comic mediation of class disparity" (Murphy 2008, 108). Brennan's one-act plays portray tenement families seeking upward mobility, one through a daughter's marriage, the other through that most plucky of means, a leprechaun. Both plays are noteworthy for the author's adoption of stereotypes—the use of which stands in opposition to the tenets espoused in the ILT's mission statement to neither show Ireland as "the home of buffoonery" nor to stage material that ignores an audience "weary of misrepresentation" (Gregory 1913, 9).

*The Young Man from Rathmines* is a play of mistaken identity. Set in a tenement on Dominick Street, the play opens on the Dowd family engaged in an absurd staging of their home for the arrival of Mary's suitor, George Jackson. Mrs. Dowd is wearing a "faded black silk dress [with a] large piece of cheap lace" around her neck. Mr. Dowd is struggling to put on a collar at the insistence of his wife. A neighbor is in costume as their maid (Brennan [1923], 5). Mary has been exchanging letters with a recently arrived medical student, George Jackson, since answering his newspaper advertisement for "a nice, refined girl" to correspond with him. Because of his studies and Rathmines mailing address, George is considered a promising potential husband who can lift the family out of poverty. What the family fails to consider is the possibility that George is not white. When George arrives, Mary and her mother are reduced to tearful confusion, and the father to violence: "An' it was for a black haythen that I was made put on this. Just wait a minit, me buckoo, an I'll give ye such a pair of black eyes that the rest of yer face'll look white" (ibid., 23). Played by a heavily made up Gabriel Fallon, Jackson was described in the April 7, 1922, *Evening Herald* review as "an Indian half caste." His race and the family's reaction to it are as central to the comedy as the mother's obsession with upward mobility through her daughter's marriage to an educated man.

Kathleen Heininge finds a progression of the marriage play in Irish drama, tracing its evolution from straightforward to concerns about inheritance to "the ritual of courting and matchmaking where the final result is marriage out of economic necessity . . . for men and women" (2009, 160), often in the comic genre. She argues that "as socialist ideas began to take hold in Ireland . . . the marital plot becomes less straight forward. The efficacy of marriage as the best economic solution is uncertain" and the "road to [marriage] is less direct, less familiar, and less comic" (ibid). For all of its offensiveness, *The Young Man from Rathmines* might be read optimistically as a parody of the marriage comedy. However, the play lacks any observational character who might provide commentary on the cruel reception George receives. Brennan's next play, *A Leprechaun in the Tenement*, does not make the search for a positive interpretation any easier.

*A Leprechaun in the Tenement*[3] opens on Mrs. Reilly and her daughter, Mary Kate, discussing marriage and lamenting Mary Kate's

3. Script and promptbook of *Leprechaun* remain missing (possibly destroyed in the 1951 Abbey fire). Summary notes are derived from reviews and synopses that can be found in NLI MS. 25,505.

inability to keep a boyfriend. Mr. Reilly returns from fishing on the banks of the Liffey to announce that he has a leprechaun in his basket who is prepared to grant his wish of wealth and a home on Merrion Square. With two wishes remaining, Mary Kate asks for a new dress, and this is granted. The son, Mickey—described in the September 6, 1922, *Irish Times* opening night review as "a painfully portrayed imbecile"—wishes for the family to remain in the tenement because his only friend is a dog that lives in the building and he does not want to leave it behind. While the plans are under way to move to Merrion Square, an argument breaks out among the parents, Mary Kate, and their neighbor. During the commotion, Mickey steals the basket containing the leprechaun and flees. The dog eats the leprechaun, ending Reilly's hopes for an upscale life but fulfilling Mickey's dream to remain in the tenement, and the play ends.

It is all but impossible to explain Brennan's intentions in his use of negative stereotypes. Brennan is something of a ghost of Abbey history, marginalized in published Abbey histories and the Abbey archives, and barely noticed by drama critics of the day. Apparently stereotypes about unintelligent "labouring" fathers, marriage-obsessed mothers and daughters, and meddling female neighbors were, as the September 6, 1922, *Irish Times* found, "true to a type" that was acceptable on the national stage during this time. Even though the characterizations are overwhelmingly negative, none was commented on as such in the press reviews of the plays. However, several critics specifically cite the "buffoonery" of *Leprechaun*. The word *buffoonery* appears in reviews of *Leprechaun* from a wide variety of newspapers. Its use suggests that critics were not reproaching the playwright as much as they were condemning the Abbey management for staging such a work. Why did they stage such a play? The answer might be found in the economics of 1922.

On January 2, 1922, Yeats wrote Gregory that the new year might well see the Abbey have its political problems replaced by financial ones. It turned out to be both. The Anglo-Irish Treaty was accepted in Dáil Éireann on January 7, Anti-Treaty forces occupied the Four Courts on April 13, and the Free State Army shelled the Four Courts on June 28, marking the beginning of the Civil War, which would last into 1923. Throughout this period, curfews disrupted theater operations and impacted the box office. No doubt the directors were strategizing on how to most effectively negotiate their request for state subvention with the new Free State government. As Lauren Arrington argues, "while the Abbey directors were lobbying the new government, the theatre was caught between warring Free State and Republican forces" (2010, 51). Both repertoire and finances were under considerable pressure, repertoire because the directors were attempting to placate both sides and finances because attendance was down. The staging of *The Young Man from Rathmines* suggests that the Abbey team did not know which way to turn. Their uncertainty is reflected in running the play at all, but even more astonishingly, running it twice on shared bills with *Cathleen ní Houlihan*: from August 7 to 9 and on August 15, in both cases to dismal box office receipts, £138.15.10 in the first instance and £42.12.9 in the second (ATA ATC/FIN/6). In total, *The Young Man from Rathmines* was revived four times in 1922 and additional productions were staged as late as 1924. *Leprechaun* ran its scheduled six nights, but was never revived to fill future double- or triple-bills, which was usual practice for one-act comedies of the time.

If one reads the Brennan plays as employing satire and exaggeration in order to challenge urban society, then the targets become social standing in *The Young Man from Rathmines*, and dogmatic reliance on the mythological and fantastic in *Leprechaun in the Tenement*. Yet it appears that Abbey audiences found it acceptable to lampoon a man of foreign birth and to present the urban poor as intellectually inferior, but drew a line when it came to a young handicapped Irishman serving as a foil. Both plays ironically take the "buffoonery" condemned in the charter of the National Theatre and put it center stage.

The irony of the tenement plays is how central these portrayals of poverty were to the Abbey's attempts at financial stability. The emergence of a Dublin repertoire and tenement genre, particularly the Trilogy, sustained the Abbey in its early decades and became staples in later seasons. The staging of tenement drama may have begun as an attraction to domestic audiences, but its popularity grew beyond the local. The tenement play has toured extensively throughout the world and been staged during many summers, when tourist audiences comprise a significant percentage of the Abbey audience.

Along with the tenement plays came a second group of dramas also based on the real estate holdings of the time: boarding-house plays. Kevin Kearns notes that after the Act of Union, "not all affluent Dubliners were eager, or even willing, to relinquish their established roots. Many tenaciously clung to their former world, hoping that conditions would stabilize and they could find security in the new social and political order" (Kearns 1983, 42). Those holdouts included those for whom their homes were a primary money-making asset. This boarding-house segment is portrayed in Matthew Brennan's *The Big Sweep* and Brinsley MacNamara's *The Grand House in the City.* In both plays, the boarding houses are run by female owners who use the Georgian space to problematize shifting socioeconomic relationships. *The Big Sweep* does so from the point of view of lower- and middle-class Dubliners and *The Grand House in the City* from the point of view of the Ascendancy. These plays feature a segment of the Ascendancy seldom included in the Dublin repertoire.

*The Big Sweep* concerns the declining fortunes of the Ascendancy (in the character of O'Grady) and incorporates the sympathetic and antagonistic receptions received from non-Ascendancy Dubliners. The initial antagonistic reception slowly recedes, as O'Grady proves himself to be a decent, caring man worthy of his new neighbors' affections. In the end, the play champions the role of the Ascendancy in the life of early independent Ireland and unites it in a loving union with the downtrodden of the inner city. The keeper of the boarding house, Mrs. Hayden, is a miserly widow who resents her unemployed brother Pat and stepdaughter Kitty, treating them both with contempt and using her economic power as property owner to enslave them. The other residents include Gerald O'Grady, the newest arrival, who is described as "the last of an impoverished line" (Brennan [1933], 1); Miss de Lacey, a fifty-year-old music teacher; Dermot Sullivan, a civil servant and ardent nationalist; and Michael Rooney, a childless widower and retired country shopkeeper "who has decided to spend the remainder of his days in the city" (ibid., 7). *The Big Sweep* establishes a convention of the boarding-house plays representing a safe and congenial home, but lacking family ties. This convention contrasts the tenement set, which tends to lack any sense of physical security, but often presents strong familial alliances.

This is the first Dublin play not to have a traditional family relationship central among its primary protagonists. The one blood relationship, between Mrs. Hayden and her brother Pat, is tenuous at best. Mrs. Hayden only allows her brother and Kitty to remain boarders in exchange for their help in maintaining the property. With the boarders, we see the emergence of what would, in contemporary terms, be deemed an "urban family," one constructed by people whose common denominator is the city that has become an adopted home either by choice or by circumstance. Brennan identifies his characters by their ages, creating an allegorical family that maps against the traditional and encompasses conventional stereotypes. The fifty-year-old Miss de Lacey and sixty-year-old Rooney embody the sage reason and sympathetic tones of kindly grandparents. Pat is the fallible but good-natured uncle, and Sullivan the demanding adolescent. This leaves the orphaned Kitty and O'Grady as the outsiders destined to be united.

The action reveals that O'Grady had to sell everything, including his family home, in order to pay off debts on the property. He is now down to his last £125 and in search of employment. Despite this hardship, Sullivan is antagonistic toward O'Grady from the start. Eventually, Sullivan's hostility softens, and he becomes somewhat sympathetic to the new arrival's situation. O'Grady's attributes are echoed by de Lacey throughout act 1 and focus largely on his generous nature and willingness to face odds that are stacked against him in the new social order of the nation.

By the end of act 1, O'Grady and Kitty are aligned as the play's pacifists, against Sullivan and Mrs. Hayden as the play's aggressors. Sullivan is a young Catholic nationalist who romanticises the past decade's fighting, as though he regrets not having been a part of it. De Lacey defends Sullivan as best she can to O'Grady, who has been given the cold shoulder by the young nationalist: "You mustn't take all he says too seriously. He's young enough to hold the old idea that the world can be made a better place by chopping off heads, or blowing them off, or getting them off in some violent way" (ibid., 25–26).

When O'Grady is made aware of the brutality Kitty suffers at the hands of Mrs. Hayden, he becomes determined to help her. Realizing he holds two tickets to a sweepstakes (the "big sweep" of the play's title), he tells Kitty to go to his room and take one for herself. Kitty's is a winning ticket. It is worth £600 and the chance to win an additional £30,000 at the next week's horse race. O'Grady asks for no share of the winnings, but only offers his sincere congratulations. This is one more method by which this scion of the old guard is elevated to sainthood by all around him, and he grows more beloved in the eyes of Kitty. Sullivan also draws a winning ticket, effectively pitting altruistic ascendancy against violence-loving nationalist in a game of chance. When Sullivan realizes good fortune has landed in his lap, he faints, suggesting that the young nation is incapable of handling opportunity. Before the curtain falls on Kitty and O'Grady, who have professed their love for each other while awaiting the race results and are now engaged to be married, Mrs. Hayden has been revealed for the horrible human being she is, and the sage elders (de Lacey and Rooney) have restored harmony to the chaotic household.

Rather than using the boarding house as a site of unification, *The Grand House in the City* uses it to examine the State's post-independence redistribution of wealth. The new socioeconomic climate has resulted in one Ascendancy family's financial hardships. That situation is significantly marginalized in favor of presenting a neighboring non-Ascendancy landowner as an avaricious figure who attempts to manipulate the fallen Ascendancy out of their property. The set is described as "distinguished from the sitting room of the average city boarding-house by some lingering sense it seems to hold of the North side of Dublin in the spacious days of Grattan's Parliament. This note of faded splendour has a dwindling reflection in the present appointments of the room, which have a certain faded grandeur" (MacNamara [1956], n.p., 1.1). The majority of the boarding-house tenants are Ascendancy members who cling aggressively to their old status and view nonmembers as "peasant creatures from the country" and "upstarts" (ibid., n.p. 1.4). Class divides are never breached in this house. As various Ascendancy characters struggle to legally reclaim their former homes and the house owner, Diana, struggles to keep up the house's appearance, the house itself becomes a metaphor for an old way of life. Resolution of all claims occurs in the countryside of Westmeath. It is not until Diana decides to sell the Dublin house, thereby letting go of the past, that she too finds solace. With its use of the faded Georgian metaphor and its plot resolution occurring in the countryside, *The Grand House in the City* uses an urban domestic setting to fuse the rural and the past onto an urban set.

*Apartments* (1923) bridges the gap between the Ascendancy-focused *The Big Sweep* and *The Grand House in the City* and the tenement plays. Written by Kathleen Cruise O'Brien, the setting takes a comedic look at women's labor.[4] In addition to running the boarding house, Mrs. MacCarthy has a hand in the operation of a local grocery, a bookshop, and—reflecting her never-ending need to beg, borrow, and trade—a pawn shop. All of her outside work is undertaken to keep her own family fed and clothed. Her malapropism-prone husband, Mick, is a loafer with lofty ideas. Together they are precursors to Jack and Juno Boyle of *Juno and the Paycock* (which would premiere the following year), but without any of the Boyles' tragedy. The tragedy of domestic life is largely left to the tenement setting.

With the overwhelming majority premiering during the years when revivalism was a continuing influence, the domestic plays—more than any other subgenre of the urban repertoire—present a microcosm of the Abbey's active engagement with the movement. These plays exemplify that "Irish revivalism, by and large, was a modernizing force [that] sought to enter into history and record it at the same time" (Castle 2011, 293). Such simultaneity is present not so much in the form but in the subject matter and settings of the Dublin domestic plays. Showcasing internal class divisions in the home is a bold

4. *Apartments* is unpublished. See NLI MS. 21,434 for script.

move that both exemplifies how deeply personal revivalism was as a movement and critically points out its shortcomings. With the shortcomings being articulated mostly in domestic settings of the poor or otherwise marginalized, the Abbey does not shy away from the elitist criticism that was often laid at its door.

# 7 Labor Pains

## *Staging the Lockout*

ON AUGUST 22, 1913, workers from the Dublin United Tramways Company approached Irish Transport and General Workers Union (ITGWU) leader James Larkin for assistance in negotiating better terms. Their grievances concerned rates of pay, the desire for "one day off in every eight instead of one day in every ten; time and a half for Sunday work; and that the weekly payday be a Friday" (Keogh 1982, 188). Larkin met with Tramways management on August 26, but they refused to hear the workers' grievances since they were presented through the ITGWU rather than by the workers directly. That the workers had previously attempted to present these requests directly was not deemed relevant. Larkin immediately called for a strike, and it quickly spread to other ITGWU members in companies throughout the city. But Larkin's strategy of syndicalism, a general strike of sympathy by ITGWU members across the city rather than one specific to the Tramways Company, was challenged on September 3 when the Dublin Employers' Federation[1] (DEF) passed the following agreement: "We hereby pledge ourselves in future not to employ any persons who continue to be members of the [ITGWU], and any person

1. The DEF, modelled on the Cork organization that was founded to defeat a sympathy strike in that city in 1909, was an association of 404 Dublin business owners led by Tramways chairman William Martin Murphy. Before the Lockout, the DEF had succeeded in breaking the ITGWU strike of the Great Southern and Western Railway (of which Murphy was a board member) in 1911.

refusing to carry out our lawful and reasonable instructions, or the instructions of those placed over them, will be instantly dismissed, no matter to what union they belong" (Nevin 1964, 42). So began the Dublin Lockout. In a city where poverty and unemployment of general laborers were already among the highest in Europe, approximately 25,000 more (an additional 15 percent over the first half of 1913) were out of jobs.[2] With none of their objectives realized, workers began to return to their jobs in January 1914, if permitted by their employers. The ITGWU ended strike pay in February, and the DEF officially ended the Lockout in March.

In the end, even the British unions, whose members had supported the Dublin workers with cash and food, were alienated by Jim Larkin's aggressive condemnation of their less radical philosophy of organized labor. As the ITGWU's James Connolly wrote in the February 9, 1914, *Forward*, working-class Dublin was "isolated." They were isolated from the rest of Britain's organized labor force and from the majority of middle- and upper-class citizens in their home city, including some nationalist communities. John Hutchinson believes the fractured relationship with nationalists was owing in large part to labor's exposing class conflict: "Urban class-conflict subverted cherished nationalist stereotypes of Ireland as a spiritual rural community opposed to the materialist urban-class society of England, and it exposed the failure of the revival to reach the large working-class population" (1987, 186). Labor positioned itself as a part of the cultural nationalist community, and Larkin and other rank-and-file leaders considered the ITGWU a component of the movement. This view was shared by, among other established nationalists, Standish O'Grady, D. P. Moran, and Arthur Griffith, all of whom initially supported the notion of a general union based within Ireland. As Hutchinson notes, "the modernizers,

2. The Dublin unemployment rate of general laborers was 10 percent for the first half of 1913. General laborers and their dependents numbered approximately 100,000 or one-third of the Dublin population. See O'Brien (1982) and Yeates (2000) for census figure analyses of this period.

Griffith and Moran, were at first not unsympathetic to the formation of a union run on Irish lines, believing that there was no essential antagonism between capital and labour and that it could work for the regeneration of Irish industry. Moreover, since the bulk of Dublin employers were Protestant unionists and led by William Martin Murphy, whom because of his factionalism they regarded as embodying all that was worst in nationalist Ireland, they were supportive of a just consideration of the workers' claims" (ibid., 186–87). Both Moran and Griffith withdrew their support as the Lockout progressed, and they were not alone among nationalist leaders in sending mixed messages of support. Such vacillation reflects the problematic place organized labor held within the movement, a situation echoed by the labor plays staged at the Abbey.

During the twenty-two weeks of labor unrest, Dublin workers were invisible on the Abbey stage. Ervine's *The Critics, or a New Play at the Abbey* was the only Dublin play to premiere during this time. It did so at the height of the Lockout, in November. Although not portraying Dublin's labor movement, it did (as discussed in chapter 5) reflect a widening social schism. The strike may have failed in attaining its objectives, but the subsequent Lockout and formation of the Irish Citizen's Army succeeded in maximizing communal solidarity among Dublin's laborers. This community, deeply concentrated in the north inner-city neighborhood surrounding the Abbey, was eventually represented on the Abbey stage and portrayed with great sympathy. However, union leaders were harshly criticized and the rank-and-file were presented as taking retributive actions against members who did not support their cause.

Frederick Ryan's *The Laying of the Foundations* is primarily concerned with corrupt city government, but organized labor is an underlying component. Labor organizer Nolan is a pivotal character. He serves as the catalyst for protagonist Michael O'Loskin's awakening to the municipal corruption that his father, a construction company owner, participates in and to which O'Loskin is expected to acquiesce. Nolan makes O'Loskin aware of unfair labor practices within the construction business, as well as the deplorable living conditions in the tenements owned by O'Loskin's father. When O'Loskin learns that his father's investment income is derived primarily from his owning tenements that house poor workers, institutional poverty becomes the focus. Business owners who perpetuate the existence of tenements and Dublin Corporation members who create rules that favor tenement owners are targeted. Nolan is the first character to personify the organized labor movement in Dublin and one who is modeled on James Connolly. When *The Laying of the Foundations* premiered in 1902, Connolly was a close friend of Ryan's. Their friendship was largely the result of a shared interest in workers' rights. *The Laying of the Foundations* is not dogmatic on the subject of unionization; Nolan is a strident but altruistic figure on the urban scene, and the only organizer to be portrayed in such a positive fashion in the Dublin repertoire. Future Dublin labor organizers would be portrayed with much less sympathy, beginning with those portrayed in *The Lord Mayor.*

Edward McNulty's *The Lord Mayor* opened in March 1914, and is set shortly after the ITGWU suspended strike payments and the DEF officially ended the Lockout. The comedy moves from the office of Gaffney, a Dublin solicitor and backroom controller of the Mansion House, to the Mansion House itself and finally to the office of the Lord Mayor. Each of these settings follows the political climb of O'Brien, an ironmonger and meek City Council member who ascends from the brink of bankruptcy to the title of Lord Mayor. With its comedic elements often undermined by stinging commentary on corruption in city government and a younger generation questioning the status quo, it contains subtle parallels to *The Laying of the Foundations.* The character of O'Brien ultimately shares O'Loskin's predisposition toward self-sacrifice for the common good. Ending with O'Brien's vowing to be "the independent champion of the peoples' rights" and "the citizen's Lord Mayor" (McNulty 1917, 50), the conclusion of *The Lord Mayor* echoes the conclusion of *The Laying of the Foundations* in which O'Loskin vows to help build "a city whose foundations are laid in Liberty and Truth" (Ryan 1970, 37). However, *The Lord Mayor*'s younger characters, Moira and Kelly, do not believe in self-sacrifice.

Instead, they choose to marry against elders' wishes and challenge nationalist ideologies that permeate the Mansion House.

Moira, O'Brien's daughter, and Kelly, Gaffney's assistant and O'Brien's speechwriter, introduce economic issues into the nationalist discourse. In doing so, they challenge the position of Arthur Griffith and other conservative nationalists of the period. They reflect the schism between labor and nationalist leaders that existed throughout the strike and Lockout period:

KELLY: There are plenty of Gaffneys in Ireland, plenty in England. The world is all the same . . . everywhere rich and poor. England has done me no harm. England doesn't sweat me. England hasn't kept me on starvation wages. Gaffney has. England doesn't hang all around my life and choke down my soul like a nightmare. Gaffney does. What's the good of being patriotic if it doesn't raise my wages?

MOIRA: If Ireland was free and a Republic you'd be better off.

KELLY: Not a bit. I'd be just the same. There would be a change of government officials, but that wouldn't change me. (McNulty 1917, 32–33)

Kelly's view of his economic and professional standing, and the unlikelihood of either changing with the establishment of a republic, is particularly stinging. His example that Gaffney actually embodies imperialism shatters the illusion that nationalist leaders are independent of corrupt capitalism and draws them directly into the debate that Larkin put forward during the Lockout. Describing Gaffney as "the greatest bully and tyrant that ever [walked] the earth" (ibid., 33), Kelly's comments are blatantly oppositional to Griffith's "Sinn Féin and the Labour Question," which was published the previous fall. His remarks place him clearly in support of organized labor and "alienated from the nationalist struggle" (Levitas 2002b, 210). This position makes him an outsider at the Mansion House, where the Lord Mayor's office had been a bastion of nationalism since 1881. In earlier years, there had been a gentlemen's agreement that the Lord Mayor position be rotated between conservatives and nationalists. But that changed in 1881 when conservative Lord Mayor George Moyers refused to award a Freedom of the City honor to Charles Stewart Parnell; "thereafter, none but those with the necessary nationalist credentials attained the highest municipal office" (O'Brien 1982, 71).

In his examination of *The Lord Mayor*, Ben Levitas notes that in a letter to Yeats three days after the play's premiere, Lady Gregory reported that Kelly's comment about patriotism not having a significant purpose if it does not raise his wages was "one of the most applauded" lines of the play (2002b, 211). Like Nolan in *The Laying of the Foundations* and, later, the Covey in *The Plough and the Stars*, Kelly taps into an underlying working-class discontent at the expense of the nationalist cause. Groups such as Sinn Féin and the Irish Republican Brotherhood redressed this situation by 1916. Both the sentiment and the redress would be echoed by the Covey when, at the start of the Easter Rising, he demands to know what the use of freedom is "if it's not economic freedom" (O'Casey 1998, 100). This sentiment's popularity in *The Lord Mayor* at the conclusion of the Lockout is likely not a coincidence. Although the play's appeal endured for almost two decades, *The Lord Mayor* was very much a play of its time. By the mid 1920s, its subtitle in Abbey programs changes from being "A Comedy" (ATA ATC/MPC/1914) to "A Satire of the Past" (ATA ATC/MPC/1924) a notation retained in programs through the final production in 1934. The subtitles indicate a synergy between the Abbey and the national political climate. It holds the subjective, benign descriptor of "comedy" when the Abbey is under its most direct scrutiny from and—some might argue, undergoing its greatest efforts to placate—various special interests, but gives way to the more self-congratulatory moniker in the aftermath of the Civil War, with the Irish Free State a member of the League of Nations.

Although *The Laying of the Foundations*, *The Lord Mayor*, and *The Plough and the Stars* all touch upon Dublin labor issues, only two Abbey plays before 1951 deal specifically with the Lockout: A. Patrick Wilson's *The Slough* and J. A. O'Brennan's *Scrap*. These plays serve as bookends of a sort. *The Slough* deals with the Lockout in near-real time, and *Scrap* examines its ramifications decades later. In both instances, the workers and their families are portrayed as victims of an aggressive labor movement that stigmatizes those who do not support its objectives. *The Slough* is the first work to tap into the drama of the Lockout while simultaneously exposing life in Dublin tenements. Perhaps more significant to the urban drama of the national theater, it is the first step in creating the Dublin world that would be established by O'Casey as emblematic of urban Ireland in terms of tenement setting, language, and characterization. Although one cannot help but note the plot structure and character similarities between this and O'Casey's early works—most notably *Juno and the Paycock* and *The Plough and the Stars*—Christopher Murray finds no evidence that O'Casey saw *The Slough*, ultimately concluding that if he did, "he kept quiet about it" (2004, 95).

*The Slough* operates on a dual trajectory with the labor action framing an underlying allegorical representation of an individual's struggle to remain free of a mob dictate. The laborer, Hanlon, wants to remain an individual in a community that insists he join their efforts. The author's program note explains the play's allegorical framework, citing the following lines from part 1 of John Bunyan's *The Pilgrim's Progress*: "They drew near to a very miry slough that was in the midst of the plain . . . This miry slough is such a place as cannot be mended . . . It is not the pleasure of the King that this place should remain so bad . . . But it is the Slough of Despond still, and so will be when they have done what they can" (ATA ATC/MPC/1914). Labeling this passage "the Argument" of the play, Wilson establishes *The Slough* as an exploration of what would have become of Christian (Hanlon in *The Slough*) had he never found release from The Slough of Despond and made his way to the Celestial City. In citing the reference that the slough "cannot be mended," and titling the second act, which is set in the Union Committee Room, as "the Mending of the Slough," he asserts that organized labor is no answer to the woes of city laborers and that it wears a false face, pretending to offer salvation when it cannot.

This play never identifies its setting as 1913 Dublin, but the allusions are numerous. Considering that *The Slough* is often incorrectly cited as the Abbey's first Dublin play, the fact that the playwright never states the location as Dublin is noteworthy. The setting, following the play's allegorical framework, is simply "a City." The script contains no direct references to Dublin, nor is there any evidence that such a reference existed in the original Abbey production. The Lord Chamberlain's office reviewed it for consideration of performance by the Liverpool Repertory Theatre to open December 10, 1914, and in its November 30, 1914, Recommendation for License, the office refers to it as "a gloomy sordid little tragedy of an abortive strike in the North," presumably the North of England. This setting was assumed even though the Liverpool program, like that of the Abbey's, only identifies the location as "a City." The play's setting seems open to interpretation by the locale where it is staged.

Considering the many allusions to 1913 Dublin, it is not surprising that the play was seen by Abbey audiences and critics as being set in the city in that year. The labor leader Allen bears many similarities to Larkin, and the events are markedly similar to the Lockout. Like Larkin, Allen is a proponent of temperance and renowned for his oratory skill, and the strike is described as being syndicalist in nature, with Allen echoing Larkin's desire for "one big Union" (Wilson 1914, 45). The character of Peg is equally reflective of 1913 Dublin. She is the eldest daughter of the Hanlon family and supplements her shopgirl wages with part-time prostitution. Young women were among the most vulnerable workers in the city at the time, and shopgirls in particular were notoriously underpaid. This was a situation not overlooked by Larkin. As Dublin historian Joseph O'Brien notes, "their condition was often offered as evidence for the prevalence of prostitution [and the Larkin-edited] *Irish Worker* was especially active in exposing the 'slavery' imposed on these young girls" (O'Brien 1982, 205). For Dublin audiences, *The Slough* was a thinly disguised portrayal of the 1913 strike and Lockout, with the challenges and consequences of tenement living serving as a backdrop to the labor action. *The Slough* is harshly critical of the tactics of organized labor and of the Larkinesque labor leader, reiterating the point made by Larkin's detractors that he used poor workers to keep himself in a "soft" job. This negative portrayal of organized labor confronts Larkin's (and the ITGWU's) self-professed position as an element of the cultural nationalist movement.

As his few defenders in the union comment, Hanlon was once "a good trade unionist" (Wilson 1914, 39), but "has been victimized through the callous action of . . . the Union's officials" (ibid., 37). It is revealed that Hanlon's refusal to pay his union dues (which led to his blacklisting and eventual expulsion) was the result of being denied union-controlled employment because he "scabbed" during a previous strike in order to pay his sick wife's medical bills. The union provided no help during his time of need and prevented him from earning a living once his wife recovered. His downward spiral of drink, bitterness, and poverty permeates his family: his daughter Peg leaves the city to become a prostitute in Liverpool; his son, Jack, unleashes his frustration and anger on his sisters and mother before leaving home, shutting off one of the family's few steady sources of income; and his daughter Anne endures harsh factory work that contributes to her death from consumption. Anne's demise predates Mollser's in *The Plough and the Stars* by more than one decade and its treatment is radically different, but it serves a similar purpose. Mollser's death occurs between acts and is used in tandem with the stillbirth of Nora's child to emphasize a symbolic lost generation of the city. In *The Slough*, Anne's death occurs on stage and, in conjunction with Peg's emigration to Liverpool and the son's desertion, emphasizes a generation lost to one immediate family that cannot maintain unity amid poverty and lack of opportunity.

By act 3, in which Peter is assaulted by union workers and dragged off to jail while his daughter lies dying in the tenement, the hypocrisy within the trade union movement is clearly complicit in their circumstances. As Hanlon's neighbor states solemnly before the closing curtain, "Pray. It is the only thing left for poor people like us to do" (ibid., 76). Only a few years later, with the premiere of *Blight*, the notion of a tenement family turning to prayer is ridiculed. But in 1914 Dublin, this somber conclusion remained fitting for the tragedy onstage. It echoes the conclusion of Wilson's earlier one-act *Victims*, in which a couple's only child dies of starvation. This labor tragedy premiered in 1912 at Dublin's Liberty Hall, the home base of the IGTWU. Considered "the first known play to depict working-class Dubliners" (Pierse 2011, 96), *Victims* presents tenement dwellers Jack and Annie Nolan in dire straits as Jack faces his tenth week of unemployment. Jack was the leader of a failed attempt at unionization and is being blacklisted by the Masters Federation, a recently organized group of employers who have joined forces to keep any suspected labor organizers out of their ranks. Jack is horrified but also begrudgingly admiring of their focused determination in "tossing on the scrap heap the men who they think will endanger their profits by demanding a living wage" (Wilson [1916], 11). The blacklisting of employers being transferred to union men is a peculiar change of pace for Wilson, who was a dedicated trade unionist and columnist for the *Irish Worker*.

*The Slough* was a critical and popular success, revived three times within the first year of its debut in November 1914. Critical reviews were overwhelmingly favorable and focused on the timeliness of addressing the strike and Lockout. The *Irish Times* acknowledged the point of view presented in "the strike play" as that of "the underdog," but its critic appeared relieved to note that "the author does not intrude his sympathies" into the work (Wilson was a well-known figure and his politics no secret in Dublin). For Joseph Holloway, the tenement setting on the Abbey stage resonated more than the strike plot. He noted on its opening night, "the slum play was a complete success" (Holloway 1967, 167). The combination of strike plot and tenement set underscores the play's ability to portray the inner-city community that had been in the fore of Dublin's consciousness since the Lockout. Dramatic representation of Irish organized labor on the Abbey stage had been seen before, but only in the second-city plays *Mixed Marriage* and *The Labour Leader*. When *The Slough* combined the Dublin tenements with the labor movement for the first time, it challenged union leadership.

The Lockout was revisited eighteen years later in J. A. O'Brennan's one-act tragedy *Scrap*. Here the tenement set is replaced with a more habitable council house, but the family is as fractured as the Hanlons, and their demise is also the result of the father's refusal to join a union. *Scrap* considers that uncooperative union members' desires may have survived the "big strike" unscathed at the time, but that eventually loyal union members will have their revenge on any workers who "scabbed." *Scrap* presents organized labor as a force that destroys familial solidarity and implicates union revenge as a factor in forced emigration.

When the play opens, three of the four Tobin sons have already emigrated to America, and the youngest, Billy, is packing to leave that night. The father, Ned, enters the house and announces he has been fired from his job. With this news, the mother urges Billy to stay in Dublin to help support the family. Ned is beyond middle aged and unlikely to secure a new position. The parents appear oblivious as to why their boys have all left, until the mother's urging compels Billy to voice what had previously remained unspoken: "Don't you know why I must clear off out of this? Don't you know why the others went—Tom and Pat and Michael? It wasn't that they wanted to go. I'm going away for the same reason as my brothers went. It was always thrown up at them as it is to me—the Tobins—the sons of the man—that broke the strike" (O'Brennan [1931], 22). Because of Ned Tobin's behavior, the community has socially and professionally ostracized the sons. None of the boys has been able to secure steady employment, let alone build a career.

Billy's departure leaves his parents alone and overwhelmed at the prospect of their future. Ned had enjoyed the comfort of a steady job because his company's chairman rewarded him for not joining the strike. But the chairman's death ends Ned's job security. It is implied that the late chairman's son, who succeeded his father, now runs a union shop and the union does not want Ned on its rolls as payback for his past behavior. The shock of his situation brings out Ned's memories of the strike: "Now they can mock me—now they can jeer me. Yeh, I see them . . . ould Tobin, ould Tobin the fool . . . your turn now" (ibid., 19). As he clings to a now-worthless letter of promised job security that the late chairman wrote in thanks, his self-pity gives way to a flood of guilt that he has harbored for decades: "I broke the strike . . . I broke the hearts of good men. (*pause*) Aye, I met them many times after . . . Poor devils, they hadn't a smoke. An' the women! Hunger, fear, dread—wrote all over them" (ibid., 24). The play closes on the couple alone and in anguish. Ned was fortunate to survive for many years after the actual event, but the strike's legacy on this family is ultimately the same as on the locked-out workers about whom he reminisces: complete obliteration.

Aligning itself with the sentiment of many cultural and political nationalists of 1913, *Scrap*, like *The Slough*, is sympathetic to the plight of working men and their families but harsh in its treatment of the labor movement itself. When reminiscing about the "big strike," Ned's wife timidly comments on the foolishness of the workers who heeded the union's call. Ned's passionate reply judges the union for leading metaphorical sheep to slaughter: "they went out because they were brought out . . . and they never went back. Good men, men years in the job—men with homes, and wives. And they never got back. Never. Never got a job anywhere—after . . . died on the scrap-heap" (ibid., 19). Like many who tried to return to work after the failed 1913 strike, those workers Tobin alludes to in *Scrap* found they were unemployable because employers banded together to blacklist strike sympathizers. Once unions gained traction in the decades that followed, the balance of power shifted. Those workers who did not support the strike in 1913 received, like the character of Ned, their comeuppance.

The retribution imposed on Ned is the final action in a progression that began with the blacklisting of his sons and their subsequent forced emigration. The theme of *Scrap* is that the union eventually triumphs but it is a victory *over* a working-class family rather than a victory for them. As in *The Slough*, the union of *Scrap* does not forgive any man who did not support the failed strike. Such a position assumes these men had a choice, and should have chosen labor solidarity over medical care for a sick wife (*The Slough*) or a roof over the heads of a growing young family (*Scrap*).

There is an evolution of labor representation in the Dublin repertoire that reflects when the plays premiered. Organized labor was segmented into many small unions and trade associations at the turn of the century, and there was relative harmony with Dublin business owners. This harmony was reflected in *The Laying of the Foundations*, when the altruistic Nolan encourages O'Loskin to devote himself to fighting city corruption. By 1914, with the Lockout a prominent memory, labor politics become more pronounced and radical. As *The Lord Mayor* demonstrates with the character of Kelly, the public began to wonder how far nationalist ideology could deliver in its assertion that independence from England was the answer to their desire for better lives. When the Lockout is most directly addressed, as in *The Slough* and *Scrap*, family becomes the conduit through which Dublin's social divisions are portrayed. *The Slough* and *Scrap* share many similarities, but the method by which each portrays union rank-and-file retribution is quite different. When *The Slough* union members seek revenge on Hanlon, it is physical and immediate, almost a reaction to the Lockout itself, which had concluded only nine months before the play's premiere. The union members of *Scrap* are more deliberate and, it could be argued, more sadistic. They attack Tobin slowly, removing his sons from his life one by one before leaving Tobin and his wife alone to face destitution in their old age.

The evolution of retribution parallels the evolution from powerlessness to power that unions held in Dublin from the period of 1913 to 1931. *The Slough* premiered at a time when the ITGWU was decimated by the Lockout. Larkin left Dublin in 1914 and James Connolly assumed leadership, but he failed to bring the union back to its previous dominance and unemployment remained high. It was not until 1916 that the ITGWU began to rebuild. By 1919 the ITGWU had more than 100,000 members and was the largest union in the country. In 1923, Larkin returned to Dublin and eventually founded the Workers' Union of Ireland (WUI). Combined, the ITGWU and the WUI were dominant general unions by the time *Scrap* premiered in 1931.[3]

3. The history of organized labor becomes much more protracted in the 1940s, but eventually the ITGWU and the remnants of the WUI joined forces in 1990 to become what remains known as SIPTU, the largest union in the Republic of Ireland.

*Scrap* reflects the tenacity and sometimes dubious methods employed by trade unionists to gain or maintain dominance. In the end, one can reflect on the labor repertoire as being very much theater of its time, and allegorically reflective of labor's own place within the nationalist movement.

Larkin's opinion on labor as a nationalist component is made clear in the *Irish Worker* of January 4, 1913, where he writes, "the Irishizing of everything within the four seas of Ireland is our objective." The industrial movement was, like the Abbey Theatre, prone to challenges from factions both within what represented this mandate of "new nationalism" and from external forces, most notably the Catholic Church. Although the members of many organizations—including the Gaelic League, the Gaelic Athletic Association, the Abbey Theatre, and Sinn Féin—supported the locked-out workers with donations of time and money, neither official condemnation of the DEF's tactics nor official support of the ITGWU was forthcoming from the leaders of these groups. Like employers who objected to Larkin, it was less a reaction to organized labor (which had existed in Ireland for decades) than a response to his being viewed as an "agitator who adulterated bona fide trade unionism with the syndicalist sympathetic strike" (O'Connor 2002, 31). However, Church opposition to syndicalism and the "Kiddies Scheme" compelled many leading figureheads to become vocal on the subject.

The Kiddies Scheme involved a Larkin-supported plan initiated by Dora Montefiore, a British woman supportive of the union's efforts. She organized volunteers in England to provide passage and homes for workers' children so they could be cared for during the Lockout. She came under fire by the Catholic Church, but "Dublin's progressive intellectuals [including several associated with the Abbey either socially or professionally] came to Montefiore's aid: Frank Sheehy Skeffington, Constance Markievicz, William Orpen, Bernard Shaw defended her in London [as did] George Russell (AE) . . . James Connelly and Jim Larkin's sister, Delia" (McDiarmid 2005, 137). The Catholic Church declared it an outrage that children would be cared for by non-Catholics, challenged the morals of parents who were willing to allow their children passage, and sent clergy to the docks from where children were to depart to physically challenge the organizers and parents. Lucy McDiarmid brings the Church response to life: "Over a period of several days, beginning on October 22, outraged priests and angry mobs recruited by the Ancient Order of Hibernians grabbed many of the children from the hands of the social workers washing them at the Tara Street baths; pulled others off boats at the North Wall of the Liffey or off trains at Kingsbridge station; attacked anyone attempting to leave Dublin with a child; and marched triumphantly along the quays singing 'Faith of Our Fathers' after each day's successful 'rescues.' Although eighteen children made it to Liverpool, plans for getting three hundred more out of Dublin were abandoned" (2005, 125).

Church leaders made contributions toward children's funds during the Lockout and attempted to organize several "peace meetings" between the DEF and the ITGWU, but attacks on parents persisted. Nelson Ritschel traces the Church's animosity toward organized labor in Dublin back to 1910, when "the Catholic Church in Ireland took steps [including Lenten sermons reprinted in the *Irish Catholic*] to stifle socialism and the radical trade unionism that was emerging since the formation of the ITGWU" (2011, 98). One explanation for the Church's opposition to the labor movement can be found in Pope Leo XIII's encyclical *Rerum Novarum*, which critically addressed the spread of socialism in Europe and was read by the Dublin clergy as supporting its anti-syndicalist position. Issued in May 1891, the *Rerum Novarum* focused on "the integration of Catholics into modern society" (Furlong and Curtis 1994, 4), including the fields of politics and labor. Like most Vatican-issued encyclicals, it has more than one interpretation, but it was read by the Catholic Church in Ireland as being a mandate not to acquiesce to the liberal movement that was gaining momentum throughout Europe and advocating a separation between church and state. Asserting that Catholics cannot separate their faith from their role in society, Irish dioceses put the *Rerum Novarum* forward as evidence of syndicalism's being a form of socialism, something that the Vatican unequivocally identified as a form of godless society. The irony of the Church's position was not lost on James Connolly, who observed that the Church's practice of excommunication "applied the principle of sympathetic action with a thoroughness and ruthlessness that the Labour movement could not hope to equal" (Fox 1946, 158).

The September 6, 1913, edition of the *Irish Catholic* described the strikers as "members of the very lowest and most degraded section of the unemployable class who came out from the slums attracted by plunder" (Daly 1984, 115). The allusion was to Larkin as a pied piper leading the lowly to do his bidding, namely to raid the profits of Dublin businessmen. According to the *Irish Catholic*, both the unemployed and the ITGWU were unworthy of assistance. The ITGWU's acceptance of assistance from British union sympathizers appears to have only further aggravated the Church. It would take several weeks (October 25) before the *Irish Catholic* softened its position and "emphasised that the clergy must become involved in slum improvement" (ibid.). But the clergy's intent, as revealed in a series of pamphlets published by the *Irish Messenger* the following year, appears to have been, ironically like Larkin's, based on membership expansion/retention. As one of the early pamphlets stated, "Destitution is reducing thousands of our fellow Catholics to a condition of which the loss of Faith is a natural sequence" (ibid., 116).

The Church's actions during the Kiddies Scheme compelled many to speak out on the topic of the Lockout, including Abbey director W. B. Yeats. But the seeds for Yeats's reaction had already been sown during Tramways chairman, DEF leader, and Dublin Corporation member William Martin Murphy's opposition to the Lane proposal. In September 1913, the Dublin Corporation announced its decision to reject Hugh Lane's offer to donate his extensive art collection to Dublin if the city would build a gallery to house it. This ended a debate that had endured since Lane first offered the collection in 1905. Lane enlisted an architect whose proposed design would span the Liffey in the city center, replacing the Ha'penny Bridge. It was this final proposal presented by Lane in the form of an ultimatum that ended the corporation's consideration.[4] Lane was the nephew of Lady Gregory, and Yeats enthusiastically supported the project (as did Jim Larkin). Yeats assisted Gregory in her fund-raising efforts to defray the cost to the city should the plans be approved.[5] It was at the city's rejection of the proposal and during the early days of the Lockout that Yeats penned "September 1913" and stated that he "had not thought [he] could feel so bitterly over any public event" (Gregory 1921, 129).

Yeats passionately believed that Dublin and Ireland were on the precipice of a cultural downfall in the fall of 1913, and he targeted Murphy as representing the root of this problem. As one of his biographers observed,

> For Yeats, Murphy personified all that he most feared and loathed about the ignorant materialism of the Dublin Roman Catholic middle classes. Here were those who showed 'how base at moments of excitement are minds without culture.' Not only did they threaten the artistic life of the city and the nation at large, but events were to convince Yeats that they threatened the basic liberties of the people, too. This he believed had been particularly clearly shown when Murphy and his fellow members of the Employers' Federation obtained written undertakings from their men that they would not join trade unions such as the [ITGWU]. (Coote 1997, 330)

Yeats's disdain for the middle classes did not compel him to be overtly supportive of the workers or the union. Although it has been argued

4. At the time, Lane's collection was housed in the Dublin Corporation–owned 17 Harcourt Street, a building that the corporation acknowledged was structurally inadequate to maintain the collection. Proposed sites rejected by the city for various reasons included St. Stephen's Green and Merrion Square.

5. See the Yeats poem "To a Wealthy Man who Promised a Second Subscription to the Dublin Municipal Gallery if it were Proved the People wanted Pictures," for his most direct poetic commentary on this subject. See also Lucy McDiarmad's "The Abbey, Its 'Helpers,' and the Field of Cultural Production in 1913" (2009) for details on Gregory's Lane fund-raising efforts.

that "Yeats and Larkin were on the same side" (Cullingford 1981, 78), Yeats's direct commentary on the Lockout is scarce, reflecting what has been referred to as his disposition toward a "disillusioned detachment from public events" (Yeats 1975, 406). His comments at a Mansion House meeting in October and his "Dublin Fanaticism," published in the *Irish Worker* on November 1, are the only substantial public comments on the issue. Yeats opened his Mansion House remarks by stating that he could not "imagine a more difficult task than being impartial on the lockout," but he managed to sidestep it nonetheless:

> No man who walked through the slums of Dublin, and saw the tumbling rabbit warrens of misery, could easily be impartial. The dispute has done untold damage not only to the financial but also the moral interests of Dublin. Every one of us has a right to speak here, even those who have no part in the dispute, like myself, and whose selfish interests are suffering. I am one of the directors of a theatre, which is suffering every week as a result of the dispute. (*Laughter.*) Those who went into the conference would have to think of those outside, who are not combatants. I do not complain of the fanaticism of Dublin. I do not think that we can have strong religious feelings anywhere without fanaticism; but I have not words sufficient to express my contempt for the press of Dublin. (Yeates 2000, 296–97)

Yeats criticized the Church and zealots for their fanatical reaction to the Kiddies Scheme without naming them directly, and lambasted the mainstream press and the Murphy-owned *Irish Independent* for providing them a platform. However, his "contempt for the press of Dublin" also included the Larkin-edited *Irish Worker* for publishing the names of those who crossed the picket lines, and nationalist newspapers for fueling unrest with their opposition to Larkin. His only direct commentary is reserved for the inhabitants of "the slums of Dublin," a large percentage of whom were the locked-out workers and their families. Yeats's sympathy for those most directly impacted by the Lockout would be echoed in both *The Slough* and *Scrap*.

Like Yeats, Lady Gregory had a personal interest in the Lockout. She disdained Murphy for his leadership on the Dublin Corporation's rejection of the Lane gallery and for the manner in which his *Irish Independent* relentlessly featured articles discrediting the project in an effort to sway public opinion. Like Yeats, she remained largely silent on the issue.[6] However, she shared Yeats's distaste for the state of affairs in Ireland and the public's complicity. One of Gregory's few visits to Dublin in 1913 was to attend the Dublin Corporation meeting announcing its decision (in a fairly close vote of 32 to 25) to reject the Lane proposal. Afterward she commented, "it is the fault of the system that puts our precious things in the hands of a democracy" (Kohfeldt 1985, 240). Clearly her disdain for the city officials extended to the public that elected them. It is reasonable to read her comments as those of a woman exhausted by the failure of many years' effort, and in line with Yeats's exasperation over cultural decisions being swayed by a short-term "bottom line" mentality rather than a grander long-term vision.

The Abbey was not unique in its official evasion of the subject.[7] Except for the Gaelic Athletic Association, leading cultural organizations remained silent. The Gaelic League primarily supported the

6. Gregory was absent from Dublin for most of 1913. She toured North America with the Abbey players from January to April (spending a considerable amount of this time fund-raising among Irish-Americans for the Lane project) and spent most of the remainder of the year in Coole, convalescing from an injury she suffered while sailing back to Europe and to be with her family following the birth of her grandson, Richard.

7. Several nonmanagerial members of the Abbey were directly supportive of organized labor. One who played a significant part in the events of 1913 was the actress Helena Moloney. A friend of Larkin, it was Moloney who helped (with Casimir Markievicz) create his disguise so he could evade police in an effort to address the workers' rally on what would become known as Ireland's first Bloody Sunday. Moloney was also with Larkin when he was arrested at the Murphy-owned Imperial Hotel on O'Connell Street before the police attacks began. Although Sean O'Casey was an ITGWU member and supporter of Larkin during this time, these events predate his affiliation with the Abbey Theatre.

locked-out workers via its London branch, rather than through its Dublin headquarters. On the other hand, more overtly political groups were quite vocal. Sinn Féin president Arthur Griffith was one of the loudest critics of the ITGWU. Griffith questioned any organization that was deemed, or deemed itself, part of the nationalist movement, be it cultural or political. Although originally a supporter of Yeats and his notion of establishing a national theater, he officially distanced himself from that effort after viewing Synge's *In the Shadow of the Glen* in 1903 at Molesworth Hall. Referring to the INTS decision to stage it as "ill-advised" in the October 17, 1903, *United Irishman*, he claimed, the play "is no more Irish than the Decameron. Synge's play purports to attack 'our Irish institution, the loveless marriage' . . . according to Mr. Synge, marry lacking love, and, as a consequence, the woman proves unfaithful. Mr. Synge never found that in Irish life." Thereafter, Griffith kept Yeats, Synge, and eventually the Abbey under watchful eye in attempts to discover further evidence of plays that presented an Ireland outside of his vision.

In "Sinn Féin and the Labour Question," Griffith claimed that the ITGWU was missing the point. Capitalism was not the enemy, as Larkin opined, England was because it instilled the capitalist economy in Ireland. Griffith considered Larkin's stance unnationalistic in its attack on Dublin employers—many of whom were considered nationalist in their political stripes, albeit of the parliamentary kind in Murphy's case[8]—and in its service to what they considered an apolitical cause. In many respects, Griffith's article, published in the October 25, 1913, issue of *Sinn Féin*, is, as Lockout historian Pádraig Yeates suggests, an "incantation against the forces of modernism" (2000, 355), be those forces capitalist or socialist in scope: "It is the right and function of the Nation to say to Labour: you are Labour. You shall sell your services to Capital for a lawful price, and a lawful price is

8. Murphy was an MP from 1885 to 1892 and a nationalist, conservative Home Ruler. Like all Home Rulers, he believed nationalist tenets and a place within British parliament need not be mutually exclusive.

that which will enable you to live in decency and comfort and provide against the material ills of the world. For I am the Nation—your father and the father of Capital also, and in my house my children shall not oppress the other—it shall not be a house divided against itself." This passage is reflective of the overall tone of the article, and, ironically, not very different from the Catholic Church's position. The nation is God-like and must be served equally by all factions within society. Every faction's service must be to the nation and to serve anything else (union leader or labor collective) above that is to do so at the detriment of the whole. As Yeates observes, "this elevation of the nation to a deity, and the insistence that only through identification with a religion, a culture and a nationality could an individual hold any rights, was the stock in trade of most nationalists throughout Europe. Griffith's denial of the right of Larkin . . . to claim Irishness was also a denial of [his] right to a political existence" (2000, 355). Officially, Sinn Féin leadership opposed the union's efforts (Eamonn Ceannt was the only vocal detractor to Griffith's position) as did the Irish Republican Brotherhood (IRB). But the IRB was less adamant, and Pádraig Pearse and Tom Clarke were on record as supporting the ITGWU's cause. Just as the Kiddies Scheme aggravated the Catholic Church and compelled Yeats to voice an opinion on the Lockout, Larkin's willingness to accept "charity" from England may well have contributed to the animosity directed at him from groups like Sinn Féin.

Largely ignored by cultural revivalists and attacked by the political nationalists, the Lockout left Larkin and the labor movement as "isolated" as the Dublin workers. Parties would converge a few years later during the Easter Rising, but the chief convergence at that time occurred between nationalist groups and the laboring classes. Nationalist organizations saw the potential of tapping into the disenfranchised laborers who had initially rallied behind Larkin, and these groups made significant efforts to redirect that passion to their mutual causes. For the Abbey Theatre, this effort took the form of supporting the plight of the workers with plays sympathetic to their living conditions, while simultaneously portraying union leadership as complicit in circumstances. This opportunistic staging reflected the political climate, but it also reinforces how urban plays often demonstrate the Abbey's engagement with current events. In examining these labor plays, one wishes that there was a way to determine if pro-union plays were submitted and rejected by the theater. Sadly, there is no comprehensive record of the works the Abbey declined during this time period.

Organized labor was one of the more problematic components of early twentieth-century nationalism, partly because it blurred the operational lines between political and cultural efforts. As Hutchinson observes, political and cultural organizations tend to operate by distinctively different strategies. The political effort focuses on a top-down effort in order to construct a state from above with "one overriding goal—political autonomy" (Hutchinson and Smith 2000, 591), while the cultural effort "perceive[s] the nation not as a state but as a distinctive historical community. Since a community is a spontaneous order of different groups and individuals . . . it cannot be constructed like a state from above, but can only be re-animated from below" (ibid., 591–92). Under Larkin's leadership, these two systems of operation were crossed with each other. Larkin rallied a community from a grassroots level and fulfilled the objective of educating and building cohesiveness, but by highlighting the disenfranchised workers who were either alienated by or unmoved by the nationalist project, he inadvertently highlighted shortcomings. Furthermore, the ITGWU operated in strictly hierarchical terms: it was a top-down structure with Larkin orchestrating all efforts. Considering these dichotomies, it is perhaps neither surprising that the strike failed nor that the plays on the subject staged by the Abbey were negative in their allusions of the event (*The Slough*) and its legacy (*Scrap*).

It is quite plausible that *The Slough* was staged, in part, for purely commercial reasons. Under the leadership of Yeats and Gregory, the urban plays were often the works that sustained the company through tough financial periods, and late 1913 into early 1914 was the start of very lean times. The American tours of 1911 and 1912 "were so successful . . . that the theatre did not run into serious financial difficulties again until 1914" (Flannery 1982, 259). They learned in 1908 with the Casey plays that putting Dublin on the stage sold tickets. But the play's success was also owing, as Ben Levitas notes, to advantageous timing, which he finds an "essential aspect of *The Slough*'s success" both for its being "performed next to a war, in which ground gained by socialists was swiftly being eaten up by issues of international conflict . . . when *The Slough*'s battered personae left the stage for the last time their departure was an appropriate reflection of labour's depleted forces" (2002b, 219). It also, as recent scholarship so convincingly argues, reflects a need to consider that Hutchinson's demarcations have evolved, with the benefit of time, to reveal that cultural revivalism and cultural nationalism, although they share some qualities, are two separate things. Furthermore, as Levitas and others have suggested, there are moments when the cultural and political arms of the nationalist movement were one and the same.

*The Slough* was well received enough when it premiered in November 1914 to have an additional one-week run staged later the same month. It was revived again in February 1915, and also became part of the Abbey tour to the Cork Opera House and Manchester's Gaiety Theatre later in the year. But this is where *The Slough* ends: roughly at the same time as laboring classes and republican movements converge and begin their trajectory toward 1916. It is as though the Abbey and its audiences lose their appetites for representations of division between these two segments of the population, again, likely a reflection of the political climate.

The revivalist movement was well over by the time *Scrap* premiered in 1931 and the Abbey was comfortably receiving its state grant. Thirty percent of the plays to premiere at the Abbey in 1931 were set in urban Ireland: Robinson's adaptation of Sheridan's *The Critic, or a Tragedy Rehearsed* (set in Dublin), Hugh Quinn's *Money* (Belfast), and *Scrap*. The majority of new works were written by the old guard (including the Yeats plays *The Cat and the Moon* and *The Dreaming of the Bones*) and set primarily in the west of Ireland. As the Free State was embarking on a period marked by the leadership of a now firmly established Catholic bourgeoisie—and on the precipice of the de Valera–led Fianna Fáil decades—this was no time for revisionism. Rather, it was a fine time to reinforce a failure on the part of an upstart segment of the population that by 1931 had either been partly absorbed into what would be the minority political party[9] or further marginalized in Dublin's societal structure. Although not political animals, the Tobin family of *Scrap* are certainly a reminder of what ultimately happened to those who did not acquiesce to the pressure imposed by a now-rising class. Although cultural revivalism was, by 1931, no longer a dominant presence, it had entrenched itself so thoroughly into the national psyche that it was part of the governing fabric.

9. Cumann na nGaedheal and the Labour Party were united in their attempts to prevent Fianna Fáil from gaining power.

# 8 Getting Personal

## *The Dublin Biodramas*

IN 1913 Lady Gregory expressed her "hope to see a little season given up every year to plays on history and in sequence at the Abbey" (Gregory 1913, 91). Gregory offered no formal definition of what she considered a history play; but in the broadest sense, it is not limited to the dramatization of a "real" historical figure or event. In the Abbey's early years, history plays often blended a mythical narrative through ancient text with timeless concerns of lineage or freedom. No matter what they were based on, the early history plays consistently portray, as Christopher Murray notes, a narrative duality that criticizes public timidity and advocates self-sacrifice, traits he points to in support of *Cathleen ní Houlihan* as possibly "the archetypical Irish history play" (1988, 271). Gregory's inclination toward realism and her desire for history "in sequence" suggests that she was interested in what might be considered the modern expectation of a history play: one that either depicts a significant event through characters who witness the action or focuses on the life of a historical figure. It also suggests a season containing plays that chronologically examine Irish history. Each of the four men who went on to be subjects of Dublin-set biographical drama at the Abbey—Robert Emmet, Jonathan Swift, James Clarence Mangan, and Jeremiah O'Donovan Rossa—could conceivably have been part of such a season.[1]

1. Charles Stewart Parnell was the subject of the most biodramas at the early Abbey. However, these plays are not set in urban Ireland and are not included here.

In his examination of the Irish historical novel, James Cahalen suggests that "if every Irish novel with history in it were to be included, just about every Irish novel ever written would have to be examined" (1983, xiii). The same might be said of Irish drama in the first half of the twentieth century. The Abbey's propensity for staging myth-based plays in (to varying degrees) a realist manner complicates the search for drama that fits the modern expectations of a work labeled *historical*, stifling the impulse to limit identifying "historical" drama only to those that portray the "real." Nevertheless, this is an impulse toward which we tend to gravitate: "whether we stress a work's closeness to or independence from its sources, we are thinking within a framework based on a play's relationship to the external historical reality it purports to imitate" (Lindenberger 1975, 3). There is no shortage of "external historical reality" in the Dublin plays, from the illusory in the Lockout plays and direct armed conflicts in the O'Casey Trilogy to the Phoenix Park murders in *The Invincibles* and the courtroom drama of *Trial at Green Street Court House*. But these are driven by events rather than biography. The biographical was, as Murray notes, "a form somewhat neglected in the early years of the Abbey, probably because the Queen's was still very actively turning out melodramas on Irish patriots and competition was not in question" (1988, 272). The tradition of such melodramas was long-standing, and the volume so substantial that plays addressing the 1798 rebellion alone have been identified as a genre, with subgenres (in dramatic and cinematic form) extending forward to include "the Robert Emmet play, with its tragic love thwarted" (Morash 2002, 155) by an informer. The notion of Emmet's failing because of an informer is not a staple of the early Abbey's Emmet plays, but the convention of "tragic love" certainly is.

---

The Parnell plays are: *The Parnellite* (Seumas O'Kelly, 1917), *The Lost Leader* (Lennox Robinson, 1918), *Parnell of Avondale* (William Robert Fearon, 1934), and *Moses' Rock* (Frank O'Connor and Hugh Hunt, 1938). Considering its allegorical references to Parnell, one might also include *The Deliverer* (Lady Gregory, 1911) in this list. Also omitted is Maura Molloy's Emmet play, *Summer's Day* (1935), which has no scenes set in the city. For the Molloy play, see NLI MS. 29,367.

Indeed, love interests dominate the early biodramas, the majority of which are set in the city of Dublin, simultaneously reflecting its centrality to politics and culture, and the idealistic or idealized legacies of its subjects.

Cahalen ultimately defines the *historical* as that which deals with "political events in modern Irish history prior to the author's own experience" (1983, xiii). This chapter adapts Cahalen's definition by categorizing the Dublin biodrama as a character-driven play that focuses exclusively on the life of a historical figure who lived "prior to the author's own experience." There are surprisingly few plays that fit this definition in the early repertoire. This is surprising because, as Lionel Pilkington points out, the founders' interests in developing original historical plays when they first conceived of an Irish theater included, among other considerations, Yeats's desire to develop "a history play dealing with the life and death of the Irish patriot Robert Emmet" (Pilkington 2001, 10). This desire might be traced to Yeats's own biography: he claimed his "great-grandfather has been Robert Emmet's friend and was suspected and imprisoned though but for a few hours" (Yeats 1955, 21) following the failed rebellion. Frank Fay, who had worked with his brother, Willie, on a production of James Pilgrim's *Robert Emmet* at St. Teresa's Hall in 1900 (Hogan and Kilroy 1975, 85), was also looking for a new Emmet play. He wrote to Yeats on July 25, 1902, that "having a play on Robert Emmet" was a "*necessity*" (Hogan and Kilroy 1976, 31), but, since it would be staged at the Queen's, "it must be a melodrama; [the Queen's] audience wouldn't, *at present*, understand anything else" (ibid.). Yeats never did write an Emmet play of his own, but the INTS did stage one, Henry Connell Mangan's *Emmet and Napoleon* (1903), for the Cumann na nGaedheal Celtic Literary Society's Emmet Centenary in the Rotunda in 1903. Yeats's not authoring an Emmet play might be explained by his goal in the early years to differentiate the Abbey repertoire from that of populist theaters (and such theaters' dominance of the melodramatic biodrama) or to the apolitical promise made to Annie Horniman and, later, to the shifting powers of political parties while he lobbied for and strove to maintain state subvention. This might also be why the majority of Abbey biodramas, all of which addressed the lives of republican-oriented figures, were not staged until after the Horniman subsidy was on its way to revocation. Although the subsidy did not officially end until 1910, the Abbey directors knew it was likely in its final year when they staged their first biodrama, Conal O'Riordan's Emmet play, *An Imaginary Conversation* (1909). Over the next four decades, Swift, Mangan, and O'Donovan Rossa were also singled out for attention in the Dublin repertoire.

The most obvious link between these men is their political, paramilitary, or literary connections to republican causes, but they also had relationships with Dublin that continue to be recognized in various forms of cultural tourism (such as literary and walking tours). Although O'Donovan Rossa was not a Dublin man, the trial that led to his imprisonment and forced emigration took place in the capital and his burial at Glasnevin makes him very much a son of the city. Emmet was a Dubliner tried and executed in the city. He and O'Donovan Rossa were both icons of the republican movement in their lifetimes and their status has only increased over time. Dublin native Mangan's stripes were earned through his republican-leaning poems, including "Dark Rosaleen" and contributions to *The Nation*. Swift's work on behalf of Dublin's poor and his satirical writings made him a much-loved figure in his later years, but he was most heartily embraced by the nationalist community in the centuries after his death. Each man was also known for physical or philosophical uniqueness that set him apart from the society in which he lived. Such character quirks would be useful in developing dramatic characterization for the stage; but the timing is critical as well. Terence MacSwiney's *The Revolutionist* (staged in 1921) is an example of how, as in the case of *Cathleen ní Houlihan*, the political climate contributes to a history play's reception. *The Revolutionist*'s director, Lennox Robinson, recalled,

> MacSwiney, Lord Mayor of Cork, had undertaken a hunger strike in England lasting 74 days. This play had been published some years before [1914]. It was so pertinent to the situation that the Abbey was determined to produce it, though the country was in the teeth of the

> 'Black-and-Tans' war. . . . At the dress-rehearsal . . . I was met by a couple of lads with revolvers sagging from their hands, who said that I couldn't pass . . . their only object was to prevent an English paper, which had sneered at MacSwiney's hunger strike, from getting a photograph of the rehearsal. The English photographer surrendered his camera in terror and the incident closed. (1951, 122)

History plays were not new to Dublin; they had been performed in local theaters for decades. But such plays were largely apolitical until after the Acts of Union passed. It is at this point that historical plays "tended rather to attack than to reinforce establishment beliefs" (Murray 1988, 270), and this attack included staging biodramas about the lives of men revered in republican circles. The lives of these men are the focus of each play, but the city setting is more than a background. In most of the plays, Dublin's commerce and political centrality—legal and otherwise—is portrayed as constant, but the players as ever-changing. The city does not, though, serve as an excuse for atrocities or an agent of change. Rather, it inspires, with the exception of *Rossa*, by the nature of its cosmopolitan climate.

The republican movement's invocation of its past is mirrored in the construction of cultural revivalism, which can be said to have begun with the nineteenth-century antiquarian studies of Sylvester O'Halloran and Charlotte Brooke. In asserting the value of Irish manuscripts, they undertook a resuscitation of the dead on the printed page, beginning a dialogue carried forward by the Gaelic League and others. "Literature, however," as Adrian Frazier so eloquently posits, "arises not just from the author, but from the entire human struggle for power through articulation—more specifically, in the case of literature on the stage, from the actors who raise the text to life, the audiences in whom it takes shape, the patrons who foster it, and all the economic and political stresses in which it is lodged" (1990, xv). That dialogue was present at the Abbey from the start, but the politics of the day (both external in the form of Dublin Castle and internal in the form of the Horniman contract) required a certain amount of circumvention. One way around the politics was to infuse it with the mythological (*Cathleen ní Houlihan*, for example), which also fit Yeats's aesthetic. When it came to the urban plays, one had to tread more carefully since an urban setting contained less room for a dreamscape and, therefore, fewer linguistic hiding places.

In 1909 a dialogue between the past and present was familiar, but no less radical an act than when O'Halloran and Brooke began the conversation almost a century earlier. As Freddie Rokem states, "there is room for historians only in a world where it is possible to establish relations between the past and the present. And history can be performed, in the world and on the theatrical stage too, when different structures of time (besides the daily reappearance of the sun), can be distinguished, making it possible to ask not only if the things that appear again are natural phenomena but if they are triggered by some kind of agency, creating a pattern, not just a mechanical repetition" (2000, xi). The agency that triggered the first Emmet play was the emergence of playwrights fortified by the coalescence of the various scholars and organizations such as the Abbey that took dialogue with the past and lifted it toward the stage.

Robert Emmet's short, eventful life caught the attention of several playwrights in Europe and the United States long before the Abbey opened its doors in 1904, most of whom wrote plays that "were more concerned with dramatic effect and patriotic sentiment than any historical regard" (Geoghegan 2002, 269). That same description applies to Conal O'Riordan's *An Imaginary Conversation* and Lennox Robinson's *The Dreamers.*

Since *An Imaginary Conversation* concerns an imagined meeting between the poet/composer Thomas Moore and his Trinity College classmate Robert Emmet in equal measure, it is really a dual biodrama. Moore's reputation was already undergoing revisionist consideration at the time,[2] and this is reflected in the play along with Emmet's iconic altruism. The play was well received on its debut and revived

2. Moore is also mentioned in act 2 of the Mangan play *The Man in the Cloak*, with the character of Blythe, presumably a man of literary circles, describing Moore

several times as late as the 1920s, with most of the leading Abbey players—including Sara Allgood, J. M. Kerrigan, Fred O'Donovan, Barry Fitzgerald, and Eileen Crowe—performing in this three-hander at some point. The one-act tragicomedy is set in May 1797 and centers around Emmet, Moore, and Moore's sister, Kate, with Emmet presented at his idealistic best somewhat at the expense of the Moore siblings. The Moore family's Catholicism is repeatedly mentioned, as is their passivity toward the British: Kate gently reprimanded for admiring the British soldiers on College Green and Moore chastised for living in fear of his mother's admonishments for his political interests. The play's message is an unsubtle call to action for young Catholics who espouse a nationalist ethos. While Emmet speaks of liberty as "the most beautiful mistress a man can have," Moore counters with her being "a cold, cruel devil, worse than the Assyrian queen that has been killing her lovers all the time" (O'Riordan 1935, 134). When Moore defends himself to Emmet—"I love liberty as well as you"—Emmet responds with the play's only overt cynicism: "yes, you've given her words [as opposed to actions] in plenty" (ibid., 135). This sarcasm is buffered, however, when Emmet is inspired by Moore's singing of "The Red Fox." This air fits what Emer Nolan identifies as Moore's "real achievement in the *Melodies* . . . to convert the military and political disaffection of the past into an appealing form of lamentation for the world that such disaffection had failed to recover. The history of Irish resistance is thereby converted into *cultural* opposition, and the music itself pleads Ireland's case for recognition and justice" (2007, 5). This "appealing form of lamentation" is present in many of the Dublin biodramas, contributing to their inherent romanticism. The tone is pointedly hopeful or bittersweet, even in those biodramas that are decidedly tragic. The optimism is conferred by the legacy of the subjects. The audience knows the history of these men and that their contributions endured beyond the physical and mental hardships that are laid bare.

---

as "the worst punster in Dublin," reflecting the negative opinion not uncommon at that time.

Robinson's *The Dreamers* is a more traditional historical play, in that it focuses on a specific event and figure. It was also rather personal to the playwright. Robinson said, "the whole play is an attempt to say what I think about Robert Emmet" (1918, 5). Christopher Murray has argued that on a political level much of Robinson's work, including *The Dreamers*, contains a pointed disdain of public apathy in relation to active leaders. Murray points to act 2 and its focus on "the fecklessness of Emmet's supporters [as throwing] the whole enterprise of Emmet's attempt at rebellion into disarray and disrepute" (Murray 1986, 120) as a primary example of Robinson's position. Robinson called it his "attempt to write a 'natural' historical play, not detracting from the nobility of the noble characters but, as in Emmet's case," to Murray's point, "not glossing over the cowardice and treachery that led to his defeat nor omitting to note the failings in his own character" (1942, 105–6).

*The Dreamers* dramatizes the months leading up to the Emmet-led Rising of 1803 and ends with his capture at Harold's Cross. The lengthy act 2 is devoted to the day of the failed Rising when Emmet acknowledges that "the preparations are not as complete as [he] would have hoped" (Robinson 1915, 28), surrounded as he is with a small group of drunk volunteers and too few arms. As has been well documented, everything that could have gone wrong with the 1803 Rising did, and most of these issues are dramatized: volunteers waiting in the pubs turn to drink, ammunition stored at a local depot is damaged or improperly handled, and the Wicklow volunteers never receive word to join the efforts in Dublin. Focusing so much on the volunteers' incompetence elevates Emmet and reflects the entrenched metaphorical Christ imagery—a young man who died so that his people might live—of the Emmet legacy. This metaphor is overt in this tripartite act, in which Emmet is let down by a key volunteer in each scene, paralleling Judas's warning of three betrayals. The metaphor is extended when Emmet speaks in threes near the act's conclusion: "Had I another week—had I one thousand pounds—had I one thousand men, I would have succeeded . . . there was failure in all—plan, preparation and men" (Robinson 1915, 58).

The play further adheres to the Emmet legacy with its inclusion of Sarah Curran, the young woman to whom Emmet was secretly engaged. Inclusion of a sentimental subplot is something of an anomaly in Robinson's canon, but the inclusion of a lost, temporarily absent, unrequited, or problematic lover is present in all of the Abbey's Dublin-set biodramas except *An Imaginary Conversation*. This might be read as a reflex to extend the melodramatic tradition of history plays at area theaters or as evidence of the urban plays' position within the Abbey repertoire to reach a wider audience, perhaps both. In the biodramas based on the literary figures Mangan and Swift, references to a love interest serve primarily to offer one explanation for the men's eccentricities. With the political Emmet and O'Donovan Rossa, however, the romantic subplots of lost love in the former and estranged love in the latter represent the sacrifices each man made for the sake of his political convictions. This lack of cohesion between the personal and political, be it permanent or temporary, is not uncommon in republican narratives and anticipates what would become a convention of Troubles-themed drama, fiction, and film in later decades when republican figures become more commonplace. John Hill notes a cinematic tendency to accentuate "a firm opposition between the public world of politics and violence (which is associated with tragedy and fatalism) and the private world of romance, home and domesticity (which is linked with the avoidance of politics and the possibility of redemption)" (Hill 2006, 192). This simultaneously reinforces the commitment of the republican figure and elevates his sacrifice. In the case of *The Dreamers*, it extends the Abbey's propensity for portraying self-sacrifice to its urban repertoire.

The play's title appears to refer to both Emmet and Curran, who are presented as believing in the possibility of being married in a free Ireland up to the very last minute. This youthful optimism is portrayed entirely free of cynicism. As Sarah comments to her sister near the play's conclusion, "he said he hoped and dreamed . . . and so did I, so did I" (Robinson 1915, 68). Such wistfulness echoes the lamenting tone of *An Imaginary Conversation* and indeed of the Emmet legacy overall. When examined in tandem, these Emmet plays suggest that the Abbey was invested in a specific version of Emmet that adhered to the romantic legacy and would, therefore, avoid the questioning of that legacy's martyred rhetoric that was to become more readily voiced in Irish drama in the 1920s, most famously in Denis Johnston's *The Old Lady Says "No!"*, a play whose rejection by the directors—and ultimate 1929 staging by Hilton Edwards and Micheál MacLiammóir for their Gate Theatre—is the stuff of Abbey legend.

Although the Abbey saw fit to stage two O'Casey plays that provocatively incorporate challenges to the martyr motif, *The Shadow of a Gunman* and *The Plough and the Stars*, neither play contains a plot or theme that has the language issue at its core. In the former, parody of Cathleen ní Houlihan is evident (as was discussed in chapter 4), but it is the figure of her and what she represents more than the language of her that is challenged and, of course, she is a figure of Irish mythology, not historical reality. The pub scene of *The Plough and the Stars* interrogates the rhetoric of nationalism with its direct quotations from Pearse, but the impact is more that we see those enraptured and question them than that we are put in a position of questioning the rhetoric itself. In *The Old Lady*, on the other hand, the rhetoric of martyrdom is embedded into every scene, with its direct use of the writings of Emmet, Pearse, Mangan, and others central to the rhetorical history of nationalism used so generously that it becomes a cacophony of what Johnston called "intentional clichés" (Johnston 1992, 53). Other factors clearly contributed to the directors' rejection of *The Old Lady*—including its expressionist form and Johnston's letter to the editor in the February 27, 1927, edition of the *Irish Statesman*, in which he challenged the directors to be more open to submissions made by "younger and less-established playwrights of the city" (Adams 2002, 86)—but reducing the Emmet rhetoric to cliché was directly in conflict with the Emmet apparently favored by the early directors.

Even more than Emmet, Clarence Mangan was of significant interest to Yeats, who wrote extensively about him, hailing Mangan as "the greatest" of the Young Irelander poets who filled the pages of the *Nation* in the mid-nineteenth century (Yeats 2004, 98). In his early essays on Mangan (including "Clarence Mangan (1803–1849)" and

"Clarence Mangan's Love Affair"[3]), Yeats generously refers to John Mitchel's biographical introduction to *Poems by James Clarence Mangan* (1859). Louis D'Alton's *The Man in the Cloak* appears to have used the Mitchel notes as a source, particularly in its construction of what Ellen-Shanon Mangan refers to as the "myth of Mangan": "child of an abusive father, sad subject of unrequited love, talented writer who took to drink and opium to deal with his mental and physical ailments and lived his late years in abject poverty" (1996, 80). D'Alton's portrayal of Mangan has been described as "effectively understated rather than romanticized" as a result of the character being drawn as "a weak-willed sponger who knows the limitations of his talent" (Hogan 1967, 46). However, the play's entrenchment of the myth forces it into the sentimentality that permeated the Young Irelander school of which Mangan was a part. As such, it does contain a romantic sensibility, much like the Emmet plays.

Set in a Bride Street dosshouse in June 1849, *The Man in the Cloak* borrows heavily from Mangan's last days as described by Mitchel. The author's directions make clear that the set of Mangan's last known address should reflect absolute squalor: "There should be nothing missing that will convey the aspect of utter poverty, neglect and desolation. Whatever is absent, such as the door from the frame on the left leading up to the stairs, and two panes of glass from the window (patched with cardboard), assists the appearance of terrifying penury" (D'Alton 1971, 4–5). The structure is progressive: advancing from Mangan's outer world (act 1) to his inner world (act 2) and, when the two cannot be reconciled, to his death (act 3). The first and third acts are filled with O'Caseyesque dialogue; characters engage in boisterous banter that becomes more serious as a cholera epidemic advances toward Bride Street. The most compelling portion of the play is the opium dream of act 2, which is the only act told entirely from Mangan's point of view and serves as a sort of memory play (within the play).

3. "Clarence Mangan (1803–1849)" in the *Irish Fireside*, March 12, 1887, and "Clarence Mangan's Love Affair" in *United Ireland*, August 22, 1891. See Yeats 2004.

4a and 4b. *The Man in the Cloak* by Louis D'Alton (1937). Courtesy of the Abbey Theatre Archives.

The opium dream is divided into three parts—an idealistic dream that gives way to nightmare—and contains three sets: one representing Mangan's adolescent home; one the home of Catherine, a young woman to whom Mangan has been giving German lessons; and the third a pub. Each set houses one part of the Mangan myth: his family's poverty and his father's volatile combination of self-loathing and dismissal of his son as a "scribbler" who "will come to nothing" (ibid., 31); his unrequited romantic life; and the physical eccentricities and addictions that created barriers between him and the literary establishment, even though he published in several of Dublin's leading journals and newspapers.

In the dream Mangan vows to stand up to his father's oppressiveness, asserting that he "will not run into a mouse-hole from him as he boasted others of his family have done" (ibid.). The presence of Catherine represents Mangan's unfulfilled romantic life, but includes her as a loyal supporter of his talents: "your writings will yet make you known, I am sure. It will be a fine thing for you to awaken some day and find yourself famous" (ibid., 32–33). The public house, in which he is met by two publishers, represents his dealings with the Dublin literary establishment and is, as in the earlier sequences, mostly positive. The two men make promises of introductions and one loans him money. The sets eventually merge into what becomes a nightmarish vision as Mangan comes down from his opium high. The nightmare dramatizes the stifling impact that poverty and loneliness had on his mental and physical well-being and, as a result, his creative productivity. In the merger, Catherine dies, even his previously sympathetic mother insists he place a clerical salary ahead of writing in order to support his parents and siblings, and the literary men dismisses him as "a prostitute poet and a procurer of illicit rhymes" (ibid., 48).

The nightmarish vision, in which the positive commentary of the dream merges into negative voices against which his attempts at self-defense struggle to get through, has at its center a gendered paradox in which Mangan is simultaneously victim of patriarchy and eager to join its ranks. Central to this paradox is Mangan's father, whom Mangan confronts as "my greatest enemy" and "the sources of all my misfortune . . . you crippled me" (ibid., 44). The implication is that Mangan was emasculated as a young man and this carried over into his inability to find romantic love or assert himself in the masculine world of the nationalist movement. His delirium gives way to attempts at asserting his literary merits, but he is shouted down by character recitations of ballads celebrating the men of 1798 ("The Ballad of Michael Dwyer" and "The Boys of Wexford") and by Emmet's speech from the dock. Mangan claims he has "a song more worthy of [the nationalist] cause" (ibid., 45), but his recitation of "The Nameless One" is drowned out by the insults hurled at him from his father and the literary agents. The play is sympathetic to Mangan's plight, and this is largely conveyed in the dreamy act 2. With this act's departure from realism, the play "focused on the necessity of confronting one's past honestly" (O'Farrell 2004, 194). This didactic element is emblematic of many of the biodramas, particularly the Emmet plays and Yeats's *The Words upon the Window-Pane* (1930), one of a trio of biodramas to focus on the life of Jonathan Swift.

The early Swift plays are G. Sidney Paternoster's *The Dean of St. Patrick's* (1913), Arthur Power's *The Drapier Letters* (1927), and Yeats's *The Words upon the Window-Pane*. These corroborate Robert Mahony's observation that by the late nineteenth century, there was "growing favour for the Dean among popular writers [and] even the story of Stella and Vanessa . . . had begun to attract more positive sentimental attention" (1995, 128). Most of the plays touch upon the Stella and Vanessa sagas, but they all also draw attention to Swift's nationalist status and attempt to locate him firmly in the city of Dublin. In doing so, they stabilize the problematic nature of Swift's relationship with the city. *The Dean of St. Patrick's Cathedral* and *The Words upon the Window-Pane* only minimally present Swift in a nationalist light, although they do rely on romanticizing his biography. *The Drapier Letters*, the sole play to present Swift as an overtly nationalist figure, does not actually include the character of Swift onstage. Instead, Swift's nationalism is reflected in the reactions of Dubliners toward him and his writings. On the early Abbey stage, then, Swift only appears as an Irish nationalist hero in absentia.

Paternoster's melodrama premiered on January 23, 1913, for a four-night run and was revived three times in the same year. Each act features incidental political references, but these moments are overshadowed by the play's overt emphasis on Swift's relationships with Stella and Vanessa. Stella frames the play, energetic in act 1 and dying in act 4; and Vanessa is a disruptive presence in the middle acts. Act 3 is the only one in which both women are present. Set in St Patrick's Cathedral in 1716, Swift is about to marry Stella when Vanessa interrupts the proceedings. Furiously, Swift banishes Vanessa, but Stella cancels the wedding. The play, as Mahony notes, received relatively positive notices from Dublin critics, suggesting "that Dublin playgoers were receptive to the presentation of [Paternoster's] tragic Swift" (Mahony 1995, 130).

This Dean is a man forever distracted by the two women, and their removal is required before his political, social, and literary accomplishments can be acknowledged. The final act finds the Dean in the company of Archbishop William King of Dublin and Henry St. James, Lord Bolingbroke. With the women absent, the archbishop praises Swift's contributions to Ireland and the city of Dublin: "The Dean is greater in his retirement [from court life] than in the days when the Queen's ministers were proud to do him honour. Then he but directed a party. Now a nation does him reverence" (Paternoster 1923, 64). Swift then mentions the donations to Dublin's poor he will make in his will, and, responding to Bolingbroke's query "Why trouble about the knaves?" Swift exclaims, "A true Englishman's question. Why trouble about the dogs? Poverty's their natural state. In laziness and ignorance they were begotten, knaves and brutes they have become. So grind 'em down and keep 'em down. They are even foolish enough to believe in their dean" (ibid., 65). This pronouncement of England's responsibility for having created the very conditions cited as evidence of Irish inferiority is the first positioning of Swift as a destabilizing nationalist figure. The Dean's sarcasm highlights this responsibility for having turned the streets surrounding his parish into slums and its inhabitants into beaten citizens. Taking the role of the oppressor, Swift demonstrates how easy it is for him to manipulate the poor: crowds are gathered outside to witness a lunar eclipse but disperse when informed that it "has been postponed by order of the Dean" (ibid., 66). In claiming that Dubliners are "foolish" to believe in him, Swift proclaims his own ambiguity as leader of the downtrodden. His nationalist credentials are resolutely (re)established, however, by the quotation of a passage from his *Character, Panegyric, and Description of the Legion Club*,[4] in which he famously paralleled the Irish Parliament with a lunatic asylum. Offering Swift's writings as evidence of his pro-Dublin, pro-republican position became a constant feature of all future Swift plays.

Arthur Power's *The Drapier Letters*, the first Swift play set entirely in Dublin, is the most nationalist of the early plays. In a prefatory note, Power claimed that his play was "an attempt to invent a reason why [Swift] changed from calling [Ireland] a 'land of slaves where all are fools and all are knaves' to . . . the noble sentiment" (Power 1927, 5), enunciated in *A Letter to the Whole People of Ireland*.[5] This fourth part of Swift's *Drapier's Letters*, which Yeats identified as the installment that "passed from the talk of study and parlour to that of road and market" (1967, 188), most directly speaks of Swift's nationalist ethos.

In the drama, set in a slum tenement near St. Patrick's Cathedral in 1724, a young woman, Mary-Bridget, is accidentally shot by the authorities as they search her flat for the author of *A Letter to the Whole People of Ireland*. In her subsequent delirium, Mary-Bridget recalls her invocation of Ireland's glorious Celtic past as encouragement for the Dean to recognize that it was the loss of such glory that led to Dublin's ever-expanding slum conditions. At the same time, the Dean's own "pride," she laments, amounts to a rejection of his Irish heritage: "To be warring against your own Kind . . . is to bring disease . . . Sure

4. This quoting of *The Legion Club* (1736) in an act set in 1728 is one of many examples to disrupt chronology for dramatic effect.

5. W. B. Yeats. *Prose Works*, 10:63. Power's note ignores that Swift wrote of "fools" and "knaves" only in 1727 (see *Poems*, ed. Williams, 2:421, ll:1–2), that is, after penning the *Letter to the Whole People of Ireland*, the only lapse in chronology. The play itself sets the action in 1724, the year the *Drapier's Letters* was actually published.

weren't we all great once; great—aye, and had bracelets and crowns, and robes, and all manner of geegars, like any old prince or queen . . . I don't think we were always like this—living in slums the way we are" (Power 1927, 30–31). Mary-Bridget's vision harkens back to Stella's dream in Paternoster's *The Dean of St Patrick's Cathedral*, in which Ireland is presented as a stark "wilderness" and England a "kingdom": "I dreamed of you [Swift], revered Father. You were standing alone in a wilderness and of a sudden there came one to you . . . he was clad in glowing colours . . . he offered you all the kingdoms of the world. I was beside you holding you back. But you broke away from me, and in my despair I awoke" (Paternoster 1923, 8). This contrast between ancient royalty (Mary-Bridget's Ireland) and modern sovereignty (Stella's England) parallels the advancement of Swift's nationalist credentials on the Abbey stage.

After conferring with Swift's servant, who has come to check on her condition, Mary-Bridget confesses to her mother that "it was I who made him write those letters . . . He was beginning to understand, I tell you . . . I would have made him love us, and he would have changed the face of the whole nation" (Power 1927, 32). In its somber conclusion, with Mary-Bridget dead and her mother keening as the curtain falls, this one-act play presents a vision of constructed history. Although such a constructed Swift fit in well with revivalist tenets, the play failed to appeal to its audiences. It was staged only twice: during its premiere one-week run opening on August 22, 1927, on a double bill with George Bernard Shaw's *Arms and the Man*, and in February 1928, on a double bill with Edward McNulty's *The Lord Mayor*. The Shaw plays were championed by Lady Gregory and popular at the Abbey during the 1920s,[6] and opening *The Drapier Letters* with Shaw's *Arms and the Man* suggests that its directors originally had high hopes for the Power play. McNulty's *The Lord Mayor* was likewise popular with audiences, and pairing it with *The Drapier Letters* seems to imply

6. See *Shaw, Lady Gregory and the Abbey: A Correspondence and a Record*, (Laurence and Grene 1993).

continued support for the Power play and an attempt to help it find a larger audience. However, it failed to do so and was pulled from the rotation after its 1928 run.

*The Words upon the Window-Pane* premiered in November 1930 and was staged seven additional times through 1947, making it the most frequently performed Swift play. Yeats's Swift is a man consumed by fear, "afraid of solitude, afraid of outliving [his] friends—and [himself]" (Yeats 1934, 54). Nonetheless, Swift overcomes his fear long enough to meditate on the contrast between affairs of the heart and those of reason. As Richard Allen Cave observes, "Swift's Rome-inspired philosophy argues for a resoluteness that rises above human needs; the very gift of love is consequently a threat to his mind's rule. Swift's cursing like Job the day of his birth is an attempt to deny those human needs, all part of the hope that he will commit to posterity nothing but the fruits of his intellect. But as the play shows, it is Swift, the man, that exerts a powerful fascination over future ages" (1986, 24–25). Yeats demonstrates the way in which Swift "exerts a powerful fascination" by having his spirit take over the play.[7] The people gathered for the séance in a Dublin boarding house are attending for private reasons of their own: from Mrs Mallet's desire to contact her dead husband for advice to Cornelius Patterson's desire to find out whether he will enjoy the earthly pleasures of food and drink and the company of his favorite dog in the afterlife. Only the Cambridge student, John Corbet, is interested in reaching Swift. But the Dean's spirit thoroughly disrupts the gathering. His presence recalls the eighteenth-century satirist who both entertained and upset the status quo. It also reflects the divisive controversies among nineteenth-century historians and critics who had been unable to agree on where to position Swift in the canon of Irish nationalism.

7. The most thorough survey of the whole issue of Yeats's relationship with Swift is Donald T. Torchiana's "Imitate Him if You Dare" (1966), 120–67. See also, for *The Words upon the Window-Pane*, Rollins 1983, 103–15.

The Swift plays reflect the evolution that the Dean's status as a nationalist icon underwent in Ireland during the course of the twentieth century. Only *The Drapier Letters* presents an overtly nationalist Swift, and this is done without Swift on stage. Set in a tenement, it is the only play that connects Swift with the poor. When juxtaposed with the Paternoster and Yeats plays, both of which go to great lengths to portray the intellectual and moral stature of the man, *The Drapier Letters* highlights that class of Irish society that emerged during the Lockout and gave the nationalist movement the populist support it needed to rise in 1916. As such, the early plays reflect Swift's foundation in the republican movement.

Roger McHugh's *Rossa* premiered in 1945 and was awarded that year's Abbey Theatre Prize for best historical play. As the author noted in his preface to the published edition, he "kept close (possibly too close) to the historical facts" (McHugh [1946], n.p.), resulting in what is the most straightforward and least melodramatic biodrama of the repertoire. Since the extensive writings and public speeches of O'Donovan Rossa were widely available at the time the play was written, there was an abundance of historical record to excavate. The play has multiple settings, including Rossa's home in Co. Cork, the British prison in which he was interred, and the New York City apartment where he briefly lived following, as a condition of his release, his forced emigration to America. The Dublin sets, which are of interest here, are his Glasnevin gravesite, a Mountjoy Street rooming house, and the courtroom in which he was found guilty of high treason and given a life sentence of penal servitude.

The play opens with "the curtain ris[ing] on a darkened stage. Three things can be seen dimly: a gravestone with the inscription ROSSA in large lettering; on its right, the figure of the speaker; on its left, a bugler in the uniform of the Fianna. He blows a single short call on his bugle" (ibid.). The speaker delivers the opening of Pádraig Pearse's graveside oration and concludes it in the epilogue. Framing the play with Pearse's elegy creates the quality of a memory play, and giving Pearse ownership of the memory evokes the esteem in which the leaders of the Easter Rising held Rossa and the inspirational role he played in their efforts. In the end, it becomes a national memory play as a result. It is interesting that this play premiered while Ireland was still under the Emergency Powers Act, a period that falls within the country's more isolationist decades. There is an irony to the Abbey's staging a play about an inspirational, forward-looking figure who was a catalyst for other forward-looking leaders at a time when the country, at least politically, was looking inward and growth was at a standstill. It mirrors the role Ernest Blythe, managing director at the time of the *Rossa* premiere, played in the Abbey's own evolution. Here was a man instrumental in securing the theater's future by being among the most vocal government supporters for its state subvention, yet whose tenure as a managing director was noted, in part, for a rejection of experimental or controversial new writing. Such irony was likely not lost on McHugh, a noted academic whose critical writings on a range of Abbey figures, including Yeats, O'Casey, and O'Connor, demonstrated the solid grasp he had on the Abbey's past and contemporary history.

The somber tone of the Glasnevin prologue is not carried over into much of the play, where Rossa is frequently in the company of family and supporters or, as in the British jail scenes, his progressive thoughts. Those moments all reflect the optimism noted in so many of the biodramas. However, the third scene of act 1, set in a Mountjoy Street rooming house where his wife awaits news of his trial, is more reminiscent of the tenement plays. This domestic set contains women we have seen before in such works: a worried, pregnant, young wife whose husband is facing trouble for his political convictions and a sympathetic, elder woman who is full of reassuring words. The courtroom scene mimics the construction of McHugh's own *Trial at Green Street Courthouse*. As in that earlier play, character histrionics and set design are both minimized and the public reaction is included (here, through the occasional shouts of unseen observers). The audience is addressed directly by Rossa as he gives evidence for his defense (largely by pointing out the Crown's lack of evidence), putting them in the jurist position that was assumed in *Trial at Green Street Courthouse*.

The scene concludes with the judge's passing a life sentence for high treason and a fade to curtain.

All three Dublin sets share an optimism that can be found in the earlier biodramas: the graveyard prologue, with its reminder of Rossa's legacy; the rooming house, with its glimpse at domestic concern and support; and the courtroom, with its focus on Rossa's determination to express his convictions no matter the consequences. The graveyard epilogue is equally representative of this optimism. Here the speaker addresses the audience directly from a darkened stage after delivering a significant portion of the closing part of Pearse's oration, to deliver a poem penned by Thomas McDonagh for the Rossa burial ceremony in 1915:

> Grieve not for him: speak not a word of sorrow
> Although his eyes saw not his country's glory,
> The service of his day shall make our morrow:
> His name shall be a watchword in our story.
> Him England for his love of Ireland hates:
> This flesh we bury England's chains have bitten:
> That is enough: for our deed now he waits:
> With Emmet's let his epitaph be written. (McHugh [1946], 70)

This conclusion and so many other moments in the play place Rossa firmly in the company of inspirational republicans. In linking him with the Easter Rising, through the Pearse and McDonagh references, he is also firmly located, as were Emmet, Swift, and Mangan, within the city of Dublin.

Eamonn Hughes writes that "autobiography allows us to see how individual self-understanding was constructed and functioned" (2003, 32) during the revival period. Likewise, biodramas provide insight into how the Abbey fashioned its identity as a revivalist institution. Taking 1922 as the end of the Revival, *An Imaginary Conversation*, *The Dean of St. Patrick's Cathedral*, and *The Dreamer* comprise the Abbey's revivalist biodrama plays. All three "prioritize the nation over the self" (ibid., 33), in line with Hughes's findings of the autobiography. Interestingly, so do *The Drapier Letters* and *Rossa.* Only *The Words upon the Window-Pane* and *The Man in the Cloak* stand apart, with Swift putting himself first and Mangan attempting to. But the results are regret and solitude, suggesting that these plays also fit the revivalist ethos. This is one way to understand why the biodramas feel so similar to the nonurban canon, where revivalist characteristics were most on display.

# Conclusion

THE ABBEY THEATRE has undergone many changes over the years: managing and artistic directors have come and gone, as audiences have vocally supported or decried its repertoire. Calls for more Irish-language offerings have alternated with calls for less of the same (sometimes simultaneously), and the theater has struggled for financial support and been lambasted for how it appropriates its state funding. But, except for the years between July 1951 and July 1966 when it operated out of the Queen's Theater while being rebuilt following the fire, it has always been based on approximately the same plot of land in Dublin's north inner city. Although plans are under way for it to relocate in the future, to date its location has been the Abbey's only constant.

In light of the early Abbey's reputation for being a bastion of the peasant quotient (PQ), this project—undertaken to answer the question Where was Dublin, home to the Abbey and central to the political movements that emerged during its early decades, on the Abbey stage?—was approached with restraint. The expectation, to be honest, was that only a handful of urban plays would be unearthed and that they would largely mimic O'Casey. It became an archival delight to be so wrong and to discover patterns that made a city quotient (CQ) just as applicable to the Abbey's early repertoire as the PQ. The archival work broadened my appreciation for how the early directors kept pace with the city and the changing times from the Abbey's inception until its destruction on the evening of July 17, 1951, ironically during a run of one of the most Dublin of Dublin plays, O'Casey's *The Plough and the Stars.*

The original theater was, to quote Sean McCann, a "derelict vaudeville hall and morgue that were put together to give Dublin its best known and most criticized establishment outside the Catholic Church" (1967, 53). Anybody interested in the Abbey's history would be hard-pressed to argue with the less quantitative portion of that statement. The space on which the old Abbey stood did have a theatrical history, and both real and potential fire hazards played roles in its structural evolution. Originally, the Theatre Royal Opera House was built on the plot in 1820, but it burned down a few years later. The Mechanics' Institute purchased the site in 1849, and they constructed a multipurpose building that included concert rooms. The Institute eventually converted the concert rooms into a theater, but their patent application was denied when other Dublin theater patent holders (whose permission was part of the process) vetoed the application. It operated as various entertainment venues in fairly quick succession:

> As the Princess's Theatre the building entered a new phase and later, under the management of a Dublin comedian, Pat Langan, became The People's Music Hall . . . Over the years its status gradually declined to that of a penny-gaff and at one time the hall was used as a boxing arena. Finally, in 1901, J. B. Carrickford and Madame Louise Grafton, forbears of several generations of touring "fit-up" actors, reopened the hall as The National Theatre. They generally employed English stock actors but, as the theatre did not have a patent, their repertoire was confined to one-act pieces. The rival theatre, the Queen's, objected to Carrickford's procedure and, under threat of fines . . . the repertoire was changed to vaudeville and music hall. (Robinson and Ó hAodha 15–16)

The National Theatre eventually closed in 1903, because of a combination of poor attendance at variety shows and notice from the fire department that improvements were required in order to address potential fire hazards. The building was still derelict when Annie Horniman leased it in 1904. At the same time, she also purchased the adjacent Penny Bank (previously a city morgue), at Two Marlborough

Street, giving the original Abbey its L-shaped structure. Like her predecessors, Horniman faced patent permission before the Abbey could open as a theater:

> It was . . . necessary for Miss Horniman and Yeats to apply to the courts for this patent. All the other theatres in the city objected in court to the application because they thought the new theatre would be competing with them. Yeats' statement that the new theatre would be strictly non-commercial did not satisfy them. When they saw that the patent was likely to be granted, they agreed only on condition that a provision be inserted to the effect that the new theatre be permitted to produce only plays by Irish authors in the Irish or English language and all standard works in any language written not less than fifty years before the date of the patent. (Kavanagh 1984, 46)

These creative restraints on the patent were contributing factors to the shape the Abbey repertoire took during its early years.[1]

Since neither Horniman nor Yeats was a resident of Ireland in 1904, the patent was issued in the name of Lady Gregory, who, along with Yeats and Synge, gave a rurally dominated emphasis to the theater's repertoire, an emphasis that would keep the urban marginalized on a stage dominated by Dublin actors and Dublin-based writers, and for a particularly urban domestic audience. Although marginalized,

1. The first patent was for a six-year period. Upon Horniman's departure, a new patent was issued (for the standard twenty-one-year period) that altered these creative restraints considerably. They were now allowed to produce "all acknowledged masterpieces of English dramatic literature of the eighteenth century and earlier" and to produce such plays "as shall be selected by the Board of Directors of the National Theatre Society" (Kavanagh 1984, 79). The third and final patent, issued in 1932, again for twenty-one years, eased the creative restraints further. The patentees (Gregory and Yeats) could now perform plays by Irish authors "and works by authors of any nationality on Irish subjects and works by foreign (not including English) authors" (ibid., 154).

the urban repertoire would become a significant popular force at the early Abbey. But it was and remains marginalized.

These plays are marginalized, in part, because they do not fit easily into the standard Abbey story. The O'Casey Trilogy is the only exception, and there seems no end to curiosity about these three plays or the man himself. It is difficult to determine if this interest is the result of his greatness as a dramatist or a desire to feed the canon. In either case, the proliferation of Trilogy scholarship is one reason the balance of the Abbey's urban repertoire has been minimized. This canon fodder influences the study of Irish drama at undergraduate and graduate level, where students (including this former student) are given little indication that there was a Dublin presence on the Abbey stage before or after O'Casey's three pivotal works. It is as though he emerged from a vacuum and then took Dublin away with him to England, leaving the Trilogy to be played on in perpetuity on the Abbey stage as the only evidence of early twentieth-century Dublin. Examination of the Dublin plays shows that this was not the case.

The history of the Abbey, of Ireland's years as a part of Great Britain and then Free State, of the first two years of the Republic of Ireland, and key moments in Dublin's history all become relevant. The historical context informs the texts and the productions, and the rhetoric contained in the plays informs the history. It is a project of reciprocity that, it is hoped, shows that the PQ had a counterpart and that Dublin was not only present on the Abbey stage, but that the Dublin plays reflect the climates in which they premiered and offer insight into how the theater operated during key decades. Perhaps most important, it is hoped that this introduction to the early urban repertoire contributes to smoothing out one more edge in Abbey historiography.

*Appendix*

*Works Cited*

*Index*

APPENDIX

# List of First Productions

| | |
|---|---|
| *The Laying of the Foundations* | December 4, 1902 (at 34 Lower Camden Street) |
| Author: Frederick Ryan | |
| Director: N/A | |
| Cast: Mr. O'Loskin, T. C. | F. J. Fay |
| Michael | P. J. Kelly |
| Alderman Farrelly | J. Dudley Digges |
| M. MacFadden | Frank Walker |
| Mr. Nolan | N. Butler |
| Mrs. O'Loskin | Maire Nic Shiubhlaigh |
| Mrs. MacFadden | Honor Lavelle |
| Eileen | Maire T. Quinn |

| | |
|---|---|
| *The Man Who Missed the Tide* | February 13, 1908 |
| Author: W. F. Casey | |
| Director: N/A | |
| Cast: Dr. Gerald Quinn | Arthur Sinclair |
| James Walsh | Fred O'Donovan |
| Martin Kelly | J.M. Kerrigan |
| Mrs. Gerald Quinn, Moira | Sara Algood |
| Sheila Kennedy | Maire O'Neill |
| A Housemaid | Eileen O'Doherty |
| A Barmaid | Eileen O'Doherty |

| | |
|---|---|
| *The Suburban Groove* | October 1, 1908 |
| Author: W. F. Casey | |
| Director: N/A | |
| Cast: Dick Dalton | J. M. Kerrigan |
| James O'Connor | Fred O'Donovan |

| | |
|---|---|
| Mrs. James O'Connor | Sara Algood |
| Jack O'Connor | U. Wright |
| Una O'Connor | Maire O'Neill |
| Claude Callan | Arthur Sinclair |

*The Cross-Roads* (prologue only) — April 11, 1909
Author: Lennox Robinson
Director: N/A

| Cast: | |
|---|---|
| Ellen McCarthy | Sara Allgood |
| Brian O'Connor | Fred O'Donovan |
| James O'Reilly | Sydney J. Morgan |
| Sydney Doyle | Eric Gorman |
| Henry Blake | J. A. O'Rourke |
| Mrs. McCarthy | Maire O'Neill |
| Mrs. Desmond | Eileen O'Doherty |
| Mike Dempsey | J. M. Kerrigan |
| Tom Dempsey | Arthur Sinclair |

*An Imaginary Conversation* — May 13, 1909
Author/Director: Norreys Connell (Conal O'Riordan)

| Cast: | |
|---|---|
| Kate Moore | Sara Allgood |
| Tommy Moore | J. M. Kerrigan |
| Emmet | Fred O'Donovan |

*Mixed Marriage* — March 30, 1911
Author: St. John Ervine
Director: Lennox Robinson

| Cast: | |
|---|---|
| John Rainey | Arthur Sinclair |
| Mrs. Rainey | Maire O'Neill |
| Tom Rainey | U. Wright |
| Hugh Rainey | J. M. Kerrigan |
| Nora Murray | Maire Nic Shiubhlaigh |
| Michael O'Hara | J. A. O'Rourke |

*The Dean of St. Patrick's Cathedral* — January 23, 1913
Author: G. Sidney Paternoster
Director: Lennox Robinson

| | | |
|---|---|---|
| Cast: | Patrick | Michael Conniffe |
| | Sweetheart | Helena Moloney |
| | Mistress Esther Johnston | Nell Byrne |
| | Mrs. Dingley | Nora Desmond |
| | Dr. Jonathan Swift | Patrick Murphy |
| | His Grace, the Archbishop of Dublin | George St. John |
| | Mr. Joseph Addison | Farrell Pelly |
| | Mrs. Van Homrigh | Ettie Fletcher |
| | Mistress Anne Long | Una O'Connor |
| | Mistress Hester Van Homrigh | Ann Coppinger |
| | Mrs. Touchet | Nell Stewart |
| | First Lady | Kathleen O'Brien |
| | Second Lady | Betty King |
| | Henry St. John, Viscount Bolingbroke | Philip Guiry |
| | Royal Servant | Thomas Barry |
| | Mr. Congreve | A. Patrick Wilson |
| | His Grace, the Duke of Ormond | Charles Power |
| | Dr. John Arbuthnot | Eric Gorman |
| | Robert Harley, Earl of Oxford | Sean Connolly |

*The Critics, or a New Play at the Abbey* — November 20, 1913
Author: St. John Ervine
Director: Lennox Robinson

| | | |
|---|---|---|
| Cast: | Mr. Barbary | J. M. Kerrigan |
| | Mr. Quacks | Fred O'Donovan |
| | Mr. Quartz | Sydney J. Morgan |
| | Mr. Bawlawney | Arthur Sinclair |
| | An Attendant | H. E. Hutchinson |

*The Lord Mayor* — March 13, 1914
Author: Edward McNulty
Director: A. Patrick Wilson

| | | |
|---|---|---|
| Cast: | Mrs. Murphy | Sheila O'Sullivan |
| | Mrs. Moloney | Maura O'Byrne |

| | |
|---|---|
| Gaffney | Reginald Montgomery |
| Kelly | Michael Hayes |
| O'Brien | Sean Connolly |
| Mrs. O'Brien | Maureen Delany |
| Moira O'Brien | Cathleen MacCarthy |
| Scanlon | Michael Conniffe |
| Doherty | Edward Reardon |
| Mrs. Moran | Ethel Fletcher |
| Mr. Butterfield | Arthur Shields |
| Lackey | Thomas O'Neill |

*The Slough* November 3, 1914
Author/Director: A. Patrick Wilson

| | |
|---|---|
| Cast: Peter Hanlon | Arthur Shields |
| Mary Hanlon | Maura O'Byrne |
| Annie Hanlon | Kathleen Drago |
| Peg Hanlon | Eithne Magee |
| Jack Hanlon | Philip Guiry |
| Edward Kelly | H. E. Hutchinson |
| Margaret Kelly | Nora Desmond |
| Tom Robinson | Fred O'Donovan |
| Jake Allen | A. Patrick Wilson |
| Joe Moran | J. F. Barlow |
| Jim Crocker | Sydney J. Morgan |
| Tim Daly | J. A. O'Rourke |
| Bill Nolan | J. M. Kerrigan |
| Pete Riley | Michael Conniffe |
| Matt Taylor | Thomas O'Neill |

*The Dreamers* February 10, 1915
Author: Lennox Robinson
Director: A. Patrick Wilson

| | |
|---|---|
| Cast: John Brady | Arthur Sinclair |
| Robert Brady | A. Patrick Wilson |
| Martin Brady | U. Wright |
| Robert Emmet | Fred O'Donovan |
| Lacey/Quigley | Eric Gorman |

| | |
|---|---|
| Sarah Curran | Sara Allgood |
| Henry Howley/Morrissey | J. M. Kerrigan |
| Thomas Freyne | James Smith |
| McCartney/Con/Mangan | Sean Connolly |
| Hannay/Jones | H. E. Hutchinson |
| Trenaghan | Philip Guiry |
| Peter Freyne | George St. John |
| Roche/Mike | J. A. O'Rourke |
| Mulligan | William Shields |
| Julia | Kathleen Drago |
| Jerry | Tomas O'Neill |
| Jim | J. F. Barlow |
| Peter Flynn | Sydney J. Morgan |
| Felix Rourke/Larry | J. M. Kerrigan |
| Mickey | Michael Coniffe |
| Kate | Shiela O'Sullivan |
| Mary | Cathleen MacCarthy |
| Philips | Fred Harford |
| Mrs. Dillon | Ann Coppinger |
| Mrs. Palmer | Helen Molony |
| Jane Curran | Nora Desmond |
| Major Sirr | Philip Guiry |
| Other Men | Arthur Shields, Edward Reardon, Jack Dunne |

*Blight: The Tragedy of Dublin* December 11, 1917
Authors: Joseph O'Connor and Oliver St. John Gogarty
Director: Fred O'Donovan

| Cast: | |
|---|---|
| Stanislaus Tully | Fred O'Donovan |
| Mrs. Mary Foley | May Craig |
| Jimmy | Michael MacLiammoir |
| Lily | Irene Kelly |
| Miss Maxwell-Knox | Margaret Nicholls |
| Mrs. Larissey | Maureen Delany |
| Mr. Bannermann | Maurice Esmonde |
| Jimmy Larissey | P. J. McDonnell |
| A Labourer | Barry Fitzgerald |

| | |
|---|---|
| Medical Dick | Arthur Shields |
| Medical Davy | Clement Garrick |
| Charwoman | Dorothy Lynd |
| Members of the Board of the Townsend Sanatorium: | |
| Mr. Norris Galbraith | Eric Gorman |
| Mr. Tisdall-Townsley | Fred Harford |
| Mr. Morphy | Peter Nolan |
| Mr. William McWhirter | Hubert McGuire |
| Mr. Tumulty | Louis O'Connor |
| George Foley | Bryan Herbert |

*The Labour Leader* — September 30, 1919
Author: Daniel Corkery
Director: Lennox Robinson

| Cast: | |
|---|---|
| Tim Murphy | Hugh Nagle |
| John Clarke | George St. John |
| Mrs. Donovan | Margaret Nicholls |
| John Dempsey | Peter Nolan |
| Dan O'Rielly/Caretaker | M. J. Dolan |
| Jack O'Donoghue | W. Fitzgerald |
| Battie Donovan | Hubert Maguire |
| Phil Kennedy | F. J. McCormick |
| David Lombard | Paul Farrell |
| James O'Sullivan | Eric Gorman |
| Mrs. Tobin | Maureen Delany |
| Quay Laborers | Brian Herbert, R. C. Murray, A. Quinn |

*The Revolutionist* — February 24, 1921
Author: Terence J. MacSwiney
Director: Lennox Robinson

| Cast: | |
|---|---|
| Mrs. Sullivan | Maureen Delany |
| John Mangan | Barry Fitzgerald |
| Father O'Connor | Michael J. Dolan |
| Hugh O'Neill | F. J. McCormick |
| Con Sheehan | Peter Nolan |

| | |
|---|---|
| Doyle | Maurice Esmonde |
| Nora Mangan | Gertrude Murphy |
| Fan O'Byrne | Christine Hayden |
| Dr. Foley | Alan Duncan |
| Father O'Hanlon | Eric Gorman |
| Mackay | P. Kirwin |
| Bennett | J. Lynch |
| Maher | Gabriel Fallon |
| Kiely | V. Young |
| Rohan | Hubert McGuire |
| Keane | Tony Quinn |
| Lawlor | U. Wright |
| Servants, Followers | J. Barlow, P. MacDonnell, J. McCarthy, M. Gogarty |

| | |
|---|---|
| *The Young Man from Rathmines* | April 6, 1922 |
| Author: M. M. Brennan | |
| Director: Lennox Robinson | |
| Cast: Mr. Dowd | Michael J. Dolan |
| Mrs. Dowd | Mai Neville |
| Mary Dowd | Crissie Byrne |
| Mrs. Sullivan | Sheila Murray |
| Barney Reilly | Tony Quinn |
| George Jackson | Gabriel J. Fallon |

| | |
|---|---|
| *A Leprechaun in the Tenement* | September 5, 1922 |
| Author: M. M. Brennan | |
| Director: Lennox Robinson | |
| Cast: Mr. Reilly | Barry Fitzgerald |
| Mrs. Reilly | Sheila Murray |
| Alice Kate | Eileen Crowe |
| Mickey Reilly | Tony Quinn |
| The Widow Murphy | May Craig |

| | |
|---|---|
| *The Shadow of a Gunman* | April 12, 1923 |
| Author: Sean O'Casey | |
| Director: Lennox Robinson | |

| | | |
|---|---|---|
| Cast: | Donal Davoren | Arthur Shields |
| | Seumas Shields | F. J. McCormick |
| | Tommy Owens | Michael J. Dolan |
| | Adolphus Grigson | P. J. Carolan |
| | Mrs. Grigson | May Craig |
| | Minnie Powell | Gertrude Murphy |
| | Mr. Mulligan | Eric Gorman |
| | Mr. Maguire | G. V. Lavelle |
| | Mrs. Henderson | Christine Hayden |
| | Mr. Gallogher | Gabriel J. Fallon |
| | An Auxiliary | Tony Quin |

*Apartments* September 3, 1923
Author: Fand O'Grady (Kathleen Cruise O'Brien)
Director: Lennox Robinson

| | | |
|---|---|---|
| Cast: | Mrs. MacCarthy | Sara Allgood |
| | Michael MacCarthy | Michael J. Dolan |
| | Geraldine MacCarthy | Gertrude Murphy |
| | Maude MacCarthy | Irene Murphy |
| | Mr. Kiernan | Arthur Shields |
| | Mr. O'Flaherty | F. J. McCormick |
| | Miss O'Rourke | Pearl Moore |
| | Mrs. Quinn | Eileen Crowe |

*Kathleen Listens In* October 1, 1923
Author: Sean O'Casey
Director: Lennox Robinson

| | | |
|---|---|---|
| Cast: | Miceawl O'Houlihan | F. J. McCormick |
| | Sheela O'Houlihan | Maureen Delany |
| | Kathleen | Eileen Crowe |
| | Tomaus Thornton | Barry Fitzgerald |
| | Jimmy | Michael J. Dolan |
| | The Man in the Kilts | Gabriel J. Fallon |
| | The Free Stater | Arthur Shields |
| | The Republican | Tony Quinn |
| | The Business Man | U. Wright |
| | The Farmer | Maurice Esmonde |

| | |
|---|---|
| The Doctor | Eric Gorman |
| The Man with the Big Drum | Peter Nolan |
| Two Men | Walter Dillon, P. J. Carolan |

| | |
|---|---|
| *Juno and the Paycock* | March 3, 1924 |
| Author: Sean O'Casey | |
| Director: Michael J. Dolan | |
| Cast: "Captain" Jack Boyle | Barry Fitzgerald |
| "Juno" Boyle | Sara Allgood |
| Johnny Boyle | Arthur Shields |
| Mary Boyle | Eileen Crowe |
| "Joxer" Daly | F. J. McCormick |
| Mrs. Maisie Madigan | Maureen Delany |
| "Needle" Nugent | Michael J. Dolan |
| Mrs. Tancred | Christine Hayden |
| Jerry Devine | P.J. Carolan |
| Charlie Bentham | Gabriel J. Fallon |
| First Irregular | Maurice Esmonde |
| Second Irregular | Michael J. Dolan |
| First Furniture Remover | Peter Nolan |
| Second Furniture Remover | Tony Quinn |
| Coal-block Vendor | Tony Quinn |
| Sewing Machine Man | Peter Nolan |
| Two Neighbours | Eileen O'Kelly, Irene Murphy |

| | |
|---|---|
| *Nannie's Night Out* | September 29, 1924 |
| Author: Sean O'Casey | |
| Director: Michael J. Dolan | |
| Cast: Mrs. Polly Pender | Maureen Delany |
| Oul Johnny | Barry Fitzgerald |
| Oul Jimmy | Michael J. Dolan |
| Oul Joe | Gabriel J. Fallon |
| Irish Nannie | Sara Allgood |
| Robert | Gerald Breen |
| A Ballad Singer | F. J. McCormick |
| A Young Man | Arthur Shields |
| A Young Girl | Eileen Crowe |

| | |
|---|---|
| Crowd | Seaghan Barlow, F. Ellis, W. O'Hara, and M. Judge |

| | |
|---|---|
| *The Passing* | December 9, 1924 |
| Author: Kenneth Sarr (Reddin) | |
| Director: Michael J. Dolan | |
| Cast: Nann | Sara Allgood |
| Jimmie | Michael J. Dolan |

| | |
|---|---|
| *The Plough and the Stars* | February 8, 1926 |
| Author: Sean O'Casey | |
| Director: Lennox Robinson | |
| Cast: Jack Clitheroe | F. J. McCormick |
| Nora Clitheroe | Shelah Richards |
| Peter Flynn | Eric Gorman |
| The Young Covey | Michael J. Dolan |
| Fluther Good | Barry Fitzgerald |
| Bessie Burgess | Maureen Delany |
| Mrs. Gogan | May Craig |
| Mollser | Kitty Curling |
| Captain Brennan | Gabriel J. Fallon |
| Lieut. Langon | Arthur Shields |
| Rosie Redmond | Ria Mooney |
| A Barman | P. J. Carolan |
| A Woman | Eileen Crowe |
| The Voice | J. Stephenson |
| Corp. Stoddard | P. J. Carolan |
| Sgt. Tinley | J. Stephenson |

| | |
|---|---|
| *The Drapier Letters* | August 22, 1927 |
| Author: Arthur R. Power | |
| Director: Arthur Shields | |
| Cast: Mary-Bridget | Shelah Richards |
| Mrs. Cafferty | Eileen Crowe |
| Mrs. Kate | May Craig |
| Sally O'Gorman | Maureen Delany |

| | |
|---|---|
| Biddy | Aoife Taaffe |
| An English Officer | P. J. Carolan |
| Private Thomson | T. Moran |
| Private Smith | Michael Scott |
| Robert Blakely | Peter Nolan |

*Before Midnight* July 16, 1928
Author: Gerald Brosnan
Director: Lennox Robinson

| | | |
|---|---|---|
| Cast: | Patrick Kiley | F. J. McCormick |
| | "Knacker" Keener | Michael J. Dolan |
| | Det. Long | P. J. Carolan |
| | Joe Mason | Barry Fitzgerald |
| | Mike Bannon | Michael Scott |
| | Amey | Ria Mooney |
| | Civic Guard | Arthur Shields |
| | Detective | Thomas Marshall |

*The Words upon the Window-Pane* November 17, 1930
Author: W. B. Yeats
Director: Lennox Robinson

| | | |
|---|---|---|
| Cast: | Miss McKenna | Shelah Richards |
| | Dr. Trench | P. J. Carolan |
| | John Corbet | Arthur Shields |
| | Cornelius Patterson | Michael J. Dolan |
| | Abraham Johnson | F. J. McCormick |
| | Mrs. Mallet | Eileen Crowe |
| | Mrs. Henderson | May Craig |

*The Critic* January 6, 1931
Author: Lennox Robinson (a modernization of the Richard Brinsley Sheridan play)
Director: Lennox Robinson

| | | |
|---|---|---|
| Cast: | Mr. Dangle | Michael J. Dolan |
| | Mrs. Dangle | Maureen Delany |
| | A Servant | Frolie Mulhern |

| | |
|---|---|
| Mr. Sneer | Fred Johnson |
| Mr. Plagiary | Arthur Shields |
| Puff | F. J. McCormick |
| Interpreter | John Barton |
| Signora Pasticcio Ritornello | Christine Hayden |
| Anna | Geraldine Byrne |
| Nella | Jill Gregory |
| Stage Manager | P. J. Carolan |
| Cast of "The Spanish Armada" | |
| Don Whiskerandos | Arthur Shields |
| Tilburina | Eileen Crowe |
| Confidante | May Craig |
| Two sentries | Michael Finn, Michael Clarke |
| Sir Walter Raleigh | Barry Fitzgerald |
| Sir Christopher Hatton | Eric Gorman |
| Governor of Tilbury Fort | Thomas Moran |
| Master of the Horse | U. Wright |
| Knight | Denis O'Dea |
| Earl of Leicester | J. Stevenson |
| Justice | John Barton |
| Justice's Lady | Christine Hayden |
| Constable | Michael Finn |
| Son | Denis O'Dea |
| Relations | U. Wright, Michael Clarke, W. O'Gorman, Pat C. Cahill |
| Lord Burleigh | J. Stevenson |
| Beefeater | J. Winter |
| Two nieces | Frolie Mulhern, Gertie Quinn |
| The Thames | Noel de la Rue |
| Thames' Banks | Geraldine Byrne, Jill Gregory |
| The Ballet | Chris Sheehan, Doreen Cuthbert, Cepta Cullen, Thelma Murphy, V. Wynburne, Noel de la Rue |

*Money* — March 9, 1931

Author: Hugh P. Quinn

Director: Arthur Shields

| | | |
|---|---|---|
| Cast: | Mrs. McConachy | May Craig |
| | Mickey | Michael J. Dolan |
| | Aggie | Kate Curling |
| | "Ducksy" Duggan | Denis O'Dea |
| | Sam Meehan | P. J. Carolan |
| | Mr. Blaney | F. J. McCormick |
| | Bella MCCann | Maureen Delany |
| | Rosy O'Grady | Frollie Mulhern |
| | Liza | Shelah Richards |

*Scrap* — July 7, 1931
Author: J. A. O'Brennan
Director: Arthur Shields

| | | |
|---|---|---|
| Cast: | Ned Tobin | Michael J. Dolan |
| | Kate Tobin | May Craig |
| | Billy Tobin | Fred Johnson |
| | A Young Man | Denis O'Dea |

*The Big Sweep* — November 7, 1932
Author: M. M. Brennan
Director: Lennox Robinson

| | | |
|---|---|---|
| Cast: | Gerald O'Grady | Tom Purefoy |
| | Michael Rooney | Don Barry |
| | Dermot Sullivan | Joseph Linnane |
| | Miss De Lacey | Christine Hayden |
| | Mrs. Hayden | Bel Johnston |
| | Kitty Hayden | Dorothy Clement |
| | Pat Burke | W. O'Gorman |

*A Deuce O'Jacks* — September 16, 1935
Author: F. R. Higgins
Director: Michael J. Dolan

| | | |
|---|---|---|
| Cast: | Knacker Byrne | P. J. Carolan |
| | A Tin Whistle Player | J. Davenport |
| | Golden Maggie | Maureen Delany |
| | Luke Gaffney | Michael J. Dolan |
| | Harefoot Mike | Fred Johnson |

| | |
|---|---|
| Pharaoh's Daughter | Muriel Kelly |
| Yockle Brough | F. J. McCormick |
| Michael Moran | Denis O'Dea |
| A Priest | William Patterson |
| A Melodeon Player | M. Schiff |
| Jezebel | Chris Sheehan |
| The Nobbler | John Stephenson |
| Hawkers/Ballad Singers/ Corner Boys | Michael Clarke, Ann Clery, Cyril Cusak, Michael Finn, Kathleen Murphy, William O'Gorman, Nora O'Mahony, and J. Winter |

*The Grand House in the City* — February 3, 1936
Author: Brinsley MacNamara
Director: Hugh Hunt

| Cast: | |
|---|---|
| Henry Bergan | Michael J. Dolan |
| Massie Ward | Maureen Delany |
| Diana Gilsenan | Eileen Crowe |
| Walter Gilsenan | Cyril Cusak |
| Olivia Petit | Christine Hayden |
| Vincent Kelch | Arthur Shields |
| Mary Ward | May Craig |
| Brian Merriman | Fred Johnson |
| Richard Gilsenan | F. J. McCormick |
| Owen Lynam | P. J. Carolan |
| Delia Lynam | Aideen O'Connor |

*Blind Man's Buff* — December 26, 1936
Authors: Ernst Toller and Denis Johnston
Director: Hugh Hunt

| Cast: | |
|---|---|
| Laura Chavasse | Patsy Fitzpatrick |
| Mary Quirke | May Craig |
| Dominick Mapother | F. J. McCormick |
| Dr. Frank Chavasse | Arthur Shields |

| | |
|---|---|
| Dr. Anice Hollingshead | Eileen Crowe |
| Sgt. Carey | P. J. Carolan |
| John Roche | Eric Gorman |
| Theobald Thin | Michael J. Dolan |
| Liam Poer | Fred Johnson |
| Henry Harrican | Austin Meldon |
| Mr. Justice Drooley | Tom Purefoy |
| Registrar | Frank Carney |
| Seamus Ua Caoilte | Denis O'Dea |
| Juryman | Brian Carey |
| Solicitors, Barristers, Clerks, etc. | Messrs. Barror, Finn, Considine, and Hickey |

*The Man in the Cloak* September 27, 1937
Author: Louis D'Alton
Director: Hugh Hunt

| Cast: | |
|---|---|
| Clarence Mangan | Cyril Cusak |
| James Mangan | Fred Johnson |
| Kate Mangan | Ann Clery |
| John Mangan | Malachi Keegan |
| Mick Fogarty | Eric Gorman |
| Bridie Gilheaney | Josephine Fitzgerald |
| Marty Phelan | W. O'Gorman |
| Con Colgan | Seumas Healy |
| Cis Carmody | Shela Ward |
| Catherine Hayes | Shelah Richards |
| Blythe | J. Winter |
| Laurence Tighe | Tom Purefoy |

*The Invincibles* October 18, 1937
Authors: Hugh Hunt and Frank O'Connor
Director: Hugh Hunt

| Cast: | |
|---|---|
| First Fenian | Dermot Kelly |
| Second Fenian | Michael Finn |
| Publican | Victor Boyd |

| | |
|---|---|
| James Carey | Fred Johnson |
| Timothy Kelly | Cyril Cusack |
| P. J. Tynan | Frank Carney |
| Joe Brady | W. O'Gorman |
| Daniel Curley | Eric Gorman |
| Ned McCaffrey | Laurence Elyan |
| Maggie Fitzsimons | Sheila Ward |
| Caretaker | Seumas Healy |
| Mr. O'Leary | W. Redmond |
| The Publican (at Chapelizod) | Brian Carey |
| The Angler | P. H. Considine |
| Michael Kavanagh | M. Kinsella |
| Dan Delaney | John MacDarby |
| Man with Proclamations | M. Kinsella |
| Inspector Mallon | C. Barror |
| Mrs. Brady | Christine Hayden |
| Warder | Malachi Keegan |
| Governor of Prison | Gerald Hickey |
| Sister of Mercy | Ann Clery |

*Coggerers* — November 22, 1937
Author: Paul Vincent Carroll
Director: Hugh Hunt

| Cast: | | |
|---|---|---|
| | Eamonn O'Curry | Eric Gorman |
| | Mrs. Galgoogley | Josephine Fitzgerald |
| | Owen, her son | W. T. O'Connor |
| | Parnell | Fred Johnson |
| | Wolfe Tone | Frank Carney |
| | Robert Emmet | W. Redmond |
| | John Mitchel | W. O'Gorman |
| | Lord Edward Fitzgerald | P. H. Considine |

*A Spot in the Sun* — February 14, 1938
Author: T. C. Murray
Director: Hugh Hunt

| Cast: | | |
|---|---|---|
| | Denis Harman | Cyril Cusack |

| | |
|---|---|
| Rose Harman | Shelah Richards |
| Mrs. Harman | Christine Hayden |
| Annie | Ann Clery |
| First Man | Fred Johnson |
| Second Man | Malachi Keegan |

*Moses' Rock* February 28, 1938
Author: Hugh Hunt and Frank O'Connor
Director: Hugh Hunt

| Cast: | | |
|---|---|---|
| | Cady O'Leary | W. O'Gorman |
| | Kate O'Leary | Ann Clery |
| | Joan O'Leary | Shelah Richards |
| | Shuvaun O'Leary | Shelah Ward |
| | Ned Hegarty | Cyril Cusack |
| | Jer Coghlan | Fred Johnson |
| | Lieutenant Grant Fortescue | P. H. Considine |
| | Dr. Corney Jackson | Liam Redmond |
| | Biddy Lally | Christine Hayden |
| | Sorry O'Sullivan | Evelyn MacNeice |
| | Nelly | Gertrude Quinn |

*Time's Pocket* December 26, 1938
Author: Frank O'Connor
Director: Frank Dermody

| Cast: | | |
|---|---|---|
| | Abby Driscoll | Eileen Crowe |
| | Nance | Ria Mooney |
| | Patrick | Denis O'Dea |
| | Denis | Austin Meldon |
| | Martin Conlan | F. J. McCormick |
| | Sergeant Daly | Fred Johnson |
| | Corporal Dargan | W. O'Gorman |
| | Red Fahy | Victor Boyd |
| | Ned Sullivan | J. Winter |
| | Father Costello | Michael J. Dolan |
| | The General | Eric Gorman |
| | The General's Wife | Shelah Ward |

| | |
|---|---|
| Mylie Dargan | Brian McAuliffe |
| Sergeant of Police | Malachi Keegan |
| Policemen | Michael Finn, Paud Holahan |
| Soldiers | Thomas O'Gorman, Gerald Hickey |
| Orderly | Wilfred Brambell |

*Caesar's Image* February 6, 1939
Author: E. F. Carey
Director: Louis D'Alton

| Cast: | |
|---|---|
| Maria Brady | Eileen Crowe |
| Dan Brady | Fred Johnson |
| Katie Brady | Phyllis Ryan |
| Patsy Brady | W. O'Gorman |
| "Sloper" Neale | Michael J. Dolan |
| Mrs. Hogan | Maureen Delany |
| Mrs. Behan | May Craig |
| The Widow Whooley | Christine Hayden |
| Chrissie Whooley | Ria Mooney |
| Martin Powell | Denis O'Dea |
| Young Man | Victor Boyd |
| Detective | Malachi Keegan |
| Policeman | Gerard Kiernan |

*Birth of a Giant* May 13, 1940
Author: Nora MacAdam
Director: Michael J. Dolan

| Cast: | |
|---|---|
| Robert Watson | W. O'Gorman |
| Lily Watson | Eileen Crowe |
| Ruth Watson | Sheila Manahan |
| James Cathcart | Austin Meldon |
| Harry Moody | J. Prendergast |
| Mrs. Larkin | May Craig |
| Pat Larkin | J. MacDarby |
| Susan Larkin | Kitty Thuillier |
| Tommy Mallin | C. Fitzsimons |
| John Myers | Denis O'Dea |

*Trial at Green Street Courthouse* — January 9, 1941

Author: Roger McHugh

Director: Frank Dermody

| Cast: | |
|---|---|
| Ryan | Joseph Linnane |
| Jerry | Finbar Howard |
| Old Man | John MacDarby |
| Isaac Butt | F. J. McCormick |
| Frederick Falkiner | W. O'Gorman |
| Dowse | Austin Meldon |
| Armstrong | Michael J. Dolan |
| Chief Justice Whiteside | Tom Purefoy |
| Chief Baron Pigott | James Dunne |
| Dr. Stokes | Michael Walsh |
| Dr. Tufnell | Harry Brogan |
| Doctor McDonnell | Eric Gorman |
| Edmund Vesey | Denis O'Dea |
| Constable Mullen | Seumas Healy |
| Constable Grimes | J. Winter |
| Henry Talbot | U. Wright |
| Dr. O'Leary | Edward Byrne |
| Rose O'Leary, his wife | Ria Mooney |
| Clerk of the Court | Malachy Dooney |

*Remembered For Ever* — August 18, 1941

Author: Bernard McGinn

Director: Frank Dermody

| Cast: | |
|---|---|
| Roderick Brosnan | Denis O'Dea |
| Nora Brosnan | Eithne Dunne |
| Brian | Liam Redmond |
| Michael Murphy | W. O'Gorman |
| Christopher O'Connell | Austin Meldon |
| Dan Cassidy | Dermot Kelly |
| Martin O'Keefe | Michael J. Dolan |
| Guard Hennessy | Fred Johnson |
| Miss O'Sullivan | Eileen Crowe |
| A Figure | Gerard Healy |

| *The O'Cuddy* | | March 8, 1943 |
|---|---|---|
| Author: Anthony Wharton | | |
| Director: Frank Dermody | | |
| Cast: | George Posnett | Michael J. Dolan |
| | Clench | Fred Johnson |
| | Countess Pilsudska | Joan Plunkett |
| | Lord Kilfoyne | Gerard Healy |
| | Thaddeus Cuddy | Cyril Cusak |
| | Dr. McRoney | F. J. McCormick |
| | Cormac O'Cuiddeach | Denis O'Dea |
| | Michael | Brian O'Higgins |
| | A Masked Figure | Harry Webster |
| | Two Guards | Ciaran O hAnnrachain and Michael O'Brien |

| *The End House* | | August 28, 1944 |
|---|---|---|
| Author: Joseph Tomelty | | |
| Director: Frank Dermody | | |
| Cast: | Wallace MacAstocker | F. J. McCormick |
| | Saralice | May Craig |
| | Monica | Siobhan McKenna |
| | Seumas | Cyril Cusack |
| | Stewartie Pullar | Michael J. Dolan |
| | Mrs. Griffith | Eileen Crowe |
| | Constable Hanna | Harry Brogan |
| | Insurance Visitor | Christine Hayden |
| | Mrs. Fruin | Brid Lynch |
| | Policemen | Brian O'Higgins, Seumas Locke |
| | Baker | Denis O'Dea |
| | R.U.C. Sergeant | Fred Johnson |

| *Rossa* | | March 31, 1945 |
|---|---|---|
| Author: Roger McHugh | | |
| Director: Frank Dermody | | |
| Cast: | The Speaker | Seumas Locke |
| | The Bugler | H. Hossler |

| | |
|---|---|
| John O'Connell | Fred Johnston |
| Jeremiah O'Donovan Rossa | W. O'Gorman |
| A Magistrate | Fred Johnson |
| Mary Irwin | Brid Lynch |
| Parish Priest | Seumas Healy |
| Mrs. Luby | Eileen Crowe |
| Judge Keogh | Cyril Cusack |
| Governor | F.J. McCormick |
| Governor's Secretary | May Craig |
| First Warder | Denis O'Dea |
| Chaplain | Michael Dolan |
| Second Warder | Michael O'Brien |
| First Commissioner | Eric Gorman |
| Second Commissioner | Pat O'Rourke |
| Third Commissioner | Sean O Maonaigh |
| Rossa's Secretary | Siobhan McKenna |
| Mr. Lanigan | Austin Meldon |
| Mr. Madigan | Harry Brogan |
| General Ryan | Michael Cosgrave |

*Mungo's Mansion* — February 11, 1946
Author: Walter Macken
Director: Frank Dermody

| Cast: | |
|---|---|
| Mungo King | F. J. McCormick |
| Mairteen | Micheal O'Briain |
| Nellie | Siobhan McKenna |
| Winnie Gilhealy | Eileen Crowe |
| Mr. Skerret | Michael J. Dolan |
| Mowleogs | Harry Brogan |
| Jack Manders | Denis O'Dea |
| Mrs. Manders | Brid Lynch |
| The Doctor | Fred Johnson |

*The Drums Are Out* — July 12, 1948
Author: John Coulter
Director: Ria Mooney

| | | |
|---|---|---|
| Cast: | Mrs. Sheridan | Eileen Crowe |
| | Sgt. Sheridan | Brian O'Higgins |
| | Jean | Maire ni Dhomhnaill |
| | Nixon | Philip O'Flynn |
| | Denis | Raghnall Breathnack |
| | Matt | Harry Brogan |
| | Three Men | Reamonn Mac an Fhailghigh, Micheal Ó Duinn, and Labhras Ó Gallchobhair |

*Design for a Headstone* April 8, 1950
Author: Seamus Byrne
Director: Ria Mooney
Cast:

| | |
|---|---|
| Political Prisoners: | |
| Conor Egan | Michael Hennessey |
| Aiden O'Leary | Eddie Golden |
| Kevin Shields | Ray MacAnally |
| Tommy McGovern | Ronnie Walsh |
| Jim O'Shea | Sean Mooney |
| Ructions McGowan | Walter Macken |
| Bill Dunne | Michael Dunne |
| Joe Fitzpatrick | Thomas MacAnna |
| Micheal Breathnach | Michael O'Brien |
| P. J. Corrigan | Hugh Gunn |
| O'Sullivan | Traolach Hennessey |
| Prison Warders: | |
| Pat Gerachty | Philip O'Flynn |
| Mouth Phelan | Geoffrey Golden |
| Charles Grimes | James Carty |
| Principal Warder | Noel Guy |
| Criminal Prisoners: | |
| Jakey | Brian O'Higgins |
| Muscles Rogan | Harry Brogan |
| Butcher Healy | Leo Keogh |
| Bayer | Michael J. Dolan |

| | |
|---|---|
| Father Maguire | Bill Foley |
| Kathleen Egan | Brid Lynch |
| Other prisoners, warders, etc: | Michael O'Herlihy, Colm O'Kelly, Harry O'Reilly, Tom Dullaghan, Pol O'Meara, Finbar Howard, Michael Conway, Joe Cooney, and Joe Nolan |

*Sources:* The Abbey Theatre Archives; National Library of Ireland (NLI) Dept. of Manuscripts; and Lennox Robinson, *Ireland's Abbey Theatre: A History 1899–1951* (Port Washington, NY: Kennikat Press, 1951). Where the Robinson text contradicts either the Abbey Archives or the NLI, the latter sources are used.

# Works Cited

ABBREVIATIONS

| | |
|---|---|
| ATA | Abbey Theatre Archives |
| BL | British Library |
| NLI | National Library of Ireland |

UNPUBLISHED SOURCES


Abbey Theatre Box Office Receipts. ATA ATC/FIN/6 (Vol. 1: 1920–1925); ATA ATC/FIN/5 (Vol. 2: 1925–1932); and ATC/FIN/34 (Vol. 3: 1932–1951).

Abbey Theatre Programs. ATA ATC/MPC/1914 (*The Lord Mayor*, Mar. 13, 1914); ATC/MPC/1914 (*The Slough*, Nov. 3, 1914); ATC/MPC/1917 (*Blight*, Dec. 11, 1917); ATA ATC/MPC/1924 (*The Lord Mayor*, Jan. 15, 1924); and ATC/MPC/1937 (*The Invincibles*, Oct. 18, 1937).

Brennan, M. M. (Matthew Michael). *The Leprechaun in the Tenement* (reviews and synopsis). National Library of Ireland (NLI) MS. 25,505.

Casey, W. F. [1908]. *The Suburban Groove*. NLI MS. 21,315.

MacNamara, Brinsley. [1956]. *The Grand House in the City*. NLI MS. 29,346.

O'Brennan, J. A. [1931]. *Scrap*. NLI MS. 29,393.

O'Connor, Frank. 1938. *Time's Pocket*. NLI MS. 21,426.

Paternoster, G. Sidney. *The Dean of St. Patrick's Cathedral*. 1923. BL MS. / LCP 1923/32.

Robinson, Lennox. [1931]. *The Critic, or, a tragedy rehearsed by Richard Brinsley Sheridan; modernised by Lennox Robinson*. NLI MS. 29,493.

Wilson, A. Patrick. 1914. *The Slough*. BL Add. MS. 1914/35.

## PUBLISHED SOURCES

Adams, Bernard. 2002. *Denis Johnston: A Life*. Dublin: Lilliput Press.

Arrington, Lauren. 2010. *W. B. Yeats, the Abbey Theatre, Censorship, and the Irish State: Adding the Half-Pence to the Pence*. Oxford: Oxford Univ. Press.

———. 2011. "St. John Ervine and the Fabian Society: Capital, Empire and Irish Home Rule." *History Workshop Journal* 72: 52–73.

Bakhtin, M. M. 1981. *The Dialogic Imagination*. Translated by Caryn Emerson and Michael Holquist. Edited by Michael Holquist. Austin: Univ. of Texas Press.

Bickley, Francis. 1968. *J. M. Synge and the Irish Dramatic Movement*. New York: Russell and Russell.

Brennan, M. M. (Matthew Michael). [1923]. *The Young Man from Rathmines*. Dublin: Talbot Press.

———. [1933]. *The Big Sweep*. Dublin: Talbot Press.

Byrne, Seamus. 1956. *Design for a Headstone*. Dublin: Progress House.

Cahalen, James M. 1983. *Great Hatred, Little Room: The Irish Historical Novel*. Syracuse, NY: Syracuse Univ. Press.

Carroll, Paul Vincent. 1938. "The Substance of Paul Vincent Carroll: An Irish Dramatist Sets Down Some Thoughts on Ireland and Letters." *New York Times*, Jan. 30.

———. 1939. *Coggerers*. In *The White Steed and Coggerers*, 158–90. New York: Random House.

Castle, Gregory. 2011. "Irish Revivalism: Critical Trends and New Directions." *Literature Compass* 8, no. 5:291–303.

Cave, Richard Allen. 1986. "Dramatising the Life of Swift." In *Irish Writers and the Theatre*, edited by Masuru Sekine, 17–32. Gerrards Cross: Colin Smythe; Totowa: Barnes and Noble.

Clarke, Brenna Katz. 1982. *The Emergence of the Irish Peasant Play at the Abbey Theatre*. Ann Arbor, MI: UMI Research Press.

Coote, Stephen. 1997. *W. B. Yeats: A Life*. London: Hodder and Stoughton.

Corkery, Daniel. 1920. *The Labour Leader*. Dublin: Talbot; London: T. Fisher Unwin.

Coulter, John. 1971. *The Drums Are Out*. Chicago: DePaul Univ. Press.

Cullingford, Elizabeth. 1981. *Yeats, Ireland and Fascism*. London: Macmillan.

D'Alton, Louis. 1971. *The Man in the Cloak: A Play on James Clarence Mangan*. Dublin: P. J. Bourke.

Daly, Mary E. 1984. *Dublin, the Deposed Capital: A Social and Economic History 1860–1914*. Cork: Cork Univ. Press.

Deleuze, Gilles, and Félix Guattari. 1983. "What Is Minor Literature?" Translated by Robert Brinkley. *Mississippi Review* 11, no. 3 (Winter/Spring): 13–33.

Elliott, Marianne. 1989. *Wolfe Tone: Prophet of Irish Independence*. New Haven: Yale Univ. Press.

Ervine, St. John G. 1914. *The Critics*. In *Four Irish Plays*, 79–97. New York: Macmillan.

Fallon, Gabriel. 1965. *Sean O'Casey: The Man I Knew*. London: Routledge and Kegan Paul.

Fay, Gerald. 1958. *The Abbey Theatre: Cradle of Genius*. Dublin: Clonmore and Reynolds.

Fay, W. G., and Catherine Carswell. 1971. *The Fays of the Abbey Theatre: An Autobiographical Record*. New York: Benjamin Blom.

Feeney, William J., ed. 1980. *Edward Martyn's Irish Theatre*. Dixon, CA: Proscenium Press.

———. 1984. *Drama in Hardwicke Street: A History of the Irish Theatre Company*. Cranbury, NJ: Associated University Presses.

Flannery, James W. 1976. *W. B. Yeats and the Idea of a Theatre: The Early Abbey Theatre in Theory and Practice*. New Haven: Yale Univ. Press.

———. 1982. "High Ideals and the Reality of the Marketplace: A Financial Record of the Early Abbey Theatre." *Studies: An Irish Quarterly Review* 71:246–69.

Fox, Richard M. 1946. *James Connolly: The Forerunner*. Tralee. Ireland: Kerryman Press.

Frazier, Adrian. 1990. *Behind the Scenes: Yeats, Horniman, and the Struggle for the Abbey Theatre*. Berkeley: Univ. of California Press.

Furlong, Paul, and David Curtis, eds. 1994. *The Church Faces the Modern World:* Rerum Novarum *and its Impact*. London: Earlsgate Press.

Geoghegan, Patrick M. 2002. *Robert Emmet: A Life*. Montreal: McGill–Queen's Univ. Press.

Gibbons, Luke. 1996. *Transformations in Irish Culture*. Cork: Cork Univ. Press in assoc. with Field Day.

Gogarty, Oliver St. John. 2001. *Blight*. In *The Poems and Plays of Oliver St. John Gogarty*, edited by A. Norman Jeffares, 509–44. Gerrards Cross, UK: Colin Smythe.

Goldring, Maurice. 1991. *Belfast: From Loyalty to Rebellion*. London: Lawrence and Wishart.

Gregory, Lady Augusta. 1913. *Our Irish Theatre: A Chapter of Autobiography*. New York: G. Putnam's Sons.

———. 1921. *Hugh Lane*. London: John Murray.

Grene, Nicholas. 1999. *The Politics of Irish Drama*. Cambridge: Cambridge Univ. Press.

Gwynn, Denis. 1974. *Edward Martyn and the Irish Revival*. London: J. Cape, 1930; New York: Lemma.

Heininge, Kathleen. 2009. *Buffoonery in Irish Drama: Staging Twentieth-Century Post-Colonial Stereotypes*. New York: Peter Lang.

Henderson, Gordon. 1973. "An Interview with Denis Johnston." *Journal of Irish Literature* 2, no. 2–3 (May–Sept.): 30–44.

Hill, John. 2006. "It's Chaos Out There: Changing Representations of 'the Troubles'." In *Cinema and Northern Ireland: Film, Culture and Politics*, 190–243. London: BFI.

Hodos, Jerome. 2007. "Globalization and the Concept of the Second City." *City and Community* 6, no. 4: 315–33.

Hogan, Robert. 1967. *After the Irish Renaissance*. Minneapolis: Univ. of Minnesota Press.

Hogan, Robert, and Richard Burnham, eds. 1992. *The Years of O'Casey, 1921–1926: A Documentary History*. Newark: Univ. of Delaware Press; Gerrard's Cross, UK: Colin Smythe.

Hogan, Robert, and James Kilroy, eds. 1970. *Lost Plays of the Irish Renaissance*. Dixon: Proscenium.

———. 1975. *The Irish Literary Theatre, 1899–1901*. Atlantic Highlands, NJ: Humanities Press; Dublin: Dolmen.

———. 1976. *Laying the Foundations, 1902–1904*. Atlantic Highlands, NJ: Humanities Press; Dublin: Dolmen.

———. 1978. *The Abbey Theatre: The Years of Synge, 1905–1909*. Atlantic Highlands, NJ: Humanities Press; Dublin: Dolmen.

Holloway, Joseph. 1967. *Joseph Holloway's Abbey Theatre: A Selection from His Unpublished Journal: Impressions of a Dublin Playgoer*. Edited by Robert Hogan and Michael J. O'Neill. Carbondale: Southern Illinois Univ. Press.

Hornby, Richard. 1986. *Drama, Metadrama, and Perception*. Lewisburg, PA: Bucknell Univ. Press; London: Associated University Presses.

Hughes, Eamonn. 2003. "'The Fact of Me-ness': Autobiographical Writing in the Revival Period." *Irish University Review* 33, no. 1 (Spring/Summer): 28–45.

Hunt, Hugh, and Frank O'Connor. 1980. *The Invincibles.* Edited by Ruth Sherry. Newark, NJ: Proscenium.

———. 1983. *Moses' Rock.* Edited and Introduced by Ruth Sherry. Washington, DC: Catholic Univ. of America Press; Gerrard's Cross, UK: Colin Smythe.

Hutchinson, John. 1987. *The Dynamics of Cultural Nationalism: The Gaelic Revival and the Creation of the Irish Free State.* London: Allen and Unwin.

———. 1999. "Re-Interpreting Cultural Nationalism." *Australian Journal of Politics and History,* 45, no. 3:392–407.

Hutchinson, John, and Anthony D. Smith, eds. 2000. *Nationalism: Critical Concepts in Political Science.* Vol. 2. London: Routledge.

Innes, C. L. 1993. *Woman and Nation in Irish Literature and Society, 1880–1935.* Athens: Univ. of Georgia Press.

Johnston, Denis. 1977 [1956]. *Strange Occurrence on Ireland's Eye.* In *The Dramatic Works of Denis Johnston.* Vol. 1. Gerrards Cross, UK: Colin Smythe.

———. 1992. *The Old Lady Says "No!"* Edited by Christine St. Peter. Washington, DC: Catholic Univ. of America Press; Gerrards Cross, UK: Colin Smythe.

Johnston, Denis, and Ernst Toller. 1938. *Blind Man's Buff.* London: Jonathan Cape.

Kavanagh, Peter. 1984 [1950]. *The Story of the Abbey Theatre.* New York: Devin-Adair; Orono: The National Poetry Foundation, Univ. of Maine at Orono.

Kearns, Kevin C. 1983. *Georgian Dublin: Ireland's Imperilled Architectural Heritage.* London: David and Charles.

———. 1996. *Dublin Tenement Life: An Oral History.* Dublin: Gill and Macmillan.

Kelly, John. 1970. "A Lost Abbey Play: Frederick Ryan's *The Laying of the Foundations.*" *Ariel* 1, no. 3 (July): 29–48.

Keogh, Dermot. 1982. *The Rise of the Irish Working Class.* Belfast: Appletree.

Kiberd, Declan. 1996. *Inventing Ireland: The Literature of the Modern Nation.* London: Random House.

Kohfeldt, Mary Lou. 1985. *Lady Gregory: The Woman Behind the Irish Renaissance.* London: André Deutsch.

Kosok, Heinz. 1984. "The Image of Dublin in Anglo-Irish Drama." In *The Irish Writer and the City*, edited by Maurice Harmon, 18–36. Gerrards Cross, UK: Colin Smythe; Totowa, NJ: Barnes and Noble.

Krause, David. 1982. *The Profane Book of Irish Comedy*. Ithaca, NY: Cornell Univ. Press.

Laurence, Dan H., and Nicholas Grene, eds. 1993. *Shaw, Lady Gregory and the Abbey: A Correspondence and a Record*. Gerrards Cross, UK: Colin Smythe.

Levitas. Ben. 2002a. "'The Loy in Irish Politics': The Abbey Theatre in the Wake of *The Playboy*, 1907–1910." *Irish Review* 29:38–50.

———. 2002b. *The Theatre of Nation: Irish Drama and Cultural Nationalism, 1890–1916*. Oxford: Clarendon.

———. 2003. "Plumbing the Depths: Irish Realism and the Working Class from Shaw to O'Casey." *Irish University Review* 33, no. 1 (Spring/Summer): 133–49.

Lindenberger, Herbert. 1975. *Historical Drama: The Relation of Literature to Reality*. Chicago: The Univ. of Chicago Press.

Lloyd, David. 1987. *Nationalism and Minor Literature*. Berkeley: Univ. of California Press.

Lojek, Helen. 2011. *The Spaces of Irish Drama: Stage and Place in Contemporary Plays*. New York: Palgrave Macmillan.

Lyons, F. S. L. 1971. *Ireland Since the Famine*. London: Weidenfeld and Nicolson.

MacAnna, Tomás. 1971. "Nationalism from the Abbey Stage." In *Theatre and Nationalism in Twentieth-Century Ireland*, edited by Robert O'Driscoll, 89–101. Toronto: Univ. of Toronto Press; London: Oxford Univ. Press.

MacCana, Proinsias. 1982. "Women in Irish Mythology." In *The Crane Bag Book of Irish Studies (1977–1981)*, edited by Mark Patrick Hederman and Richard Kearney, 520–24. Dublin: Blackwater Press.

MacNamara, John. 1982. "The Irish Language and Nationalism." In *The Crane Bag Book of Irish Studies (1977–1981)*, edited by Mark Patrick Hederman and Richard Kearney, 124–28. Dublin: Blackwater Press.

Macken, Ultan. 2009. *Walter Macken: Dreams on Paper*. Cork: Mercier.

Macken, Walter. 1948. *Vacant Possession*. London: Macmillan.

———. 1964. *Mungo's Mansion*. London: Macmillan.

MacSwiney, Terence J. 1914. *The Revolutionist*. Dublin: Maunsel.

Mahony, Robert. 1995. *Jonathan Swift: The Irish Identity*. New Haven: Yale Univ. Press.

Malone, Irina Ruppo. 2010. *Ibsen and the Irish Revival.* New York: Palgrave Macmillan.

Mangan, Ellen-Shanon. 1996. *James Clarence Mangan: A Biography.* Dublin: Irish Academic Press.

Matthews, James. 1983. *Voices: A Life of Frank O'Connor.* Dublin: Gill and Macmillan.

Maume, Patrick. 1993. *Life That Is Exile: Daniel Corkery and the Search for Irish Ireland.* Belfast: Queens Univ. Belfast Institute for Irish Studies.

McCann, Sean, ed. 1967. *The Story of the Abbey Theatre.* London: New English Library.

McDiarmid, Lucy. 2005. "Hunger and Hysteria: The 'Save the Dublin Kiddies' Campaign, October–November, 1913." In *The Irish Art of Controversy,* 123–66. Ithaca, NY: Cornell Univ. Press.

———. 2009. "The Abbey, Its 'Helpers,' and the Field of Cultural Production in 1913." In *Irish Theatre in America,* edited by John P. Harrington. Syracuse, NY: Syracuse Univ. Press.

McDonald, Iverach. 1984. *The History of the Times.* Vol. 5: *Struggles in War and Peace, 1939–1966.* London: Times Books.

McGinn, Bernard. 1943. *Remembered For Ever: A Tragicomedy in Three Acts.* London: Allen and Unwin.

McHugh, Roger. [1945]. *Trial at Green Street Courthouse.* Dublin: Browne and Nolan.

———. [1946]. *Rossa: A Play in Three Acts.* Tralee: The Kerryman.

McManus, Ruth. 2002. *Dublin, 1910–1940: Shaping the City and Suburbs.* Dublin: Four Courts Press.

McNulty, Edward. 1917. *The Lord Mayor: A Dublin Comedy in Three Acts.* Dublin: Maunsel.

McNulty, Eugene. 2008. *The Ulster Literary Theatre and the Northern Revival.* Cork: Cork Univ. Press.

Mikhail, E. H., ed. 1988. *The Abbey Theatre: Interviews and Recollections.* Totowa, NJ: Barnes and Noble.

Moody, T. W., and F. X. Martin, eds. 1984. *The Course of Irish History.* Rev. ed. Cork: Mercier in assoc. with RTÉ.

Morash, Christopher. 2002. *A History of Irish Theatre, 1601–2000.* Cambridge: Cambridge Univ. Press.

Murphy, Paul. 2008. *Hegemony and Fantasy in Irish Drama, 1899–1949.* Basingstoke, UK: Palgrave Macmillan.

Murray, Christopher. 1986. "Lennox Robinson: The Abbey's Anti-Hero." In *Irish Writers and the Theatre*, edited by Masaru Sekine, 114–34. Gerrards Cross, UK: Colin Smythe; Totowa, NJ: Barnes and Noble.

———. 1988. "The History Play Today." In *Cultural Contexts and Literary Idioms in Contemporary Irish Literature*, edited by Michael Kenneally, 269–89. Totowa, NJ: Barnes and Noble.

———. 1997. *Twentieth-Century Irish Drama: Mirror up to Nation*. Syracuse, NY: Syracuse Univ. Press.

———. 2004. *Sean O'Casey: Writer at Work: A Biography*. Dublin: Gill and Macmillan.

Mustafa, Shakir. 2000. "Saying 'No' to Politics: Sean O'Casey's Dublin Trilogy." In *A Century of Irish Drama: Widening the Stage*, edited by Stephen Watt, Eileen Morgan, and Shakir Mustafa, 95–113. Bloomington: Indiana Univ. Press.

Nelson, Robert J. 1971. *Play Within a Play*. New York: DaCapo.

Nevin, Donal. 1964. *1913: Jim Larkin and the Dublin Lockout*. Dublin: Worker's Union of Ireland.

Ní Bhrolecháin, Muireann. 1982. "Women in Early Irish Myths and Sagas." In *The Crane Bag Book of Irish Studies (1977–1981)*, edited by Mark Patrick Hederman and Richard Kearney, 525–32. Dublin: Blackwater Press.

Nolan, Emer. 2007. *Catholic Emancipations: Irish Fiction from Thomas Moore to James Joyce*. Syracuse, NY: Syracuse Univ. Press.

O'Brien, Joseph. 1982. *"Dear, Dirty Dublin": A City in Distress, 1899–1916*. Berkeley: Univ. of California Press.

O'Casey, Sean. 1963. *Kathleen Listens In and Nannies Night Out*. In *Feathers from the Green Crow*, edited by Robert Hogan, 277–330. London: Macmillan.

———. 1989. *The Letters of Sean O'Casey*. Vol. 3: *1955–1958*. Edited by David Krause. Washington, DC: Catholic Univ. of America Press.

———. 1992. *Inishfallen, Fare Thee Well, Autobiographies 2*. London: Pan Macmillan.

———. 1998. *The Shadow of a Gunman* and *The Plough and the Stars*. In *Sean O'Casey: Plays 2*, 1–161. London: Faber and Faber.

O'Connor, Emmet. 2002. *James Larkin*. Cork: Cork Univ. Press.

O'Connor, Ulick. 1964. *Oliver St. John Gogarty: A Poet and His Times*. London: Jonathan Cape.

O'Donovan, John. 1972. "An Interview with Paul Vincent Carroll." *Journal of Irish Literature* 1, no. 1 (Jan.): 7–14.

O'Farrell, Ciara. 2004. *Louis D'Alton and the Abbey Theatre*. Dublin: Four Courts Press.

Ó hAodha, Micheál. 1961. *Plays and Places*. Dublin: Progress House.

O'Riordan, Conal. 1935. *An Imaginary Conversation*. In *Captain Falstaff and Other Plays*, 112–38. London: Arrowsmith.

O'Toole, Fintan. 1985. "Going West: The Country versus the City in Irish Writing." *The Crane Bag* 9, no. 2: 111–16.

Phelan, Mark. 2009. "'Authentic Reproductions': Staging the 'Wild West' in Modern Irish Drama." *Theatre Journal* 61: 235–48.

Pierse, Michael. 2011. *Writing Ireland's Working Class: Dublin After O'Casey*. London: Palgrave Macmillan.

Pilkington, Lionel. 2001. *Theatre and the State in Twentieth-Century Ireland: Cultivating the People*. London: Routledge.

———. 2004. "The Abbey Theatre and the Irish State." In *The Cambridge Companion to Twentieth-Century Irish Drama*, edited by Shaun Richards, 231–43. Cambridge: Cambridge Univ. Press.

Power, Arthur R. 1927. *The Drapier Letters*. In *The Drapier Letters and Her Ladyship, the Poet, and the Dog*, 6–32. Dublin: Talbot Press.

Prunty, Jucinta. 2000. *Dublin Slums, 1800–1925: A Study in Urban Geography*. Dublin: Irish Academic Press.

Quinn, Hugh. 1932. *Mrs. McConaghy's Money*. In *Three Plays by Hugh Quinn*, introduced by St. John Ervine, xv–83. London: Constable.

Ritschel, Nelson Ó Ceallaigh. 2000. "The Alternate Aesthetic: The Theatre of Ireland's Urban Plays." In *A Century of Irish Drama: Widening the Stage*, edited by Stephen Watt, Eileen Morgan, and Shakir Mustafa, 17–33. Bloomington: Indiana Univ. Press.

———. 2011. *Shaw, Synge, Connolly, and Socialist Provocation*. Gainesville: University Press of Florida.

Robinson, Lennox. 1911. *The Cross-Roads*. Dublin: Maunsel.

———. 1915. *The Dreamers: A Play in Three Acts*. London: Maunsel.

———. 1918. *The Lost Leader*. Dublin: Thomas Kiersey.

———. 1942. *Curtain Up: An Autobiography*. London: Michael Joseph.

———. 1951. *Ireland's Abbey Theatre: A History 1899–1951*. London: Sidgwick and Jackson.

Robinson, Lennox, and Micheál Ó hAodha. 1983. *Pictures at the Abbey: The Collection of the Irish National Theatre*. Portlaoise, Ireland: Dolmen Press.

Rokem, Freddie. 2000. *Performing History*. Iowa City: Univ. of Iowa Press.

Rollins, Ronald G. 1983. "Enigmatic Ghosts of Swift in Yeats and Johnston." *Eire-Ireland* 18:103–15.

Ryan, Frederick. 1970. *The Laying of the Foundations*. In *Lost Plays of the Irish Renaissance*, edited by Robert Hogan and James Kilroy, 23–37. Dixon, CA: Proscenium Press.

Saddlemyer, Ann, ed. 1982. *Theatre Business: The Correspondence of the First Abbey Theatre Directors: William Butler Yeats, Lady Gregory and J. M. Synge*. University Park: Pennsylvania State Univ. Press.

Sarr, Kenneth. 1924. *The Passing*. Dublin: Talbot.

Thompson, William Irwin. 1972. *The Imagination of an Insurrection Dublin, Easter 1916: A Study of an Ideological Movement*. New York: Harper and Row.

Tomelty, Joseph. 1962. *The End House*. Dublin: James Duffy.

Torchiana, Donald T. 1966. "Imitate Him if You Dare." In *W. B. Yeats and Georgian Ireland*. Evanston, IL: Northwestern Univ. Press; London: Oxford Univ. Press.

Trotter, Mary. 2008. *Modern Irish Theatre*. Cambridge: Polity Press.

Vaughan, W. E., and A. J. Fitzpatrick, eds. 1978. *Irish Historical Statistics: Population, 1821–1971*. Dublin: Royal Irish Academy.

Watson, G. J. 1979. *Irish Identity and the Literary Revival*. London: Croom Helm; New York: Barnes and Noble.

Welch, Robert. 1990. *The Abbey Theatre, 1899–1999: Form and Pressure*. Oxford: Oxford Univ. Press.

Whelan, Yvonne. 2003. *Reinventing Modern Dublin: Streetscape, Iconography and the Politics of Identity*. Dublin: Univ. College Dublin Press.

Williams, Raymond. 1973. *The Country and the City*. London: Chatto and Windus.

Wilson, A. Patrick. [1916]. *Victims and Poached: Liberty Hall Plays No. 1*. (Dublin: [s.n., West, Trade Union Printer]).

Wordsworth, William. 1944. *The Poetical Works of William Wordsworth*. Edited by E. de Selincourt. Oxford: Clarendon Press.

Yeates, Pádraig. 2000. *Lockout: Dublin 1913*. Dublin: Gill and Macmillan.

Yeats, W. B. 1934. *The Words upon the Window-Pane: A Play in One Act*. Dublin: Cuala Press.

———. 1955. *Autobiographies: Memories and Reflections*. London: Macmillan.

———. 1967. Introduction to *Words upon the Window-Pane*. In *Fair Liberty Was All His Cry: A Tercentenary Tribute to Jonathan Swift, 1667–1745*, edited by A. Norman Jeffares, 186–99. London: Macmillan; New York: St. Martin's Press.

———. 1975. *Uncollected Prose*. Vol. 2: *1897–1939*. Collected and edited by John P. Frayne and Colton Johnson. London: Macmillan.

———. 2004. *The Collected Works of W. B. Yeats*. Vol. 9: *Early Articles and Reviews*, edited by John P. Frayne and Madeleine Marchaterre. New York: Scribner.

Yeats, W. B., and Lady Gregory. 2001. *Cathleen ní Houlihan*. In *The Collected Works of W. B. Yeats*. Vol. 2: *The Plays*, edited by David R. Clark and Rosalind E. Clark, 83–93. New York: Scribner.

Zimmerman, Georges-Denis. 1967. *Songs of Irish Rebellion: Political Street Ballads and Rebel Songs, 1780–1900*. Dublin: Allen Figgis.

# Index

*Italic page numbers denote illustrations.*